Amelia McNutt is a hardworking researcher, writer, and lecturer, with a life-long passion to uncover the unknown stories and unsung heroes of America's military history. Being from the Boston area, she has always had a connection to the fascinating chronicles of the American Revolution which began in Massachusetts. She also researches World War I and World War II, often traveling to the battlefields in Europe including Normandy, France.

Her work is guided and empowered by her personal mission statement:

Learn The Stories – Don't Let Their Glory Fade.

To every man and woman of America's armed forces who unselfishly dedicated and sacrificed themselves for the grateful citizens of this great nation.

Thank you.

To those who have tolerated, inspired, and cared for me. You know who you are.

Thank you.

Amelia McNutt

AMERICA'S FIRST SOLDIERS

Very Best Wishes

Amelia C. McNutt

AUSTIN MACAULEY PUBLISHERS™
LONDON * CAMBRIDGE * NEW YORK * SHARJAH

Ordering Information
Quantity sales: Special discounts are available on quantity purchases by corporations, associations, and others. For details, contact the publisher at the address below.

Publisher's Cataloging-in-Publication data
McNutt, Amelia
America's First Soldiers

ISBN 9781649798145 (Paperback)
ISBN 9781649798152 (Hardback)
ISBN 9781649798176 (ePub e-book)
ISBN 9781649798169 (Audiobook)

Library of Congress Control Number: 2022915415

www.austinmacauley.com/us

First Published 2023
Austin Macauley Publishers LLC
40 Wall Street,33rd Floor, Suite 3302
New York, NY 10005
USA

mail-usa@austinmacauley.com
+1 (646) 5125767

I wish to thank all the helpful and supportive members of Austin Macauley Publishers. Thank you all for guidance and support.

I wish to thank, Rosanne Crowley, for endlessly listening to my accounts of military history. She has, through her patience and strength, kept me focused and on track writing this book.

Thank you to my supportive family and friends. Thank you to Sarah who edited an essay that became this book.

I have had many travels in writing this book and was inspired by the words of many authors' past – in particular, Professor Allen French. I also met more than one informative, and passionate guide along the Battle Road Trail, one in particular was very helpful. Thank you, Patrick McGarrity.

Writing a book is at times very solitary work, the underpinning of that is the understanding of family and friends. Sometimes a question asked, or a smile offered was just what this writer needed to believe in this project. Thank you all.

Table of Contents

Part 1: The Stories: 1775–6

Introduction

"These are the times that try men's souls."

The Crisis (1776)
Thomas Paine (1737–1809)

Late in the evening of 19 April 1775, a large group of British soldiers arrived on Charlestown Neck across the Charles River from the Town of Boston. Clad in their notorious redcoats, they were easy to see even in the darkest of nights, and this was indeed a dark night for the British Soldiers in Boston. On this night, the Redcoats that ran onto the Charlestown Peninsular looked different, they were in total disarray: fatigued, breathless, weary, frightened.

Some were wounded, others without weapons, or ammunition, and nearly all drained of their courage to die for King and Country. They looked like men who had been chased by ghosts.

Wednesday, 19 April 1775 was the day the American Revolution went from ideas, thoughts, conversations, prayers, and hopes to actions driven by the most ordinary and extraordinary persons in Massachusetts. The events of 19 April are further distinguished on 17 June 1775 at the Battle of Bunker Hill and on 17 March 1776 as the British retreated from Boston to never return.

Chapter I
The Road to Lexington
Part 1
General Thomas Gage

"America is a mere bully, from one end to the other, and the Bostonians by
far the greatest bullies."
General Thomas Gage
1770

It was just before dawn on Wednesday, 19 April 1775, as the lead elements of a large detachment of British Soldiers marching from Boston to Concord disturbed the Colonial residents at Lexington. The deployment of 700 British soldiers marching into the Massachusetts countryside was a loud, bold, and different stroke for the British in Boston.

This immense display of Colonial era power was begrudgingly ordered by the Commander and Chief, British Forces in North America, Lieutenant General Thomas Gage. General Gage knew better than to anger Colonial Americans, his superiors did not.

Gage arrived in Boston 13 May 1774 aboard the *HMS Lively*, a heavily armed Royal Navy ship sent to Boston to aid in the blockade the Port. General Thomas Gage was a career officer from an old, distinguished, aristocratic family that could trace its noble roots all the way back to the 15th century. Thomas attended military school, and after his school training, as was the custom purchased his commission as a lieutenant.

As a young officer, Gage was at *Culloden's Moor* in 1746, when the British Army annihilated the Scottish Highlanders in the final act of the last *Scottish Jacobite rebellion*. He also had fought alongside George Washington in the *French and Indian War*. He was very familiar with Americans, having spent nearly two decades in Colonial America. General Gage even married an American, Margret Kemble, a younger woman from New Jersey who would outlive him by thirty-seven years.

The King appointed Gage *Royal Military Governor of Massachusetts Colony,* and Commander and Chief of British Forces in North America in an effort to restore British sovereignty in rebellious Boston, and Massachusetts. Gage was the King's expert on all things Colonial American.

Gage's job was nearly impossible. By 1774, lines had already been drawn in Boston separating Loyalists from Patriots. Boston specifically, and Massachusetts as a whole was the seat of the rebellious colonial activities in British America in the waning decades of the 18th century. To his credit, Gage repeatedly tried to quell the ever-rising tensions and anti-British sentiments in Boston and Massachusetts with patience and peaceful means whenever possible.

He wanted to avoid armed conflict in Colonial America at nearly any cost. He understood his rebellious countrymen better than most of his peers. He did not want to engage the rebels and offer to them a reason for a violent exchange.

When Gage arrived, *The Boston Massacre* was a recent and bitter memory, of only four years. The *Boston Tea Party* was a current memory occurring just six months past. The famous dumping of over 300 chests of valuable British tea into Boston Harbor on December 16, 1773, incited the British Ministers in Parliament. They demanded that Boston residents pay for the lost tea. That was too extreme a remedy for the citizens of Boston.

With Boston unwilling to please the ministers in London, they devised a series of *Acts* to be imposed on Boston and Massachusetts, and General Thomas Gage was there to enforce them. These punitive Acts did not bring the Bostonians to their knees, they rather tore apart any remaining bonds of kinship between the mother county and her colonies.

The New England Colonies and their sister colonies had faced other *"Acts"* before. These Acts were nothing less than taxes. *The Stamp Act*, and *The Townsend Acts* had been imposed upon the citizens of the American Colonies unsuccessfully a decade earlier. These taxes elicited a resounding chorus from the Colonies.

Voices erupted together from the pulpits of New England's protestant churches, the hills of Pennsylvania and Virginia, the farms of the Carolinas and Georgia, responding— *"No taxation without representation."*

But this time it was different, as these acts were not taxes, they were measures that greatly curtailed the liberties of the citizens of Boston in particular and extended into all of Massachusetts. These were strong arm tactics designed to punish citizens, they had a polarizing effect as Parliament tried again, and issued four acts to be imposed on the American Colonies.

The *Coercive Acts*, or the *Intolerable Acts* as Colonial Americans called them were to take place in rebellious Boston. Intended to hurt the Colonials, these acts unintentionally created and expanded the determined Patriotic resistance. Not a languid opinion was to be found or shared in Boston. These acts began to steadily galvanize the colonial citizens of Massachusetts and beyond, swinging support to the outlaw group founded in Boston, *Sons of Liberty*.

By 1774, as General Gage arrived in Boston the Sons of Liberty had chapters in: Massachusetts, New York, New Hampshire, Connecticut, Rhode Island, New Jersey, Maryland and Virginia. In the famed Boston chapter, Gage could find: Samuel Adams, John Adams, John Hancock, Dr. Joseph Warren, and Paul Revere.

The first of the four *Coercive Acts*, or the *Intolerable Acts* was the *Boston Port Act*. The closure of the Port of Boston to commerce. This was an exceptionally cruel blow to the vital, vibrant port of Boston. Many in Boston and beyond depended upon the goods that arrived from all over the world to the wharves of Boston. Commerce was the life blood of Boston, as it was in New York, Philadelphia, Charleston, and up and down the coasts of the colonies.

If Boston was vulnerable to be put out of business, so was any other Colonial American seaport. The specter of this fear loomed larger than the British Ministers in London could comprehend. It was a fatal disease that arrived in Boston and could spread to any colony with the whim of a Royal decree.

The *Massachusetts Government Act* was debilitating to a population that had effectively governed themselves since 1620. The Royal appointment of a Military Governor of the Province of Massachusetts was unacceptable to the peaceful residents of Massachusetts. They did not want a British General acting as a royal dictator.

Eventually, the British Royal Military Governor, General Thomas Gage moved the seat of government from Boston to Salem. And to add further insult to injury, there would be no, or a very limited allowance of local town and city government council meetings. Massachusetts men had been engaging in self-determination since the Pilgrims walked across Plymouth Rock.

They had formed governing councils, established militia companies, formed communities with multi-generational roots. This was an insult that insighted many Colonials beyond Massachusetts. They understood that this same fate could easily be applied to them.

The *Justice Act* moved trials from Massachusetts to England. If the Royal Military Governor believed that a fair trial could not be had in Massachusetts for a royal official, and royal official included a British soldier, then that trial would or could be moved out of Massachusetts, and it could be moved to England.

In the same colony, in the same city that had found the seven of the nine British soldiers innocent at the *Boston Massacre,* was now seen as unjust, incompetent or both. This was a most egregious act that had the potential to allow a man charged with murder to be whisked away to a friendlier judiciary area. It also required that any witnesses travel a great distance to participate in the justice system.

It was for practical senses a desperate act designed to impugn, and even malign victims of serious crimes in Massachusetts. This was like the other two acts an affront to past practices for well over one hundred years. If justice could not be guaranteed in Massachusetts, then the next step was to dismantle the court system, requiring all legal matters to be compromised to suit an English governor. Power was slowly being acquired and centralized in a Royal Military Governor.

The *Quartering Act* was first passed onto the American Colonies in 1765. It required the residents of the American Colonies to house, feed, or help pay the costs of the British troops garrisoned in the American cities. It was an abysmal failure. When resurrected and forced upon the residents of Boston and Massachusetts in 1774–75 it was a source of frustration and only added to the hostile environment in and around Boston.

The citizens of Massachusetts understood the act to require them to house and feed the British army of occupation. Military occupation was something new and violently unacceptable in Boston as it provided the spark that ignited the *Boston Massacre.* British soldiers were there to restore order, but the residents of Boston saw the soldiers as the instruments of a military royal governor who could use them to usurp their freedoms as he wished.

The colonies had always organized, armed, and maintained local militia forces, those same militia forces were called on by the British authorities to help fight the Indians, French, or Spanish. They could be called up anytime Britain asked the Colonial Governor for help. It was a frightening and unforgiving experience for the residents of Boston to house, feed and share their private property with an army of occupation.

With the knowledge that the Colonials were now actively gathering war making materials, the conciliatory General Thomas Gage took a proactive position.

Gage ordered a secret mission to float up the Mystic River from Boston, and after landing, the troops would march in force to collect all the gun powder in the powder house in what was then Charlestown. Today, that area is known as *Powder House Square* in Somerville.

Sending troops into an area known to harbor rebels, and to have them retrieve gun powder and return it to Boston was a dangerous task. Gage fully understood his actions could have consequences, and selected the *4th Regiment, The King's Own*, a line regiment of the British Army with a storied history.

The *King's Own* was formed in 1680, and had fought on many European battlefields. It also served the Crown suppressing rebellions in England, Ireland, and Scotland. Author Trevor Royale, writing in, *Culloden; Scotland's Last Battle and the Forging of the British Empire* claims that the 4th Regiment, took the highest casualties that April day in 1746 on Culloden's Moor.

The 4th Regiment was positioned in the first line where the Highlanders smashed into the British forces. The 4th Regiment barely held the line as the Jacobite Highlanders charged straight into British muskets and bayonets. The 4th Regiment incurred 34% casualties in just a matter of minutes. 1[i]

General Gage knew the *King's Own* were battle hardened, tough, disciplined troops because Gage was a young officer who experienced the carnage on Culloden's Moor personally. The 4th Regiment was the perfect choice to complete Gage's orders.

The Colonials knew the British were coming for the powder. General Gage had been told by the man in charge of the powder house, William Brattle that the local towns had taken their share of the stored powder. This was a very troubling fact for Gage; he knew that with enough gun powder, the Colonials could begin a violent confrontation with the British Army. What remained was the King's powder, and Brattle urged General Gage to remove it before the Colonials returned to take it.

Gage had supposedly dropped the note passed to him by Brattle, and that note was secured by one of the many Colonial spies in Boston. Boston was full of Colonial spies and word got out into the countryside that the British Regulars were coming for the King's powder stored in Charlestown. The thought that battle hardened, well-armed British Regulars were going to land on the shores of Mystic River was quite discomforting to the local residents.

On 1 September 1774, nearly 300 of Gage's best troops rowed out of Boston and up the Mystic River to Charlestown. They disembarked their boats and marched in-force to the powder house systematically collecting the large store of gun powder in Somerville. Other British Soldiers marched into nearby Cambridge to retrieve some cannons.

All of this was done without incident, there were no shots fired on or by the British soldiers. They completed their orders and rowed back to Boston with the powder and cannons. The locals took their frustrations out on William Brattle, the loyalist who had begun this unsavory episode.

They formed mobs, and threatened Brattle at his home. He begged forgiveness that was never forthcoming. From those disorganized, angry mob stories grew and sparked rumors of violence that traveled throughout Massachusetts and beyond.

Stories grew quickly accusing the British troops of firing on and killing citizens as they marched through the countryside. Incredibly, mobs even told stories of Boston being shelled by the British. There was no truth to these stories, yet they influenced men as far away as Connecticut to arm themselves and head toward Boston.

Rumors sent many militiamen to Cambridge believing the King's soldiers had committed acts of war. First hundreds, then thousands of angry militiamen gathered in and around Cambridge. Eventually they learned the truth, and returned to their villages and towns. The fast reaction of the local militiamen was not lost on General Gage, and he determined that there would be no other expeditions of his forces into the countryside to secure the King's powder.

In just a few short days, General Gage had learned what he feared most, that the Colonial residents of Massachusetts had no fear of him or his army in

Boston. Gage also realized that these mobs outnumbered his forces, and they only lacked real leadership to become more than a mob—but an army.

The event remembered as the *Powder Alarm* got General Gage his gun powder and cannons, and it drove the Colonials to further suspect, and prepare themselves against British aggression. Gage handed the agitators of the smoldering rebellion what they needed to further galvanize their cause—the use of British military force.

Gage had given the Colonials an example of British power, and the Colonials had responded in kind. Gage got his powder but the Colonials found the will to fight and defend their lives and property as they organized into better trained militia units.

As the repercussions mounted, General Gage slowly became aware of the predicament he had placed himself and his army into. With a full understanding of the Colonists reaction to his powder grab, and his demonstration of British power, General Gage wrote desperately to London imploring his Ministers to send help to him and his army in Boston,

"If you think ten thousand men sufficient, send twenty; if one million is thought enough, give two; you save both blood and treasure in the end [ii] *"*

The confident General, veteran, and victor over previous rebellions against the British Crown was making a powerful point to his superiors. Do not underestimate the determination, training, experience, and the will of the armed Colonial citizens of Boston and Massachusetts. What General Gage had witnessed first-hand in and around Boston, his masters in London had not.

Gage was a voice in the darkness to those still in England, a voice of fear, not a voice of British power and resolution.

The *Powder Alarm* of 1 September 1774, along with the *Intolerable Acts* of May 1774, left the residents of Boston and Massachusetts no illusions when it came to the British Army and the use of armed men foraging into the countryside. By the end of September 1774, a few short weeks after the Powder Alarm, so angered were the Colonist that local town and villages met in secret and determined that they should drill and train their militia units.

They also actively sought to acquire the tools they would need to defend themselves if the British aggression occurred again. They tried to accumulate gun powder, bullets, and bayonets for their muskets. Men who were good on horseback were chosen to become alarm riders. They would ride into the countryside and sound the alarm to the Minutemen and Militiamen that the British Regulars were on the march.

Town councils met secretly and unlawfully gathered to authorize the purchase of cannons, and cannon shot. All of these materials of war were in short supply, so when they were gathered, they were stashed out in the countryside away from the British garrison in Boston. In essence, many Colonial residents were preparing for war.

It was time to prepare for more armed actions, and into that caldron of growing anti-British sentiments stepped two agitators to take full advantage of the heightened emotions of the time. Into the vacuum of leadership that would convert angry mobs into an army of resistance, stepped John Hancock, and Samuel Adams. The historical odd couple of the burgeoning revolution in Massachusetts.

Part 2
The Odd Couple

"Among the natural rights of the colonists are these: First a right to life, secondly to liberty, and thirdly to property; together with the right to defend them in the best manner they can."

Samuel Adams (1722–1803)
1772

In March of 1775, John Hancock and Samuel Adams were welcomed into the home of Jonas Clarke, a preacher in Lexington, Massachusetts. Lexington was where John Hancock had spent much of his youth, there he was remembered as John Hancock III. Lexington was where his father, Colonel John Hancock Jr was born in 1702.

Lexington was where Hancock's grandfather, Colonel John Hancock Sr. arrived as a teacher, and became a minister, serving Lexington for 55 years. Both his father and grandfather graduated Harvard College, were ordained ministers, were active in local politics, and achieved the rank of Colonel in the militia.

John Hancock's father, Colonel John Hancock Jr., died when John was just seven years old. He was sent to live with his uncle Thomas Hancock in Boston. Thomas was a very wealthy Boston businessman. Young John's Uncle and Aunt lived in the Beacon Hill section of Boston. They were very wealthy influential people who also owned slaves.

Like his father and grandfather John III would attend Harvard College. But he was not to be a minister, politician or militia colonel, Young Hancock would learn his uncle's business. Import and export was the expertise of Thomas Hancock, founder the *House of Hancock*. Young John was an eager and successful apprentice.

When his uncle died in 1764, John Hancock III inherited everything Thomas owned, including the business, real estate all over Massachusetts, the big house and the slaves. When John Hancock walked into Reverend Clarke's house, he was the richest man in Massachusetts, and one of the richest men in all the British American Colonies. He was the *President of the Massachusetts Provincial Congress*, *Chairman of the Committee of Safety*, and a well-respected Boston philanthropist.

He also held the honorary title of Lieutenant Colonel, *Independent Corp of Cadets*, the honor guard of the Royal Governor of Massachusetts. The new Military Royal Governor, Lieutenant General Sir Thomas Gage did not need a ceremonial honor guard. He stripped Lieutenant Colonel John Hancock III of his prestigious title and rank, a direct insult.

Hancock dressed in the best of styles, lived in one of Boston's most beautiful homes in its finest neighborhood. He rubbed shoulders with Royal officials including Provincial Governors, and business and political connections in Boston and London. Surviving portraits show Hancock dressed impeccably.

As a distinguished member of the upper class, his coat was perfect in its tailoring, and it was outlined with gold piping reminiscent of a General's coat. It covered a neat and crisp white linen shirt with a high collar, and cuffs protruding beyond his neat blue coat. His hair coiffured in white and pulled back with a stylish black ribbon that fell neatly upon his shoulders. He was the embodiment of a wealthy Englishman, as close as one would find to *Colonial Royalty* in Boston, or New England in 1774.

Samuel Adams was like John Hancock in few ways. He was a namesake son of an influential politician and church deacon. Samuel Adams Sr. was a successful Boston businessman who fathered twelve children, with only three surviving into adulthood, including his son Samuel Adams Jr. Young Samuel like John Hancock went to Harvard College, and that was the end of their similarities.

Sam Adams was fourteen years older than John Hancock and much more streetwise than the aristocratic Hancock. Unlike Hancock, young Samuel seemed to fail at every business opportunity he encountered. When he was appointed a tax-collector, he failed to collect the taxes. This endeared him to the taxpayers but not the government wanting and needing those funds. Adams managed to get out of trouble with the aid of his fellow Boston political leaders.

Samuel Adams has been described as a master propagandist. He was much more than that, as he knew how and when to influence a crowd and could easily turn that crowd into an unruly or an organized mob. Adams was a master manipulator, and present at both the *Boston Massacre*, and the *Boston Tea Party*.

He was a mover and shaker of the working class in Boston, and deeply committed to personal liberty, and the rights of British Colonial citizens in Massachusetts. Samuel Adams' influence over events leading up to the revolution was described as:

"...stimulation of events...necessary in the strategy of revolution."[iii]

Samuel Adams was dedicated to nothing less than independence for nearly all of his adult life. His writings from the time he was a young college student at Harvard reflect his desire to see the colonies independent of England and her suffocating laws and taxes. In 1743, for his Master of Arts degree from Harvard, young Sam wrote his thesis titled:

"Whether it be Lawful to resist the, Supreme Magistrate, if the Commonwealth cannot otherwise be preserved."[iv]

While John Hancock was learning to be a rich man, Samuel Adams emerged as a leader in Boston Politics. After the French and Indian war ended, Adams became vocal in opposing the *Sugar Act* and *Stamp Act*. These were taxes that the Colonials believed were unjust, and men like Adams led the successful resistance to have them repealed.

Adams was a one-man political action committee, who organized his fellow citizens and politicians into groups of resistance. Adams could cross religious divides, economic boundaries, and ideological barriers. He was one of America's first master politicians and he specialized in uniting disagreeing factions. While serving in the Massachusetts House of Representatives, Adams met newly elected delegate John Hancock.

Together Adams and Hancock would use their different bases of support to resist the latest attempt of the British Government to tax the Colonies. The

Townsend Acts were little more than a small duty imposed on goods imported into the Colonies. The revenue it collected would help support the Royal appointees, including judges.

Resistance against the acts grew from in Boston and Massachusetts. From this last act of petulance, the British Crown sent armed British troops to Boston for the protection of its loyal citizens. It was the occupation of Boston by armed British soldiers, and the *Intolerable Acts* that gave the rebellious odd couple of Adams and Hancock the fertile ground they needed to ferment their revolution.

Hancock and Adams made sure the British Government's actions toward her colonies was seen as punitive, and unnecessary, contrived by an arrogant government three thousand miles away. Adams framed the egregious acts in 1764, questioning and inciting his followers as he wrote:

"If taxes are laid upon us in any shape without our having a legal representative where they are laid, are we not reduced from the Character of free Subjects to the miserable State of tributary Slaves?"[v]

The world's most powerful land and sea forces now occupied Boston. Forces that remained at the ready to deny the rights of Englishmen living in the American Colonies. They did as much as anyone or anything to ignite passions of liberty. These acts, and their enforcement including the startling event of armed British soldiers marching into the peaceful Colonial countryside was seen as no less than tyranny. A tyranny that should never be tolerated again.

This historical *Odd Couple*—John Hancock and Sam Adams are remembered for what they did together as much as how different they were. One wanted to fight, and be the equal of a father and grandfather, each a colonel in the militia. The other wanted to start the fight, knowing his voice should not be silenced on a battlefield, but be preserved to insight the next battle.

One was a debtor, who was once on the edge of insolvency and prison, the other one of the richest men in the New England colonies. One was groomed in appearance, manner, and education and was eager for his own vain glory. The other, a working-class street ruffian who could unite fighting factions into a single organized mob with a voice stronger than any single man.

One was a Ladies's man, the envy of many of his peers, the other a man's man, someone you wanted to have a beer with, complain with, or fight a fight with. And one was consumed by protecting his fortune, the other consumed by protecting the fortunes of others. They were the right two men, in the right time and when they walked into Jonas Clarke's house in Lexington, they were in the right place.

The Reverend Jonas Clarke opened the door to his Lexington home to his fellow Harvard College alumni, and revolutionaries, Hancock and Adams. Clarke had married John Hancock's cousin, Lucy Bowes and lived in the house John Hancock's grandfather built. It was Jonas Clarke who succeeded John Hancock Sr. as Reverend at the Church of Christ in Lexington.

The Revered Clarke raised ten children on his very successful 60-acre farm. Jonas Clarke was every bit the revolutionary Samuel Adams was, with a powerful church pulpit to preach from, Clarke possessed just the right mixture of fiery temperament and ice-cold intellectual calculation. Into the small town of Lexington, Clarke brought the word of God, while Hancock brought his fortune, and Adams his powerful rhetoric.

The Reverend Clarke, like Adams and Hancock, was very vocal in his opposition to the various British acts imposed on Colonial America. Of these acts or taxes, Clarke would write on behalf of the Lexington Selectman to their representative in Boston describing them as:

"...a door to numberless evils, which only time will discover,"[vi]

Clarke continued his vilification of British mandates from both the pulpit and the selectman's seat in Lexington. The Reverend Jonas Clarke added a voice somewhere between Hancock's aristocratic tones and Adams' street speech. Reverend Clarke's voice was draped in theology, espousing a philosophy that the people of Lexington understood.

Clarke's words expressed a logical conclusion concerning the rights of the Colonial citizens. In 1774, as the Intolerable Acts were administered, and the armed, intimidating British Army marched into the countryside Jonas Clarke united the voices in Lexington as it was concluded:

"...that the time had come to prepare for rebellion."[vii]

Reverend Jonas Clark was the outspoken, well educated, influential voice of the Patriot cause in Lexington. But he was not a soldier. From the pulpit Reverend Clarke addressed the soldiers that would soon defend the rights of free men in Lexington, and beyond. Clarke preached:

"LOVE to GOD, which contains the essence of religion, is a source of every virtue, every grace; and inspires the soul with the noblest principles of action…which excites men, for the public good, for the safety and happiness of society, of their country, to sacrifice anything, everything dear in life—yea, life itself…TRUE Valor is, therefore, to be considered as a moral virtue…And where courage, valor or fortitude, has reason for its basis, and is encouraged, cultivated and supported, by the principles of religion, it becomes a virtue of the highest rank, and prompts and leads men on to the most heroic…"[viii]

Very early on the morning of 19 April 1775 John Hancock, Samuel Adams and Reverend Jonas Clarke walked down to the town green from Reverend Clarke's house. Clarke's house was, and remains just a few hundred yards from Lexington Green. They were there watching as the Minutemen and Militiamen gathered to answer the alarm.

Reverend Clarke was prodded by his companions as they watched the gathering of *America's First Soldiers*. Clark was asked, *"…if the men of Lexington would be ready if it came to a fight?"*

The good Reverend's response was more like a General reviewing his troops than a country pastor watching the men of his flock on a cold, dangerous night in New England. Reverend Clarke stated:

"I have trained them for this very hour"[ix]

Captain John Parker was the man in charge of the 120-man Lexington Militia company. Most of the Lexington men were kin of sort, family, marriage, etc. In April of 1775, Captain John Parker and his men had only one complaint, they did not have enough gun powder.

But they did have the courage and the support of their town to defend life, liberty and property. General Gage was unaware of Captain Parker, and his valiant citizen soldiers. Gage wanted all his problems to go away, but he was about to find out his problems had just begun.

Part 3
Those Waiting for Gage

"The attractiveness of North America as a refuge and opportunity was no new thing...the increase in immigration became so great that it constituted a social force itself."

Bernard Bailyn
Voyagers to the West
1986

Gage's even-handed patience was very unusual for a British General in the 18th Century. It was lost on the Colonial citizens and their leaders who saw Gage and his troops as a source of British tyranny. They saw their liberties disappearing, and eagerly blamed General Gage and his Regulars. To make matters worse, General Gage's moderate approach was also lost on his ministers in London. They now insisted on an aggressive stance in Boston and Massachusetts.

British authority was to be asserted at any price. Like a curtain slowly descending between acts in a tragedy, Gage's hope of peace and reconciliation was extinguished by those he wished to save, and those he wished to please.

On 14 April 1775, Commander and Chief, General Thomas Gage received a letter from Lord Dartmouth, *Secretary of State for the Colonies from 1772–5.*

William Legge, *2nd Earl of Dartmouth,* was a very well connected and powerful force in the government of King George III. Known to be a generous man, he was the namesake of *Dartmouth College,* in Hanover, New Hampshire. Lord Dartmouth's powers reached deeply into Colonial America, and he and his peers in King George's Court had grown quite frustrated with Boston.

Dartmouth believed the time had come to end the treachery in Boston, and put down the rebellious behavior by force. Lord Dartmouth demanded that General Gage take immediate and harsh actions. He no longer wished to see Gage, *"soothe the griefs"* [x] of the Colonial Americans. The April 14, letter from the mighty Lord was driven by angry members of the British Parliament. They chastised Gage's inaction and ordered him into action, Lord Dartmouth wrote:

"A smaller force now, if put to the test, would be able to encounter them [American Colonists] *with greater probability of success than you might expect from a greater army. The only consideration that remains is in what manner the force under your command may be exerted, to defend the constitution and restore the vigor of the Government…the first and essential step…would be to arrest the principal actors and abettors…"*

Thomas Fleming,
Bunker Hill, Page 52

General Gage's diplomatic efforts were ignored, and his policies of moderation, and patience were abruptly abandoned. General Gage's attitude and intentions of a peaceful solution have often been discounted in some historical reflections. Gage's knowledge of Colonial America and its inhabitants had inspired the King to position him to end the growing chorus of rebellion in Massachusetts.

With his 20 years of service in Colonial North America, personal experiences fighting alongside Colonial Militiamen, and his American wife, Gage understood well the American mindset in 1774. He grasped that force was a response that Colonial Americans understood very well. *They did not fear armed men; they are armed men.*

Many served a lifetime in local militia groups filled with family and friends. Colonial Americans had established local governments, abided by British laws, and bravely entered the new world creating: successful cities, towns, villages, farms, schools, and churches.

The British residents of the American Colonies had been defending themselves for over 150 years from the Indians, Spanish, French, and the

British. Many immigrated to the American Colonies to escape the very same British tyranny that was descending upon Massachusetts in the 1770s.

Some estimates have the population of the American Colonies in 1775 as 2.4 million people. Of that number, an astounding 85% were British [Celtic] in origin.[xi] The following is an appraisal of immigration to the American Colonies by 1775:

"In the years after cessation of war in North America [The Seven Years War (1756–63) aka French and Indian War] *the colonies experienced an extraordinary burst of expansion…The attractiveness of North America as a refuge and opportunity was no new thing…the increase in immigration became so great that it constituted a social force itself. A force that added strain to the established relationship between the Colonies and Britain…the greatly increased flow of immigration…presented problems to the British rulers…that could not be solved within the limits of their ideas of the time…and* [the English] *administrative capacity…"*[xii]

Many of these new arrivals came to the Northern colonies including New England, an area known for its religious tolerance. In one account gathered from many sources, estimates of *"245,000 Scot, Scot Irish, and Irish people"*[xiii] had immigrated to the American Colonies from 1700 to 1775. Immigrants from these Celtic regions were very familiar with British tyranny.

Some of these immigrants escaped poverty in England, while others fled brutal subjugation in Ireland. The Scots had an entire way of life intensely eradicated by the repressive, totalitarian British monarchy. A 2002 assessment of Scottish emigration notes:

"The great Scottish Rebellions of 1715 and 1746, and the persecution and repression that followed their failure, caused large numbers of Scots and Scotch-Irish to enter the Colonies…The violent repression of the Scottish highlanders after the Battle of Culloden drove many more immigrants to the Colonies…"[xiv]

Massacred at Culloden's Moor on April 16, 1746, the Scottish people were then *"pacified"*[xv] by the Duke of Cumberland, a man remembered as the *"Bloody Butcher."* The pacification of the Highlands was nothing less than the

British engaging in 18th century ethnic cleansing. Cumberland was the second son of England's German born and raised King George II and is remembered for wiping out the Highlanders and their way of life.

The British saw the Highlanders as no more than tribes of treasonous barbarians. Their tartans, bag pipes, broadswords, and language all became illegal after Culloden and the pacification. Seeking a new life, some of the Clans men and their kin immigrated to Ireland, and many others beyond to the American Colonies.

According to one Scottish archeology center:

The eviction of Highlanders from their homes peaked in the 1740s and early 1750s as the Highland economy had collapsed...From 1753, however, 50% of emigrating Scots chose to settle in the United States. "[xvi]

Further examination of the records of these immigrating new citizens finds, *"39% of the English* [Scot and Scotch-Irish] *immigrants were between 25 and 59 years old...35% were older teens and young adults (15–24 years old)*"[xvii]

These were prime ages for settlers to be able to preserve their new lives in Colonial America. Gage did not underestimate that fact, but many other British officers came to lament their time underestimating and fighting the Colonists in Massachusetts.

Gage knew the Americans would fight. Gage had been at Culloden, he knew he was not facing the same sword wielding, shield carrying, tartan wearing, charging Clansmen of 1746. He was facing men who could and would fight with muskets and a committed strategy to destroy his Majesty's soldiers.

It was General Gage himself who offered the best explanation of the New England spirit that had flustered the British in Massachusetts. One evening Gage said to a fellow officer:

"It is impossible to beat the notion of liberty out of these people" [xviii].

Gage would try to *beat the notion of liberty* out of the King's subjects in Massachusetts. He approached the Colonial residents of Massachusetts carefully, for he knew many had already tasted British tyranny, and held it in contempt. But the King and his Ministers ignored General Gage and decided their own course to follow in Colonial America in the spring of 1775.

The actions the Ministers demanded, created the actions Gage half-heartedly undertook. And when British aggression was mixed with years of tensions, the inevitable result was a deadly exchange on a peaceful New England field.

Part 4
Marching into History

"The summer soldier and the sunshine patriot will, in this crisis, shrink from the service of their country; but he that stands by it now, deserves the love and thanks of man and woman."

The Crisis (1776)
Thomas Paine (1737–1809)

Just about as the 18th of April was becoming the 19th of April two lanterns were visible in the steeple of an old Boston church. They shone but for a brief moment and it was long enough for the simple message to reach Paul Revere.

The moment immortalized by Harvard professor, Cambridge resident, Henry Wadsworth Longfellow:

"If the British march
By land or sea from the town to-night,
Hang a lantern aloft in the belfry arch
Of the North Church tower as a signal light,—
One, if by land, and two, if by sea;
And I on the opposite shore will be... "[xix]

The Midnight Ride of Paul Revere (1860)
Henry Wadsworth Longfellow (1807–82)

The British were on the march, headed out of Boston. Paul Revere was only one of over two dozen riders that would multiply into nearly 60 riders from Boston through Massachusetts, into New Hampshire, Connecticut and Rhode Island.

The rides that began in the Massachusetts countryside ended in the far corners throughout the New England Colonies. No chances were taken that the message that the *"Regulars are Coming"* would not get out to the militia companies long before the Redcoats arrived in Lexington or Concord.

Paul Revere was dispatched by Dr. Joseph Warren, unlike the other messengers he had a special job to do. Revere was to find John Hancock and Samuel Adams in Lexington and warn them that they may be the target as well as the materials in Concord. It was suspected they were to be arrested by Gage's men and held on the charge of treason against the British Crown. Revere knew exactly where Hancock and Adams were, he had ridden out to Lexington on Sunday, 16 April 1775 and found them.

Just days before the Wednesday battle of Lexington Green, Revere met with Hancock, Adams and Clarke, he passed to them the information that had been gathered in and around Boston the last few days. Revere was directed by Dr. Joseph Warren to inform the rebellious trio that:

"...the Boats belonging to the Transports were all launched, and carried under the Sterns of the Men of War. (They had been previously hauled up and repaired). We likewise found that the Grenadiers and light Infantry were all taken off duty. From these movements, we expected something serious was [to] *be transacted."*[xx]

The men who wanted revolution now knew how close it could be. A British armed force was to move in the next few days. It had a specific target—war materials in Concord, and the men who could inspire others to go war—John Hancock and Samuel Adams.

After many years of chasing that elusive aspect of courage that resides in those facing conflict, of finding inspiring words and organizing protests, of facing mobs and creating mobs, of tasting the joy of successes and bitterness of failures, Samuel Adams, the most dedicated, most radical, of all Patriots had his opportunity within reach.

Like a man who had endured a week of rainy, raw, gray New England skies, suddenly the sun came out and warmed Sam Adams to his very soul. His gift was to be hand delivered by the man he least expected to help him, Lieutenant General Thomas Gage, the military master of all the King's soldiers in North America, and the commander of the army of occupation in Boston.

Gage's force of 700 light infantry mixed with grenadiers was an imposing force to march into the countryside. First to march were the light infantry. The grenadiers followed; they were the intimidating element of the British Army.

They were large, strong, imposing men, and they were purposely segregated into intimidating groups, recognizable by their eye-catching bear-skin high hats. The light infantry was smaller and grouped together because of their speed on the battlefield and were identified by their unassuming short black helmets. The light infantry could chase down a fleeing enemy and finish them off with their bayonets.

The grenadiers and light infantry exited the boats onto marshy beach soil at the mouth of the Charles River. The soldiers waded through the water and mud, some sinking over their high black boots. It was just after midnight and the restless soldiers had wet pants and boots, and that was just the first problem on a day of problems. Still, they gathered themselves together, formed their lines, and marched down the road toward Concord.

The horse-mounted senior officer was Lieutenant Colonel Francis Smith. Lt. Colonel Smith was fifty-two years old and had spent his adult life in the British Army. Surviving paintings portray Smith as a large, portly man, quite dissimilar to the dashing, red-coated, British mounted officers, captured in many eighteenth century images.

Smith was part of the *10th Regiment A Foot*, an infantry regiment that had been in service to His Majesty for ninety years when they landed in Boston. Smith has come down through history as unprepared for the events that important day—he was reactive in Lexington, Concord, and the march back to Lexington on Battle Road. He was at no point proactive in his command on April 19 and seems to have shown little initiative beyond closely following his orders from Gage. He was a very poor choice.

General Gage, not wanting to expend an entire regiment from his garrison in Boston, had chosen to assemble a group of companies to march on to Concord. Smith was at the rear of the column, nearly a quarter mile behind the forward elements of his massive 700-man column.

Lt. Colonel Smith had been saddled with a mixture of forces as he marched toward Concord. The result was a non-coherent group that presented many challenges to Smith's command. Simply put, Lt. Colonel Smith was the wrong man in the wrong place on April 18–19, 1775. Although he would do his best, he was the type of commander who lacked imagination, and the ability to read his enemy and the Battlefield, and he lacked initiative.

Smith exited Boston with specific orders from General Gage. Smith, like men of his times, was trained to obey orders, not to offer questions or resistance. While he moved slowly at the rear of his column, history was unfolding as the lead elements of the British column reached Lexington.

Smith had sent 200 men out from the main body of his force. They were to get to Concord and hold the two bridges over the river, therefore protecting the largest element of the column moving behind them to search and destroy weapons in Concord.

These were Gage's orders to Lt. Colonel Smith, and marching onto Lexington Green was not found in those orders dated 18 April 1775:

Thomas Gage
British Commanding General and Governor of Massachusetts,
Orders to Lt. Col. Smith, 10th Regiment of Foot

"Having received intelligence, that a quantity of ammunition, provision, artillery, tents and small arms, having been collected at Concord, for the avowed purpose of raising and supporting a rebellion against His Majesty; you will march with the Corps of Grenadiers and Light Infantry...with the utmost secrecy to Concord, where you will seize and destroy...But you will take care that the soldiers do not plunder the inhabitants, or hurt private property.

You have a draught [map] of Concord, on which is marked the houses, barns, etc. which contain the above military stores... [cannons] must be spiked, and the carriages destroyed. The powder and flour must be [dumped] into the river...And the men may put balls of lead in their pockets, throwing them by degrees into ponds...You will open your business and return with the Troops, as soon as possible, which I must leave to your own Judgment and Discretion.[xxi]

Lieutenant General Sir Thomas Gage drew up his orders in secret. But Gage's secret was no secret at all. Some of the British soldiers, and many Colonial spies knew of the covert countryside mission. One man who did not know where he was going was Lieutenant Colonel Smith. He did not know the objective of his march until 10 PM on April 18, as he and his troops were standing on Boston Harbor's sandy shores getting ready to enter a boat.

At 10:00 PM, the British soldiers were gathering as ordered. But due to lack of planning and communication—it was after all, a secret mission; nothing went according to schedule. It took until nearly 1:00 the next morning—three hours to ferry the British soldiers across the Harbor. A rising tide covered what was to be dry mud flats by two feet of water.

The exiting soldiers were now wet footed along with cold, and irritated by delays most of those gathered knew was unacceptable. Once they assembled on the Cambridge side, they again waited for all the troops to land and form for the march. They were late this just another in a series of fateful mistakes. When they started marching, they should have already been in or passing through Lexington.

Days before the march, General Gage had sent two British officers to ride the two possible routes to Concord. One was by land, over Boston Neck, into Roxbury, Watertown, Waltham, Lexington, and on to Concord. It was a long 21-mile journey on horseback. The other route was by sea, as his troops would be rowed across Boston Harbor and land in Cambridge. From Cambridge, it was a straight shot through Menotomy, which today is Arlington, Lexington, and on to Concord. This route that started by sea, was 16 miles long or almost 25% shorter.

Gage chose the shorter route because he was acutely aware of the dangers his troops could encounter from angry ambushing militiamen. Writing to Lord Dartmouth on 28 March 1775, just 22 days before the events of April 19, Gage fully understood the dangers that had been raised after the Powder Alarm. The veteran General, and the King's appointed expert on Colonial affairs stated:

"[Gage] *feared...the provincial militia's forming ambushments,* [ambushes] *whereby the light infantry must suffer extremely in penetrating the countryside.*"[xxii]

Gage's assessment was correct. His words fell on the deaf ears of the blinded Ministers and their delusional King, as had other words of warning General Gage had offered his King and Ministers. Gage wrote to the Earl of Dartmouth the following assessment of his command in New England:

"Your Lordship will know from various accounts, the extremities to which Affairs are brought...the disease was believed to have been confined to the town of Boston, but now it is so universal there is no knowing where to apply a Remedy...The whole country was in a ferment—many parts of it, I may say and ready to unite."

Gage was more of a prognosticator than anyone realized. When he wrote, *"...ready to unite."* he was far more prophetic than even he realized. By April of 1775, the seeds of Colonial groups combining had fermented to organized, armed, intelligent, resistance aimed at the King's General and occupying army.

The King's response, *"though the conflict is unpleasant, Great Britain cannot retract."*[xxiii]

The words of George III, the last and final authority are at once full of vanity and vacuous. George III succeeded his German born grandfather, George II to the British throne, who succeeded his German born father George I to the throne.

The Georges were the protestant Kings with a distant connection to England's throne. They had fought forces inside and outside England who wished to restore the English Throne to its Catholic heirs. George II had defeated the Jacobite revolution in Scotland, with his own son leading the victorious forces.

Scotland was a land of clans, where small bands of men had fought and killed each other for a thousand years. But the residents of the American Colonies were only alike with their Scottish ancestors in name and fearlessness. George II's modern army, led by the Duke of Cumberland had destroyed the Highland clans. Men who did not own land, were armed with swords and shields, men who spoke Gaelic, a foreign tongue to the British.

George III was facing a rebellion in the American Colonies quite different than those he and his ancestors faced in Great Britain. In the Colonies, many men owned land, had a musket, gun powder and lead shot. Men who were not afraid of a modern army, rather they could on a moment's notice, form into a modern army.

But King George III had visions of his uncle conquering Scotland, and he was now prepared for his own conquest of a rebellion in the Colonies. But unlike the royal mind that was determined to sit upon the throne of America, times, places and people had changed. Men like George and his ministers were insulated by sycophants maintaining delusions from the truths of an evolving world.

Before the British began their march to Lexington Paul Revere had arrived at the house of Reverend Clarke. His orders from Dr. Warren in Boston were very specific. He was told to alert Hancock and Adams that the British Regulars were marching to Concord and would pass thought Lexington perhaps in an attempt to arrest them.

When Revere arrived, the Clarke house was under guard. Revere's news was old news in Lexington. Riders had passed through the town all day bringing the news of Gage's plans to march to Concord, thus endangering Adams and Hancock.

Paul Revere rode from Charlestown to Lexington, a distance of about twelve miles in about one hour. He rode the fastest horse he could find once he had rowed across Boston Harbor. Revere had encountered British officers on patrol, sent out by Gage to watch for riders bearing the news of the oncoming Red Coats.

He had found ways to avoid them, and still got to Lexington just after midnight. He believed the British advance units were not far behind him, he was wrong about the timing, right about their intent to march to and through Lexington. Adams and Hancock had to get to safety away from Lexington. They would but not at this early hour, there was a battle that had to be inspired.

They would not leave until hours later when the British were very close to Lexington, and as they moved away from Lexington and the dangers growing there, they would be able to hear the first shots fired on Lexington Green, and the American Revolution.

Twenty-one mixed British Army companies eventually left Cambridge, ten companies of light infantry and eleven companies of grenadiers. They followed the direct route to Menotomy slicing through the small village nestled between Cambridge and Lexington.

In the lead of the impressive column were the light infantry, and as they marched, they put a bit of distance between themselves and the grenadiers behind them. The light infantry was led by younger lieutenants directing the fast-moving soldiers.

As they traveled, they noticed many Colonial residents watched them pass. It is impossible to hide or keep secret a large body of armed men moving with a purpose. Soon, they would intercept Colonial riders looking for them, and they would also overhear the Colonial residents gossiping about what was waiting for them in Lexington.

There was not a secret to be had or kept on the early morning hours of 19 April 1775.

Before he sent out the 21 companies of mixed infantry and grenadiers, General Gage sent out a dozen British officers on horseback led by Major Edward Mitchell. Major Mitchell and his fellow officers were light infantry men, so they were fast and kept moving about on the road from Cambridge to Concord.

These paroling officers were to keep the roads clear for the advancing column and look out for messengers carrying the alarm that the British Army was marching in-force into the countryside. Remarkably, these patrols encountered many of the messengers and scouts who were sent by the Colonials to find the marching British column.

The patrolling British officers stopped three men riding between Lexington and Concord. William Dawes saw the British officers and turned back to Lexington. Dr. Samuel Prescott, familiar with his surrounding, galloped his horse into a field and on to Concord. Paul Revere was captured.

Revere could not afford to be captured. He was losing time that was needed to spread the alarm. He also had to get back to Lexington and make sure Hancock and Adams fled to safety out of the reach of the British Army that was slowly and steadily descending onto Lexington. Paul Revere told the British officers who were tentatively holding him:

"...*because of the delay* [British leaving Cambridge late] *500 Provincials would soon be in Lexington.* "[xxiv]

Revere's wild exaggeration was expressed to alarm his captors into releasing him. It worked, but it had far-reaching consequences for the men who defended Lexington Green. The British officers immediately rode for Lexington to find the advancing light infantry and warn them that Lexington was a trap.

Lieutenants William Sutherland, Jesse Adair, and William Grant were the mounted young lieutenants at the front of Smith's Column. They had captured some of the scouts sent out of Lexington by the Militia leader, Captain John Parker. With each scout captured, Parker and his men remained blind to the

British position. But it was eye opening for the young British lieutenants riding toward Lexington.

Lexington, the young Lieutenants were told by residents they encountered on the road, was a gathering place of many Militiamen, waiting for the British army. As they got closer to Lexington, the young British officers heard wild estimates that, 500 or 600 or maybe 1,000 men were armed and waiting for them in Lexington.

These wild rumors were disturbing to the young leaders, but when one of Major Mitchell's patrolling officers stopped them and told them what Paul Revere had claimed a short while ago; they halted the column. With the British officers telling them this valuable intelligence, the entire narrative had changed.

Were they marching into a trap? Were the other stories, and more exaggerated numbers closer to the truth? Were they to be ambushed and massacred in this wild, savage place? The column was halted, and they called for their superior officer to hear what was waiting for them in Lexington.

Major John Pitcairn was the man in charge of the 200 men in the lead of the Column. Pitcairn was told of the large force waiting just a half mile away. And Lieutenant Sutherland told Pitcairn of the stories they had heard from the rebel scouts they captured on the road toward Lexington. Sutherland lastly told Pitcairn, a Colonial on horseback lowered his musket and pulled the trigger. It failed to fire but reinforced that the column was in danger.

Pitcairn through his young Lieutenants:

"Ordered his men to load, fix bayonets and move forward... but on no account to fire...without orders"[xxv]

If they were to be ambushed, they would be ready to fight. They were one step closer to Samuel Adams' moment.

Marching into Lexington, British soldiers fully expected to engage a massive mob of uncontrollable, armed, rebellious Colonials. Their adrenaline was up, their guns loaded, and their bayonets fixed, walking one beside the other, holding their formation as they approached Lexington.

Theirs was just the right mixture of courage and fear, of known and unknown, wanted and unwanted, life or death waiting just a short distance down an old colonial road, on a cold spring morning. The sun was rising, and the temperament of six companies of British soldiers was up as they marched toward Lexington Green.

The advance units were instructed to bear right by the zealous young Lieutenants. The column of soldiers suddenly turned off the road to Concord and onto the road to Bedford, beside Lexington Green. Marine Major John Pitcairn rode his horse, and quickly arrived and assessed the developing situation.

There was not 1000, 600, or 500 men on Lexington Green. But there was a small body of armed men who were gathered, and they were being watched by every window and door, from around houses and barns, over stone walls and behind trees.

Many residents had assembled to watch what was next for their beloved fathers, husbands, brothers, family and friends. Amongst those watching was the Reverend Jonas Clarke. From this moment on, it was the veteran John Pitcairn who was in charge of the British forces marching onto the Green.

Major John Pitcairn was born in Fife, Scotland in 1722. Fife is a rugged coastal area of the Scottish Lowlands, just north of Edinburgh. A place where the difficult and dangerous work of coal mining was one way to survive, a life unsuitable for John Pitcairn.

He chose to become a Marine, an elite seaborne British soldier. He spent nearly all of his adult life building a successful and distinguished career in His Majesty's Marines. His son William was also a Marine, and one of the 600 Marines under Major Pitcairn's command in Boston. Major Pitcairn had another son, Robert who served the crown in the Royal Navy.

Young Robert Pitcairn would discover an unknown island one morning when he was on watch for the Royal Navy in the Pacific Ocean. The unknown island appeared over the horizon, and it was named Pitcairn's Island, in honor of the man who first sighted it.

History would find Pitcairn's Island when a British Royal Navy ship washed ashore one day. On board that ship was the mutinous crew of the *HMS Bounty*. They beached and burned their ship on the shores of Pitcairn Island.

In April of 1775, Major John Pitcairn was well-liked and respected by his fellow officers, soldiers, and the tory residents of Boston. On the morning of Wednesday, 19 April 1775, Major Pitcairn was not commanding his Marines in Lexington. He was assigned to command six companies, the advance units of Colonel Smith's column. It was Pitcairn's sterling reputation that caused his superiors to select him for the day's secret and important mission to Concord. But in the process of selecting the Major they did not select his elite troops, and the Marines were left in barracks in Boston. It was a serious oversight.

In Lexington, a most critical time and place, John Pitcairn commanded a group of light infantry soldiers, with loaded guns, and racing heart rates. He did not know them, and they did not know him. But all knew they may be in mortal danger.

From his horse, Major Pitcairn ordered the militia men to throw down their arms and disperse. He ordered his men to hold fire, riding across the field he shouted at *America's First Soldiers*, demanding them—*"disperse, throw down your arms and disperse."* He fully understood he was a breath away from a disaster.

Some accounts describe the British Regulars on Lexington Green, as out of sync with their officers that early Wednesday morning. Soldiers bond with their commanding officers, forming a mutual alliance of respect and confidence.

Men facing other armed men need to be familiar, certain and having no doubts in the man commanding them into danger, and at sunrise on that April morning a commander and his men were strangers. The unfamiliarity amongst the British ranks with Pitcairn and he unfamiliar with them was exactly what was not needed at that on a cold spring morning, as the sun rose on history warming the faces of *America's First Soldiers,* defying the world's most powerful army.

It was the poor judgement of many in the British Government, and military that pushed Lieutenant Colonel Smith into the history books beginning as his troops formed on Lexington Green, exactly where they should not have been.

Chapter II
Lexington Green

"Stand your ground; don't fire unless fired upon, but if they mean to have a war, let it begin here."[xxvi]

Captain John Parker
Lexington Green 19 April 1775

Across from the unfamiliar was the very familiar gathered on Lexington Green. Eighty-one local Militiamen had answered the alarm on this early spring morning. Amongst their ranks were farmers, shop keepers, blacksmiths, not a single professional soldier. They were friends and family gathered to protect each other as they had for generations. The group of *America's First Soldiers* included:

4 named *Locke*, 4 named *Brown*, 10 named *Smith*, 11 named *Harrington*, 14 named *Munroe*, and they were commanded by one of four named *Parker*— Captain John Parker.[xxvii]

The time for words was over. Whether spoken by the politicians or from the pulpits of the churches from Boston to Lexington, the time for words was over. The glorious hopes of politicians were a dim memory as *America's First Soldiers* turned out before sunrise on Wednesday morning, 19 April 1775.

John Hancock and Samuel Adams were not on the Lexington Green as the sun rose on 19 April 1775. Their parts had been performed so well that the British army with all of its power and might, marched onto Lexington Green, a place it should not have been.

The men who gathered on Lexington Green were not politicians, they were ordinary citizens, and they had little to gain and everything to lose. They lined up as they had a hundred times before, with no complaints. The line that began on the Lexington Green that morning has stretched for nearly 250 years, and still protects the lives and liberties of Americans. As the overwhelming British force marched onto the Green, *America's First Soldiers* stood peacefully in position, on their Green.

Forty-five-year-old, Captain John Parker was a farmer born in Lexington. He like so many men in Massachusetts was a lifetime member of a militia company comprised of local citizen soldiers. John Parker had risen to the rank of captain and was the commander of the Lexington Militia company on April 19.

Parker had served with elite forces—*Roger's Rangers* during the seven-year *French and Indian War* (1754–63). Captain Parker answered the call to arms for his family, property and the town he had called home his entire life. Yet, he answered the call as a very sick man, Captain John Parker was dying of the infectious disease Tuberculosis. He would be dead in less than five months.

Very early, hours before the British arrived, Captain John Parker and many of his militia company gathered together on the town green, their muster field. They assembled at the alarm that the Regulars were marching toward Lexington. The Militiamen had been called to action by the famous midnight rides of Paul Revere, William Dawes, and Dr. Joseph Prescott.

The three riders warned the countryside:

"The Regulars are coming!" The countryside was alive as ever-increasing groups of residents from Cambridge to Concord turned out to answer the alarm.

When Parker and his men first turned out, it was between midnight and 1:00 in the morning. The Reverend Clarke in his remembrances of the events wrote:

Between the hours of twelve and one on the morning of the 19 of April, we received intelligence...that a large body of the King's troops...[1200–1500] were embarked in boats in Boston and had gone over to land on Lechmere's Point [Cambridge] and it was shrewdly expected they were to seize and destroy the stores, belonging to the Colony than stored in Concord...Upon this intelligence...the militia of this town [Lexington] *were alarmed and ordered to meet at the usual place of parade...not with any design of commencing hostilities but to consult as to what might be done for our own and the people's safety...in case of overt acts of violence or open hostilities should be committed by this mercenary band of armed and blood thirsty oppressors."*

Opening of the war of the revolution,
19th of April 1775. A brief narrative
of the principal transactions of that day

Clark, Jonas, (1730–1805)
Page 4.

Between 3:00 and 4:00 a Colonial messenger returned to Lexington claiming that there were no British soldiers on the road to Lexington. That of course was in direct opposition to what all the other riders and messengers had declared. Captain Parker did not fully trust what he had been told. Lexington Militiaman Nathaniel Mulliken recalled those fateful hours:

"[we] *were dismissed by our captain, John Parker, for the present, with orders to be ready to attend at the beat of the drum."*[xxviii]

In the hours that passed between Paul Revere's arrival, and the arrival of the greatly delayed British Regulars John Parker had much time to think. And he had much time to share his thoughts, and garner the thoughts of his most trusted advisor, Reverend Jonas Clarke.

One can imagine Captain Parker who is very ill, yet his illness is secondary to his duty of protecting his family, friends, and town. His very life is being threatened, as reports were filtering in of the immensely inordinate force of 1,200 to 1,500 British soldiers on the march.

Although that number is a remarkable exaggeration, Parker did not know that, and he believed his situation was breathtaking in its perilous uncertainty. As his fellow soldiers rested waiting for the British, Parker would have the time to consult Clarke, Hancock and Adams. Captain Parker gave a sworn statement on April 25, just six days after the battle of Lexington:

"[I] was informed that a number of Regular Troops were on their march from Boston in order to take the Province stores at Concord, [I] ordered our militia to meet on the common in said Lexington, to consult what to do, and concluded not to be discovered, nor meddle or make with said Regular Troops...unless they should insult us..."[xxix]

In the center of this deadly drama were the odd couple of Massachusetts politics, the driving voices of revolution—John Hancock and Samuel Adams. Hancock saw opportunity in Lexington. He was suddenly in the place where he could become the equal of his military heroes, his Colonel father and Colonel grandfather.

He spent parts of the night preparing his sword and gun for the action that was certain would unfold shortly. Here was his moment to shine in a battle, lined up with his fellow Patriots against the mighty British army. His opportunity for vain, heroic, glorious existence was close enough to taste. But his friend Samuel Adams had other plans for the dreamy eyed, glory seeking, John Hancock.

Adams would never let Hancock walk onto a battlefield, and before the firing began, Adams had himself and Hancock whisked away by carriage in the direction of Bedford. But before he departed, the master manipulator did all he could to provide that the two sides would be armed, agitated, and face to face.

This was the fertile situation Adams had wished for, a historical moment where one side could, and would blame the other, and incite men to go to war. So often, wars require a moment, a definable event that damns one as aggressor, allowing a full retaliatory response from the damaged party. American history since Lexington is full of such moments.

Lincoln had his moment when recently seceded South Carolina fired on Union soldiers occupying Fort Sumter in Charleston Harbor. It was 12 April 1861 and the destruction of the fort gave Lincoln his moment. In a few short weeks, the US was locked into a bitter, destructive, devastating Civil War that nearly ended our country's existence. William McKinley had his moment when the *USS Maine* sunk in Havana Harbor on 15 February 1898, leading to the Spanish-American War.

Woodrow Wilson was handed his moment when the unarmed passenger liner, RMS Lusitania, carrying weapons and supplies of war to Great Britain was sunk by a German submarine on 15 May 1915. That moment pulled the US into, The Great War—World War I. And Roosevelt's moment came when the *"dastardly and unprovoked"* bombing of Pearl Harbor galvanized the US into World War II on 7 December 1941. Moments, defined by their simple virtues, have always been needed to bring us to war.

The very moment Samuel Adams departed Lexington, the moment he had waited for most of his life was just moments away. Adams knew his voice and Hancock's voice could take what was about to happen and incite a war of independence. So, with the aid of Paul Revere, Hancock and Adams fled for their personal safety just as Major Pitcairn's troops marched onto Lexington Green.

Amongst those British soldiers marching onto the Green was, Lieutenant John Barker of the famed 4th Regiment of Foot, or *"The King's Own."* Barker recalled that the night was full of delays, and they were late leaving Cambridge, and therefore late approaching Lexington. But more troubling was what the young Lieutenant had heard – disturbing news from ordinary citizens as the British marched closer to Lexington.

"...about 5 miles on this side of a town called Lexington...we heard that here were some hundreds of People collected together intending to oppose us and stop our going on"[xxx]

The British march continued toward Lexington, giving the young Lieutenant and his fellow soldiers much to be apprehensive about.

Just passed 4:30, news reached Captain Parker that the British were only a half mile or so away. William Diamond a 16-year-old drummer in the Lexington Militia, stood bravely on the Green and beat his drum, heralding that the time had come for assembly.

America's First Soldiers answered that lonely drum beat and converged onto the Green. As they were gathering, a sea of dangerous men in red coats with rifles holding shinny steel bayonets marched into their town. The Lexington men gathered together and stood side by side as they had for generations.

The British troops could not believe any man had the nerve to gather before them. But the British army had never met *America's First Soldiers*. Lieutenant Barker recalled the British march onto the Green:

"At 5:00 we arrived there and saw a number of people; I believe between 200–300 formed in a Common in the middle of the Town; we still continued advancing keeping prepared against an attack..."[xxxi]

Captain Parker certainly was aware that a large, well-armed, and very dangerous group of professional soldiers was bearing down on his peaceful town. The Reverend Clarke expressed the following:

"...the drum beat to arms...the Militia were collecting together...In the meantime, the troops having thus stolen a march upon us...seemed to come determined for murder and bloodshed...provoked to it or not...the command was given to prime and load..."[xxxii]

Overwhelmingly outnumbered, Captain Parker and his family, friends, and fellow soldiers gathered on the Green. Fear was not to be displayed this day. The Lexington men and their leader had gathered in a peaceful formation, they were not on the road and not impeding the British.

The roadway from Lexington to Concord was open to travel, that was an important distinction in the eyes of the gathered Lexington men. But it was the formation itself that was a bold statement to the British traveling to Concord.

The assembly of the Lexington Militia was in defiance of a King, his unjust laws, and the powerful invading army the King sent to keep his subjects repressed. This gathering of armed locals could not be tolerated by the irritated British, they had many miles and hours remaining on their days work.

Believing themselves to be greatly outnumbered, and fearing an ambush awaited them, the King's soldiers marched onto the Green. The assembly was all the British needed to show the residents and Militiamen tolerance was not on their orders of search and destroy.

The Lexington men were a ragtag lot, and they possessed none of the intimidating presence of the British Regulars. The Lexington men watched as Major Pitcairn and other officers on horseback led the British Soldiers into formation. Their drummers loudly beat the cadence and the well-disciplined army moved off the road and onto the village Green.

They moved as one, shoulder to shoulder, row in front of row, each Regular carried a musket, now loaded and primed and a shining steel bayonet. A stunning demonstration of military power.

The outward appearance of these well-armed, equipped, and trained British soldiers was an impressive site in Colonial America. But looking closer at the British soldiers one can find a striking difference between what they looked like and in many cases who they actually were.

The reputation earned by British soldiers for over one hundred years before that march onto Lexington Green preceded them that April morning. Seen as enemies of personal freedoms, the red coated soldiers represented the repression and tyranny many Colonial immigrants had escaped in England, Scotland, and Ireland.

Most British soldiers in Colonial America were not young recruits, but men between twenty and twenty-five years old. The British Army experienced great difficulties filling their ranks by 1775, according to Professor Edward E. Curtis:

"...the crown employed two methods of obtaining men. The first of these was voluntary enlistment...A second method of obtaining soldiers was by pardoning...Vagrants, smugglers, and criminals of various kinds...Even deserters...were to be pardoned..."[xxxiii]

During the eight-year *War of American Independence* by some estimates, nearly ten percent of Regulars deserted. A high rate of failures in their civilian lives had led to a disproportionate number of discontented men to join the British army. It was written of the British Soldier in the 18th century:

"A messmate before a shipmate, a shipmate before a stranger, a stranger before a dog, a dog before a soldier."[xxxiv]

Such men were amongst those soldiers the experienced Major Pitcairn was commanding. As he led his troops onto Lexington Green what was in the good Major's heart? Leading this group of well-armed and determined British soldiers, Pitcairn had his own feelings about the men who lived in Colonial America. More specifically he had strong feelings for the Colonials who had caused him to be posted in Boston less than five months ago.

As he watched his charges march onto the Green, was Pitcairn thinking what he had recently written to a fellow officer about the Colonials?

"I assure you...I have so despicable an opinion of the people of this country that I would not hesitate to march with the Marines I have with me to any part of this country, and do whatever I was inclined. I am satisfied they will never attack regular troops."[xxxv]

Just before five o'clock in the morning, with loaded and primed muskets, rising heart rates, souls full of contempt, and minds bent on surviving what may be a trap, the British Regulars and their officers lined up on Lexington Green.

Across the Green that morning, were the hard-working citizen soldiers of a local militia. Volunteers devoted through generations of families, men of unflagging courage and commitment. Faithful as always, the men around Lexington answered the call, arriving with only their hunting muskets, powder-horns, and pockets of lead shot.

They had no uniforms, no horses, or bayonets, only the courage to stand before the world's most powerful army understanding all its predictable fury.

Watching the determined, professional army that marched onto the green Captain Parker quickly deducted his militiamen were no match for the mass of Red Coats standing across from his humble force. Parker and his men stood cautiously before the orderly line of red coated soldiers, not wanting to express a desire for conflict. They recognized that the British arrived with loaded guns and fixed bayonets, a very unusual event for men marching.

Major Pitcairn quickly processed that he was not surrounded by 500, 600, or 1,000 armed and angry men. He was facing a peaceful gathering of eighty men. Pitcairn tried to defuse the fears, apprehensions, and racing heart of men he did not know.

Riding toward Captain Parker and his men, desperate to stop the event he knew was a breath away, Pitcairn wielded his sword, moved his horse furiously, and shouted:

"Ye villains, ye rebels disperse; Dam you disperse! Lay down your arms; Why don't you Lay [sic] *down your arms!*[xxxvi]

The peaceful Lexington men gazed across the narrow Green and locked stares with their foreign, combative countrymen. Earlier, as the Red Coats marched into Lexington, Captain Parker had ordered his men:

"Stand your ground; don't fire unless fired upon, but if they mean to have a war, let it begin here."[xxxvii]

But as the minutes and images before him cascaded together he understood how feeble his well-meaning forces, and his well-meaning words had become. Greatly outnumbered, by a modern well-armed force, Parker turned to his soldiers, friends, and family desperately shouting with a voice compromised by his worsening tuberculosis.

He was hoping to avoid the carnage. He was surrounded with a whirlwind of fear and excitement. The last exhausting seconds of a life and death moment filled the air and hearts of the soldiers.

Parker shouted with all he could muster; he was after all a man with a fatal lung disease. Robbed of the breath, he needed to loudly shout his commands, Parker shouted— *"Disperse!"*

Not many moved, and those that did moved resentfully. The Lexington men had assembled as free British Colonial citizens. Their peaceful assembly guaranteed by British law, it was their last act as English citizens. They would stand, and some would die as their first act as *America's First soldiers*

Tensions which had been building for years reached the breaking point, as the British Regulars had wheeled into attack formation. Lieutenant Barker recalled in his diary:

"...on our coming near them, they fired one or two shots, upon which our Men without any orders, rushed in upon them and fired, and put them to flight..."[xxxviii]

It was too late.

One gun fired, the sound expected and yet perverse. Then many guns fired, framing the last minutes of the Colonial era in Massachusetts. Historical accounts do not report definitively who fired the first shot. Each side claiming innocence while pointing a finger of damnation toward the other. Reverend Clarke was a witness to the attack and swore:

[a British Lieutenant] *fired a pistol toward the militia as they were dispersing...brandishing his sword, pointing toward them with a loud voice said to the troops, "Fire! —By God fire!"*[xxxix]

A volley of thick white smoke, thunderous noises, and flying lead shot brought injury and death. In the split second it takes to burn gunpowder in a musket, British American Colonial citizens, and British Regular Army soldiers had crossed from the real to the surreal.

The unthinkable had occurred to the unprepared as surely as the gun smoke faded, carried off by the light spring breezes. The gathered, and the participants on each side must have held the thought—what have we done?

Unknowingly or not those men on Lexington Green were the end of the beginning as thoughts became words, words became actions, actions became battle, and battle became death, and death brought war. The Colonial era was ended by a small group of determined men on Lexington Green.

When the gunfire ended, stillness did not descend upon Lexington, rather, more primitive violence emerged as the unrestrained, enraged, British soldiers attacked with their bayonets. Those militiamen not wounded, fled to safety as the Red Coats moved to finish off their dear rebellious countrymen.

A critical, condemning, mistake had been made by the British Army that fateful April morning. A mistake that still resonates thru three centuries of American History. Shooting at your fellow citizens is one thing that had occurred at the *Boston Massacre*.

But to lose agitated men with bayonets, against wounded, and undefendable, soldiers was an act of murder. Lieutenant Barker wrote of British soldiers on Lexington Green just after the shooting:

"Men were so wild, they could hear no orders."[xl]

Lexington's citizen soldiers included just a few who managed to fire on Major Pitcairn's six companies, or over 200 soldiers of the light Infantry. When it ended Lexington counted seven dead, nine wounded, and one captured. Three named *Munroe* fell, two named *Harrington* fell, one of them died at his own front doorstep.

His shooting and crawling to his death were witnessed by his wife and very young son. One *Parker* fell wounded, only to be ran-through by a cold-blooded British bayonet. Amongst the nine wounded was *Prince Estabrook*, an enslaved Blackman.

The extraordinary carnage resulting from British Soldiers firing on and bayoneting British citizens in Colonial America on Lexington Green was memorialized by Lt. Colonel Smith. Writing his after-action report, Smith who was not present during the fighting relied on the accounts of others. Lt. Colonel Smith wrote to General Gage on April 22:

"I detached six light infantry companies to march with all expedition… these companies' arrival at Lexington…found on a green close to the road a body of the country people drawn up in military order with arms and accoutrements and, as appeared after, loaded…As our troops advanced toward them without any intention of injuring them further than to inquire the reason of their being thus assembled…one of them fired before he went off and three or four more jumped over a wall and fired from behind it among the soldiers, on which the troops returned it and killed several of them."

Lt. Colonel Smith witnessed only the result of the violent exchange between his soldiers and the Lexington Militia. Things had not gone as Gage's orders instructed. The man in charge of the light infantry as they marched onto Lexington Green, Respected Marine Major John Pitcairn reported to General Gage in writing dated April 26, 1775:

"without any order or regularity, the Light Infantry began a scattered fire, and continued in that situation for some little time, contrary to the repeated orders both of me and the officers that were present."[xli]

How badly Major John Pitcairn needed his elite, familiar Marines in Lexington. But they had been kept in barracks by the wisdom of General Thomas Gage.

The first encounter between the British army and a badly outnumbered small militia force on that fateful day ended with death, destruction, and murder. The Colonials were already labeling it a massacre. Lt. Colonel Smith immediately sent a rider back with a dispatch to General Gage. Lt. Colonel Smith urgently requested reinforcements be sent to him immediately.

Smith knew what had happened; Smith knew he and his command were dammed by an entire countryside aroused and enflamed by a massacre on Lexington Green.

When the message arrived in Boston it was sent to the respected commander of the Marines, who was not at his desk. The request sat on Major

Pitcairn's empty desk, while he was marching toward Concord. The delay caused by such a simple and avoidable mistake would have serious consequences as the day dragged on, and the fighting escalated. Another mistake on a day of British mistakes.

The blood spilled on Lexington Green, by bullet and bayonet that morning, was used to condemn a King, damn a Parliament, and set an undeniable, unalterable course for war. What was barely a spark of rebellion, had become an uncontrollable flame of revolution.

Wondering why, as many have for 245 years, Captain Parker insisted on assembling his meager force on the Green opposite an overwhelming force of heavily armed, determined, anxious, loaded musket toting, and bayonet wielding professional soldiers. I come back always to Samuel Adams. Adams wanted and needed his moment, and he understood that Lexington offered him the best chance to get what he had to have to continue his drive for independence.

He needed a tragedy that was more compelling than the Boston Massacre, a drama in real time with countless witnesses. With faces and names to be memorialized, and grieved. Victims of an aggressive, overwhelming British Army invading, conquering, attacking, unprovoked citizens of a quaint New England town. Samuel Adams had his moment.

Professor Allen French (1870–1946) was a Concord resident, a noted author, researcher and historian. A professor at Harvard College and the Massachusetts Institute of Technology. He wrote a number of books on the American Revolution, specializing on events in Massachusetts. Professor French wrote of Samuel Adams:

"The ultimate solution was independence...no one had considered independence possible except Samuel Adams...he worked for it in secret preparing men's minds for the grand change...According to a Tory accusation...Adams confessed that the independence of the colonies had been the great opportunity of his life...and had neglected no opportunity neither in public or private of preparing the way for independence."[xlii]

They were not far out of Lexington when the shooting started. And it was over in just a few minutes. They heard one shot, two shots, and then many shots. From their hideout in a quiet wooded area, John Hancock and Samuel

Adams understood those shots represented the life and death struggle that was unfolding not far from them.

A moment of uncontrolled violence, it was the struggle Samuel Adams so dearly needed, yet he did not know how dearly it was bought, the price paid in blood by the sons of Lexington. He did not know what was happening, but he knew he had his narrative to continue to preach revolution and independence.

"For Adams it was an hour of triumph. The British had fired first; the Americans had "Put the enemy in the wrong;" The two sides were committed; conciliation was no longer possible. As the sun rose there came from him one of the few exalted outbursts of his life:
"What a glorious morning is this!"[xliii]

The sun continued to rise on that historic morning. On Lexington Green, only one British soldier was wounded, and the officers quickly ordered their soldiers to assemble and prepare to march to Concord. There would be no opportunity for the Regulars to loot the town of Lexington.

The Red Coats fired a victory volley believing the fighting had ended. However, it was not an ending, it was just the beginning of a day that would stir the patriotic hearts and souls of thousands of Colonial Militiamen, who gathered and fought as—*America's First Soldiers.*

Chapter III
Concord
Part 1
A Noble Appearance

"Their flag to April's breeze unfurled,
Here once the embattled farmers stood,
And fired the shot heard round the world."[xliv]
Ralph Waldo Emerson (1803–82)
Concord Hymn, 1837

It was no surprise that the British were marching into Concord. Paul Revere, William Dawes, and Dr. Samuel Prescott all left Lexington very early on April 19, 1775, for Concord. They shouted the alarm to every house they passed, calling to arms *America's First Soldiers* on the road to Concord.

Suddenly, the mobile alarm squad ran into a group of British Officers out on patrol. Revere was captured but managed to talk and bluff his way into release. The British kept his horse, and he made his way on foot back to Lexington. Dawes and Prescott managed to get away and both eventually made it to Concord, pressing to the residents' word of the advancing British Regulars.

The alarms to gather the Concord Militiamen and Minutemen were sounded just after 1:00 in the morning. The British would not be in Lexington for nearly four hours.

The Concord Militiamen like their Lexington brethren gathered as they had whenever the alarm sounded. After the initial alarm was raised by Dawes and Prescott, the Reverend William Emerson, member of the alarm committee, grandfather of the famous author and Concord resident Ralph Waldo Emerson arrived early his musket in hand.

A month before that fateful April morning, on 13 March 1775, the fiery Reverend Emerson, a dedicated Patriot, preached to his Concord congregation of the righteousness of their struggle against the tyrannical British King and his occupying army. Emerson quoted from, Chronicles 2 13–12 (King James Bible) in his fiery sermon:

"Behold God himself is with us for our captain, and his priest with surrounding trumpets, to cry alarm against you."[xlv]

The Reverend rang the bell finishing what Dawes and Prescott had begun. Revered Emerson on that cold early morning of 19 April 1775, called his flock and all of *America's First Soldiers* in Concord. The town was soon to be full of red-coated devils—the day of Emerson's holy battle was dawning.

Concord's Militia met at the familiar site near the center of town, the field beside Wright's Tavern. The officers that had gathered in the early morning hours immediately dispatched some of the troops to continue to hide the war supplies in Concord, the known target of the British advance on Concord.

They also sent a rider out to Lexington, and as the hours faded away news came to Concord, both accurate, and inaccurate of the violence in Lexington. And as the Minutemen and Militiamen came to Concord from all the surrounding towns, they brought the stories they had heard—both accurate and wildly inaccurate.

In the early morning hours, with the knowledge that the British were advancing to Concord, Major John Buttrick, second in overall command led three companies of Militiamen out of Concord to meet the 700 advancing Regulars.

Major John Buttrick's ancestors came to Massachusetts Colony from England. Buttrick was born in Concord, so was his father, and his father's father. The Buttrick family was part of the very fabric of Concord and owned successful farms.

The Buttrick family had been in Concord since the founding of the town in 1635. When a group of English Puritan immigrants struck a deal with the local native tribe, exchanging goods for the territory of a new settlement. This was done peacefully, and the new settlers called their new home Concord.

According to Mariam-Webster, Concord's meaning is, *a state of agreement: HARMONY.* The town remained peaceful for 140 years, until it was invaded by the British Army on 19 April 1775. Concord was a large farming town, with a large religious base and a deep-rooted connection to community.

Concord had twice the population of Lexington and fielded two militia companies. It had a more developed town center, which included a courthouse. Picturesque Concord was where two smaller rivers became one Larger river, the Concord River. Two bridges cross the Concord River in the town of Concord—North Bridge and South Bridge, so named for their geographic locations.

Concord had also been a temporary meeting place for the Massachusetts Provincial Congress, a local government body General Gage believed he disbanded when he ran them out of Boston. They met secretly in Concord beginning in late March 1775.

Concord was also the site chosen to hide many of the military supplies of the growing rebellious movement in Massachusetts. Concord, like Lexington, had a fiery patriotic spirit, driven by their religious leaders - Emerson in Concord and Clarke in Lexington.

The rolls of the Concord Militiamen and Minutemen held two companies, one more than Lexington. John Buttrick was a Major in the Concord Militia forces, second in command to another venerable old resident, the aging Colonel James Barrett.

The Militia officers gathered upon hearing of the attack on the citizens of Lexington. They chose to defend their beloved town by marching three companies out of town to meet the British head-on.

Amos Barrett was a young Concord resident and Militia Corporal on the morning of 19 April 1775. Barrett fought at Concord, and later at Bunker Hill and at Saratoga, New York where the British suffered a devastating defeat.

Recollecting in 1825, on the fiftieth anniversary of the battle, then Captain Amos Barrett recalled:

"We heard they [British Regulars] *were coming...I was in town and found my captain and the rest of the company at post... We thought we could go out and meet the British... "*[xlvi]

Under the command of Major Buttrick, about two hundred of Concord's Militiamen and Minutemen marched out of the town to meet the advancing

British Regulars. Marching with their drums and fifes Concord's finest began their journey to find the world's most powerful army. They did not have to travel far. Amos Barrett remembered:

We marched out toward Lexington about a mile...and we saw them coming. We halted and stayed till they got about 100 rods [1 rod=16.5' therefore 100 rods=1,650 feet, or 1/3 of a mile] *we were then ordered to about face.* "[xlvii]

The Concord men did an abrupt about face and at once began to march back into town. With their enemies now behind them, they marched with drums and fifes playing as they stayed ahead of the determined men in red coats. It must have been an outlandish sight to behold. In one minute, in one direction they searched for their enemies, in another minute they found their enemies and marched before them, like they were leading them into Concord as conquerors on parade. Barrett finished:

"We marched into town, and over the North Bridge...to a hill not far from the Bridge where we could see and hear what was going on... "[xlviii]

Now a safe distance from the marching British army, Amos Barrett saw what others saw, that the British march into Concord was a display of power that shook some colonial residents to their core.

Seven hundred soldiers, all dressed and armed alike, moving in unison with flags flying, many drums beating, while the high pitch of fifes guided the nearly quarter mile long column of red coated soldiers. Thaddeus Blood was a member of the Concord Militia, and remembered the British marching into Concord:

"[we] saw the British troops a coming...the sun was arising and shined on their arms and they made a noble appearance in their red coats and gliding arms – we retreated in order over the top of the hill..."

The story of Patriot's Day,
Lexington and Concord 19 April 1775
George J. Varney (1836–1901) Page 84

A noble appearance, recalled Thaddeus, he was not far off. Officers, with beautiful redcoats, had white lace shirtsleeves extending beyond their red cuffed coats with shinning brass buttons against a narrow band of light tan color. They had black felt hats that gently sloped, outlined in fine gold piping at each end. And their beautiful hats each had a black knotted ribbon known as a cockade.

The black cockade was tied into place with more elegant gold piping, the cockade's presence was a symbol of Great Britain's ruling monarch, King George III. Their distinct hats fit perfectly over their trimmed pony-tailed hair tied with another black ribbon behind their heads. Gold frilly epaulets crowned one shoulder, ending as the deep scarlet sleeve followed the arm to the lace cuff.

Each officer had a narrow black sash like a scarf tied around the neck of their bleach white, beautiful high collared shirts. At their waist hung a three-foot sword, sharp enough to kill a man with one blow. A white belt held up their clean white breaches ending at the knee to an even whiter sock that filled those shiny black boots. They were imposing as well as majestic.

Such a spectacle of power had never been displayed in Concord. Even the Militiamen gathering on the hills and ridges near town were impressed with such military splendor. The long train stretched quite a distance with the soldiers marching abreast, all-in step, row after orderly row.

The enlisted men of the light infantry and grenadiers sported their faded redcoats, with wide cuffs and wide-open lapels, exposing a dusty white waist coat. They had cartridge boxes, all alike filled with plentiful ammunition on their white bandolier straps crisscrossing that trademark redcoat.

On their shoulder were long brown muskets, that fired a .75 Caliber or a lead ball 3/4" round, it was nearly five foot in length, including a nearly four-foot-long barrel. A well-trained Regular could fire his weapon at least three times a minute, and some men could fire up to six times a minute.

Attached to this state-of-the-art musket was a sixteen-inch shiny, sharp, bayonet, that would run a man through with nearly no resistance. They were more than soldiers as they marched into Concord. They were harbingers, their presence a moving omen of death and destruction looking for *America's First Soldiers.*

The Colonial Militiamen did not have cartridges, they used powder horns to pour the gunpowder into the musket firing pan and barrel, then inserted a long rod and tamped down the powder and lead shot. The process was cumbersome, time consuming and could cost a soldier his life on the battlefield.

The British soldiers had paper cartridges that contained the proper amount of gun powder and the lead ball wrapped tightly in white paper. The British soldier bit open the paper, filled the firing pan, near the flint, just above the trigger, then turned the gun upright and poured the remaining gun powder down the barrel.

Next came the bullet, or shot as they were called, and then the paper was inserted and compressed with a ramming rod into the gun barrel to hold the powder and shot in place. They were drilled to do this three times a minute under fire.

Everything about the British army that marched into Concord was impressive, modern, and designed to intimidate an enemy. They were the land based conquers of the World's largest most powerful empire of the 17th and 18th centuries. On 19 April 1775 Concord, Massachusetts was invaded by the all-powerful British army.

A recent emigrant of the inequity of life in England had arrived in Concord and settled as a country farmer. This new immigrant came to Concord and settled he thought far away from the tyranny of life in 18th century Britain. This newcomer watched the British advance into town, and decided to talk to his neighbors as to why they were there.

He approached a British officer and after a rather quick conversation walked away from the British Officer and walked away from his new neighbors. He was going home. That was the power the British portrayed as they invaded Concord. They were invincible. Reverend William Emerson also witnessed the spectacle and wrote:

"...we saw the British (sic) troops, at the Distance of a 1/4 Mile, glistening Arms, advancing toward [us] *with the greatest celerity."*[xlix]

Not all residents of Colonial Americans were as impressed as the newly arrived Englishman, and the long-settled reverend.

The stern roughly dressed Colonials had no uniforms, no pomp or pageantry to display. They knew each other, and sometimes that fact went back generations. They were what General Thomas Gage fully understood them to be—men who were little impressed by the sight of other armed men.

As Gage feared, the impact of the bold statement he made by marching into their towns, villages, farms and homes only stiffened the resolve of the men defending life, property and liberty.

Gage had been told just a month before he executed his march to Concord what was in Concord and in one case where. He rightly figured an armed rebellion is a lot less impactful when they have no: gunpowder, lead shot, artillery shells, and cannons. Gage believed his spies who told him:

"Four Brass Cannon and two Mortars, or Cohorns [sic] *with a Number of small arms in the cellar or out houses of Mr. Barrett* [Colonel James Barrett] *...and a quantity of powder and lead..."*[1]

Gage knew he had to disarm his growing enemy, and that required soldiers marching to Concord. But he did not want what had already occurred, an armed exchange with the Colonials resulting in civilian deaths.

His decision to follow the orders he received from Lord Dartmouth, and act aggressively were manifesting his greatest fears outside his low limited control miles away in Boston. Lord Dartmouth's orders, General Gage's plan, Lt. Colonel Smith's execution of the march to Concord did as much as any other event to ignite the spark that became an out-of-control conflict that led to American Independence.

As the British marched into Concord, they drew the unescapable conclusion that hundreds of militiamen were swarming in and around Concord. The site of his Majesty's Regulars did not deter most Concord men, in fact it attracted these humble colonial fighters.

They kept arriving and mustering with other unimpressed, angry local militia groups. The British officers and the more seasoned Regulars knew they were being quickly surrounded and greatly outnumbered. They were also realizing that the Colonials still held some of the high ground all around them. Concord is a town of small hills and long ridges, unlike the flatness of Lexington.

Lt. Colonel Smith, and Major Pitcairn knew they needed the high ground, and proceeded to take a number of elevated positions in the town. The gathering Militiamen peacefully retreated from their high ground, smartly keeping out of musket range from the Regulars. At the North Bridge an ever-increasing group of Militiamen still held some high ground.

Despite being steadily surrounded Smith split his forces into three groups. Smith and Pitcarin stayed in town with the largest contingent. Another group moved a short distance out of town and crossed the old North Bridge. Once over the bridge the commanding officer further divided his forces sending half his three companies' men to Barrett's Farm to look for rebel war materials.

The last group went to the South Bridge, where nothing happened. The purpose of sending troops to the South Bridge was to defend the river crossing from any perspective Colonial aggression. Once his 700-man force was split into three smaller groups, Lt. Colonel Smith, and his other officers were keenly aware that the smaller groups were becoming easily outnumbered with the gathering local militias.

The group sent to Barrett's Farm and the group that held Concord center immediately searched for any rebel materials of war that was after all the reason they had left Boston. The methods employed by the British Soldiers in some cases were less than hospitable to their fellow countrymen. The express purpose of their march to Concord was a search and destroy mission, it had begun.

They disrupted homes, businesses, farms, and barns as they vigorously worked to yield pleasing results for their commanding officers. At the farm of Colonel James Barrett, the sixty-four-year-old Concord Militia commander, the Regulars pressed as hard as they could to find what they were told was there.

Colonel James Barrett was born and lived in the house his father built. It was just about two miles out of Concord center and required that you cross the North Bridge to get there. Barrett managed a large and successful farm, the third generation of his family to work and live in Concord.

Barrett was also one of over a dozen slave holders in Concord [li] He owned a fourteen-year-old slave named Phillip who worked the farm. Hard to believe that the peaceful, liberty embracing town that would give us *Transcendentalism*, and the notable authors: *Alcott, Emerson, Hawthorne* and *Thoreau*, had slave owners amongst its residents.

In 1775, Concord like Boston was a place where outraged Colonial residents fought against British tyranny while maintaining their own despotism as owners of fellow human beings. A stark reminder of our human imperfections, and the restrictive negotiated limits inherent in the flawed American Revolution.

As the morning of 19 April 1775 was waning, the British hoped to find four valuable bronze cannons and other war materials General Gage's spies told him were hiding at Barrett's Farm. Gage's information was correct, but the Concord militia had taken great pains to hide the cannons and war supplies. And as the British searched the Barrett farm, they had to deal with Mrs. Rebekah Barrett who was every bit the patriot as her husband the Colonel.

Colonel Barrett encouraged his wife to leave the farm. She would not. Rebekah Barrett greeted the British Officers directly and cautioned them to remember they were on *"private property."* Private property ownership in Colonial America was very different then back in England, where vast tracks of land were held by the gentrified Dukes, and Lords with royal connections.

In Massachusetts Bay Colony, a great deal of property was held by working class men who owned farms and shops in towns and villages of Colonial New England.

Many Colonial men were property owners and fiercely defended their liberties as such. They had braved the dangerous Atlantic crossing, and faced the deadly enemies of man and beast that could be found in the wilderness.

The *New World* held such a grand distinction for many Colonials, as they sought the unthinkable destination of being a property owner. That is the single greatest variance as to why the American Revolution was fought so bitterly.

Unlike their brethren in Ireland, Scotland, or rural England the American Colonials often owned, and had earned property they were not prepared to surrender peacefully to a monarch, or his invading Army.

The thought of land ownership drove the dreams of many of the emigrants as they ventured across the oceans to the New World. And loosened their sense of freedom. Three thousand miles from a central government, they were in control of their lives and property and liked it that way.

To that end, in 1772 Samuel Adams drafted, *The Rights of the Colonists,* in Part III he demanded the British Crown remember the governing rule of property ownership extended to Colonial America:

"The supreme power cannot justly take from any man any part of his property, without his consent in person or by his representative."[lii]

Rights of the Colonist (1772)
Samuel Adams (1722–1803)

Mrs. Barrett, like the citizens of Lexington and Concord would not let her farm be needlessly damaged by the aggressive British soldiers. Captain Parsons was in command of the inspecting detachment and Mrs. Barrett never left his side.

She nagged the British officers as they inspected her farm. She harassed her unwanted visitors at every turn, often guiding them away from areas where hidden supplies were buried. Finally, the beleaguered British found some wooden cannon carriages and decided to burn them. That was a mistake that would only compound the fateful British journey to Concord.

With the gun carriages burning, the soldiers were not quite finished with Mrs. Barrett. They were quite hungry and they asked for some food. They had been on the march for nearly twelve hours with little food and water. She graciously gave her interrogators fresh bread and refused to take any money from the British Regulars. Meanwhile the gun carriages kept burning, sending smoke into the sky, allowing some to assume houses were being burned.

Colonel Smith and Major Pitcairn led the British troops into Concord center. The Regulars began a thorough search of houses, barns and businesses. They established their Headquarters in the building beside the militia training field.

Wright's Tavern was built by Captain Ephraim Jones and bore his name until it was sold to Amos Wright before the Revolutionary War. The tavern still sits in the center of Concord, and along with its historical significance holds an interesting irony.

Early on April 19, when the church bells bell announced the approach of the British troops, the Concord minutemen assembled at the field beside Wright's Tavern. As they gathered, their officers met in the tavern to discuss strategy. When the British officers arrived in Concord later that morning, they too met in Wright's Tavern to discuss their strategy and have some refreshments.

Of the British time spent in Wright's Tavern is an oft repeated story of the well-liked Major John Pitcairn.

"At Wright's tavern, Pitcairn called for a glass of Brandy, and stirred it up with his bloody finger, remarking, 'He hoped he should stir the Yankee blood so before midnight'."[liii]

After the carnage of Lexington, Pitcairn's blood was up.

With Pitcairn's arrival in the public square, the British, "... *found and destroyed 60 barrels of flour, broke three cannons from their wooded carriers and set them* [wooden carriers] *on fire, burnt other wagon wheels, and barrels* "[liv]

They made the mistake of burning the wooden gun carriages. Smoke was rising from Concord center, and Barrett's Farm. It was not a great leap to believe the British were burning the town, and any residence they choose.

After a long march through the cold New England night, being shot at in Lexington, surrounded in Concord the British were still determined to complete their search and destroy mission. And as news of the Lexington slaughter spread, determined Minutemen from all over Middlesex County gathered toward the smoke rising from the apparent burning of Concord.

The British officers discovered that they were surrounded by many hundreds of gathering local militias, men seemed to appear from nowhere and everywhere. The stage was set for another armed encounter, but now the Militiamen were in superior numbers, and rightfully believed that they were under attack from an invading army. At Concord, there would be no orders issued to disperse.

The rising smoke from Barrett's farm and Concord center was an ominous sign that the town was on fire, put to the torch by the Redcoats. It would exact an overwhelming response.

Part 2
The North Bridge

"Will you let them burn the town down?"

"Will you let them burn the town down?" An eager young Lieutenant admonished the aged Colonel Barrett. Barrett and his growing forces were on a high ridge overlooking the field and the road that crossed the North Bridge.

Each man understood that every minute wasted was a chance for the British to escape retribution, as they continued to burn the town. The old Colonel was already a third-generation Colonial citizen. His family service in the Provincial Militia Forces ran back to his grandfather who was also Colonel Barrett.

They had, for three generations, survived their share of frontier dangers in the 17th and 18th centuries in Colonial America. The old Colonel had already experienced enough fighting in his long lifetime, and never thought he would face British Soldiers in a battle for his ancestral town, and home.

Colonel Barrett would not let them burn the town down. From atop the hill, he ordered his men to load their muskets and begin to march toward the undermanned British position tentatively holding the old bridge. The men from Concord, Acton, Littleton, Groton, Bedford, Lincoln, Carlisle, Westford, and Chelmsford began the march down the hill toward the British Regulars at the Bridge. They marched to the fife of young Luther Blanchard as he piped, The White Cockade.[lv]

The White Cockade was an old Scottish song dedicated to the men who wore a white cockade, or ribbon on their highland soft blue bonnets. The white cockade was a symbol of the 1745 Jacobite revolution in Scotland led by Bonnie Prince Charlie that ended at the Battle of Culloden.

On 19 April 1775, parts of the British 4th Infantry Regiment, *The King's Own* were holding the old wooden Bridge in Concord. In a bittersweet irony 29 years earlier, on 16 April 1745, The 4th Regiment was part of the British

Forces that won the field at Culloden. The tune and its lyrics were familiar to many a Colonial American and the men of *The King's Own* regiment by the bridge:

"Then up with shout and out with blade,
And we'll raise once more the White Cockade.
Oh, my dear, my fair-haired youth,
Thou hast hearts of fire and of truth,
Then up with shout and out with blade,
We'll raise once more the White Cockade."[lvi]

An Cnota Ban (The White Cockade)

As noted by Arthur Tourtellot in *Lexington and Concord*:

*"The columns marching down...were the first American army under a unified commander to take the field."***57**[lvii]

At the old wooden bridge, *America's First Soldiers* fearlessly marched to an old Scottish tune into some of the very same regiment that had held Culloden's Moor and eviscerated the Scottish Highlanders and their way of life. Battlefield retribution had found *The King's Own* beside the gentle Concord River in Massachusetts.

The Red Coats, positioned at the North Bridge across from Colonel Barrett, noticed the Militiamen marching toward the Bridge. Barrett, Buttrick and their men had been positioned on the slight hill that rises from the field that abuts the river and the bridge.

Barrett had kept his soldiers a safe distance from the Red Coats at the bridge, allowing him to observe their movements, and anticipate their intentions. When the pipes and drums called the Colonials to march, British Captain Laurie ordered his men to retreat over the old wooden bridge.

Laurie had arrived at the bridge with three companies or about 200 Regulars, and his commanding officer Captain Parsons. Parsons split his command taking half his forces to Barrett's Farm, while leaving Laurie with the other half to defend the bridge.

As the Colonials moved down the hill toward the bridge, Captain Parsons was still at Barrett's Farm, putting him on the west side of the bridge.

Now all that separated invader and defender, was the width of the gentle Concord River. Making the old bridge the only way to cross the river and at that moment, the most valuable real estate in all the mighty British Empire.

"By the rude bridge that arched the flood." that was Emerson's description of the old, narrow, inclined, wooden bridge. Emerson's grandfather lived nearly beside the bridge on the April day, and Emerson himself called it his home once. You could easily see the bridge from the house. You could see all that for a brief moment, separated war and peace, freedom and tyranny, life and death.

The swelling ranks of the increasingly bitter, angry, motivated Militiamen and Minutemen aligned and singularly focused their wrath on the British Regulars at the bridge. A rage driven by the perceived burning of Concord, a display of absolute power unknown, and unimaginable in Massachusetts in 1775.

The sight of the Colonials moving down from the ridge was enough to get British Captain Laurie ordered his troops over the bridge to the east side. Laurie and his nearly 100 Regulars had spent an hour on the west side of the bridge, waiting for Captain Parsons to return from his inspection of Barrett's farm. Laurie immediately sent word to Lt. Colonel Smith in Concord Center that he was badly outnumbered, and on the opposite side of the bridge than Captain Parsons, and under attack.

Next, he ordered his men to wheel into an offensive position that was wholly ineffective for his environment. Laurie ordered a street fighting position, a formation that would be chosen in a crowded urban setting. The Regulars were stacked behind each other and presented excellent targets due to their close bunching. His act of aggression was not lost on the Militia commanders who understood that the Regulars were lining up for battle.

With each side poised for battle, seconds and minutes ticked away, no apparent voice of reason was to be heard on this day. Like events in Lexington, everything was slowly spinning out of anyone's control. History was forged in just those brief moments; that opportunity, motive, and means aligned with the disintegrated crumbling bonds of national kinship. Unlike the unlikely skirmish in Lexington, battle lines were drawn by both sides in Concord. Lines that could never be forgotten—never be forgiven.

The Colonials marched to the west bank of the river. The British fired first and two men were shot dead, one of which was Captain Isaac Davis, commander of the Acton Minutemen. Captain Davis was a thirty-year-old, well-respected leader of the Acton Minutemen. Minutemen were different from Militiamen in 18th century Colonial Massachusetts, they were closer to what we call today, *Elite Forces*. Davis' Acton Minutemen were well drilled, well supplied, and well equipped with good quality muskets.

Captain Davis was a gunsmith and he made many of the weapons his company carried onto the battlefield, including a rarity for colonial soldiers— bayonets and cartridge boxes for faster reloading. On that fateful day, Captain Davis and his bayonet wielding Acton Minutemen were afforded the honor of leading the Colonials over the bridge and into a maelstrom of British gunfire.

Unlike the enduring mystery of who fired first on Lexington Green, the British Regulars fired first at Concord. The British fire was quickly answered by the Colonials as Major John Buttrick ordered:

"Fire, fellow soldiers, for God's sake fire."

Those Colonials not on the bridge but lined up beside the river opened a deadly volley of musket fire. True to the legends and myths that have grown around the accurate fire of the Colonial Militiamen, the first British soldiers to fall were officers issuing commands.

Four of eight British officers directing Captain Laurie's columns fell first. Twelve privates were killed or wounded, and with the absence of British officers the Regulars broke. They began a disorderly retreat, abandoning their wounded soldiers, heading for Concord Center. They retreated, in disarray as fast as they could get away from the Colonials.

The British fell back, hoping to organize a proper response, they could not. They ran toward Concord and encountered the useless reinforcements they had asked for earlier. Those reinforcements were late—and led by Lt. Colonel Smith himself.

Some of the Colonists briefly pursued, with hearts full of vengeance, and scorn for the red-coated devils. One incident that was shamefully carried into history demonstrated the unbridled anger the Colonials now felt for their red coated countrymen. A British soldier had fallen wounded in the exchange of musket fire at the bridge.

Suddenly, he was attacked by a hatchet brandishing, crazed Colonial militiaman. The hatchet attack was extraordinary for that time and place, and it was an inexcusable event. Rumors spread about the Regulars that the Colonials were collecting scalps.

As quickly as the spark of violence had been ignited it faded to the new reality surrounding *America's First Soldiers*. They had successfully battled the mighty British Army into a hasty and disorganized retreat. Although vanquished, the Regulars were still formidable and dangerous.

The American dead, dying, and wounded in Concord and Lexington could account for the resolve of the British soldiers. And on the old wooden bridge many grieved the inconceivable loss, of Acton's beloved Captain Isaac Davis.

The loss of Captain Davis has been memorialized by a grateful nation. On the west side of the Old North Bridge stands a statue of a Minuteman, carved by famous sculptor and Concord resident, Daniel Chester French, the same man who chiseled the seated Abraham Lincoln in the Washington, D.C. Lincoln Memorial. The inspiration for that Minuteman sculptor was 30-year-old, Acton husband, father, gunsmith, captain, Minuteman Isaac Davis.

The dazed Colonials slowly scattered to help each other and return to high ground. They fully understood that there were many hundred volatile redcoats in Concord. But they seemed to forget Captain Parsons and his men at Barrett's Farm. The fighting at the bridge began around 10:00 on Wednesday morning and lasted but a very short while.

Remarkably, Captain Parsons who had been at the Barrett's Farm arrived and his column crossed the bridge unchallenged. The Colonials let the British pass over the bridge and onto Concord Center where the rest of the column had gathered. Incredibly, on this day, marked with such unsuspected violence, each side choose not to engage the other, it was over for the time being.

It was mournfully quiet and still at 12:00 noon on 19 April 1775. The guns, the screams, the sounds of battled just stopped, as each side gathered to decide what was the next act on this quickly unfolding, uncontrollable, inconceivable, drama thrust upon them all. Not understanding the history surrounding each one of them, they did know every minute now held life and death.

What had happened in Lexington was a one-sided bloodletting, but Concord was not that at all. Concord was a battle that had only stopped for a few moments, interrupted by soldiers who could not fully understand the seismic event that had just occurred.

Redcoats, Colonials, stately officers, and humble militia officers understood that Concord was not an ending. It would be a long day, and a last day for many still alive.

Chapter IV
Battle Road
Part 1
Back to Lexington

"As the war was thus began with savage cruelty, in the aggressors; so it has been carried on with the same temper and spirit..."

Opening of the war of the revolution, 19 April 1775.
A brief narrative of the principal transactions of that day.
Jonas Clarke, (1730–1805) Lexington Historical Society (Mass.)

Before he departed Concord with his beleaguered column, Lieutenant Colonel Francis Smith pondered his rapidly deteriorating situation. Smith was unable to fully grasp the trap closing around him. He sat for nearly two hours thus ensuring that the dangers that surrounded him increased.

He was a man used to following orders and he no longer had orders to follow. Nowhere in his orders from General Gage was there any reference to the deadly skirmish in Lexington. Nowhere in his orders was there any reference to a deadly battle over the rude arch crossing the Concord River.

Nowhere in his orders was there to be found provisions to attend his wounded and dying soldiers. Nowhere in his orders was there any reference to dwindling ammunition stocks held by his exhausted soldiers, many, many miles behind enemy lines.

And nowhere in his orders was there any instruction on how to get his column back to Boston on what promised to be a highway of death. Smith was a man with mounting problems and no orders to follow. Smith was lost.

Never was it more glaring that Smith was the wrong man to lead the march to Concord, as he sat for nearly two hours in the center of town. Time was just another enemy that Lieutenant Colonel Francis Smith could not identify and certainly could not defeat. As he waited, perhaps wishing for the reinforcements he requested hours ago, his tenuous situation became more tenuous.

As time melted away, his enemies' strengths grew minute by minute, as more men arrived with fresh stocks of ammunition, and fresh thoughts of killing British soldiers. Before long Smith and his men were surrounded by thousands of angry, determined, deadly, motivated Militiamen. Smith's troops had been moving for fourteen hours, they were exhausted, hungry and thirsty. They were being overwhelmed by fresh troops, well rested and supplied.

Somehow Lieutenant Colonel Francis Smith, and Major John Pitcairn would have to get them back to Boston.

Fifty-three-year-old Major John Pitcairn was born in the Scottish Lowlands to a landowning family loyal to the British Crown. John Pitcairn did not fight at Culloden's Moor, but if he had he would have been on the British side. They were not Highlanders, or members of an ancient Scottish Clan, they were loyal British subjects. Pitcairn was the son of a local minister, he was born and raised by the sea, and fittingly, he volunteered for the tough British Marines.

Pitcairn was a stern man who understood the necessity to control soldiers. He drilled his tough Marines constantly, and when he needed them most they were in Boston, while he was not. A glaring oversight. He was commanding scattered companies of light infantry who had ignored his orders in Lexington, an unforgivable transgression.

Pitcairn was unaccustomed to his orders being ignored and as he was preparing to leave Concord, he would be in command of British soldiers who had not listened to his orders. It compounded his impossible task of marching and surviving back to Boston. John Pitcairn did not like the rebellious residents of Massachusetts. In Boston, he was liked and well-respected by his troops, and in Concord, he was feared and loathed by the converging Colonials.

The relief column was nowhere in sight as the British began their Concord escape. The British would have to travel the sixteen miles back to Boston, and travel through Lexington where they had laid waste to *America's First Soldiers*. At Lexington, they drew blood, and they had no misgivings that in or near Lexington their blood would be demanded as retribution.

The weary British would now have to defy an inconceivable road of violence and death. A moving, ever-changing, battlefield that followed the old road between Concord and Boston. The civilized British soldiers found their predicament unimaginable as they started back to Boston.

The British Army had trained for parade ground battles, where each side lined up in an orderly civilized progression of distinct battle lines. Each country wore colorful uniforms, and had drummers, fifes, and vivid national flags to accompany their battlefield entrances. It was a grand and noble spectacle. Once positioned, each side would shoot a volley, and that volley was respectfully never aimed at officers.

The answering volleys only exchanged after the previous volley was completed. All this was done while each side kept a proper distance from their enemies. The killing beginning with musket fire would eventually devolve into a bayonet trusting, sword-wielding orgy of deadly, bloody, brutality.

Such was not the practice in Colonial America where the outnumbered, out trained, and out armed Americans chose a different tactic. The Americans chose fire and maneuver, speed and preservation, tactics learned from their native enemies. It was the overconfident British Regulars who were introduced to the future of warfare on old dusty road by *America's First Soldiers.*

Smith and Pitcairn protected the column by sending out light infantry soldiers as flankers on either side. The flankers were pressed out fifty to seventy-five yards on either side of the road. At that distance they were intended to keep the Colonials from firing at the mass of the column on the road, being that sixty to seventy-five yards was the accurate distance of an 18th entry musket.

In the columns center, on the road, was the mounted and dismounted officers, grenadiers, and the wounded. The column moved slowly, allowing the Colonists more time to deploy along the road from Concord to Lexington.

As the British moved, the Colonials had already moved, as new groups of Minutemen constantly moved into the Concord area. Word spread throughout the area of the *massacre in Lexington*, the *burning of Concord*, and the battle at the *Old North Bridge*. Militiamen and Minutemen continued to gather, as the hundreds grew to over a thousand. They converged on the road from Concord to Lexington determined to find a fight of their own.

With the British column moving in an orderly manner from west to east the Colonials were moving from all directions in a disorderly manner. They ran down roads, across streams, over walls, through farms and fields, swarming like angry hornets they brought a damming chaos to the British column.

There was no order, and no one in overall command as had been the case in Lexington and the Old North Bridge in Concord. It was all organic, as individuals and small companies of Colonials were attracted to the road leading out of Concord.

They searched for targets of opportunity, scouted for places to hide, located places of assault on the British route. Gathered where the British Column would be blind—around corners, at intersections, and behind buildings, barns, and walls.

Without any organized central command, they instinctively knew where they could be most effective killers. Many Colonial men were experienced hunters and on 19 April 1775 they were hunting a human prey who had invaded their towns, ransacked their houses, murdered their brothers, and destroyed private property.

They understood them to be invaders identified by those notorious red coats, and they knew their prey was vulnerable. The first ambush was just a mile out of Concord, at *Meriam's Corner*.

As the British approached *Meriam's Corner*, the open fields crowned by small ridges disappeared as they converged onto the road. As the ridges flattened out near the road, civilization appeared as: houses, barns, walls, trees, and an intersecting street all seemed to be in this one spot.

Without any coordinated communication, Militia forces from Reading, Billerica, Woburn, Framingham, Sudbury, and the men from Concord took positions of concealment. Along with the geography that forced the flankers onto the road with the main column was one last surprise for Smith's unprepared forces.

A small stream crossed the main road, and the small bridge over that small stream was narrower than the road. It was a deathtrap. A picture perfect funneling of the mass of the column into a single point. The slow-moving column nearly stopped as it approached the narrow bridge.

Gone were the drums and fifes of the splendid noble entry into Concord, an eerie silence was shared by all the men in the colorful red coats trying to escape to Boston. The sound of scuffing boots, rattling guns, horses and tired men complaining was suddenly shattered.

With no order to fire issued, the concealed Colonials opened fire. With memories swirling in the heads of those who had already seen action, and gory stories swirling in the heads of those who had not yet seen action, the disorder of the Militiamen delivered a murderous fury.

A thunderous sound was heard as men fired from the left, fired from the right, and from behind the shocked and trapped British column. One of *America's First Soldiers* called it a *turkey shoot*.

Amos Barrett happened onto the scene moments after the blows were delivered to the Red Coats:

"They [British Soldiers] *were waylaid and a great many killed. When I got there, a great many laid dead, and the road was bloody."*[lviii]

The disorderly Colonials used every place of concealment on the *bloody battle road*. They shot and disappeared to load or find another equally opportunistic place to shot from. They were on their home field and knew everyplace the British would be vulnerable. *America's First Soldiers* never fought by the British rules of engagement, they never assembled, never exposed or compromised their advantages. The British soldiers called it murder:

"...not only the British private but even the British officer was bewildered and indignant, thinking the method of attack dishonorable and murderous"[lix]

The Colonists set up at many ambushes for the British on the six-mile road from Concord to Lexington. From hilltops, from ridges, from behind trees, and stone walls the Colonists would emerge and deliver their retribution as if from Hell's shadows.

This was the *murderous*, inexcusable part of the day's events that unnerved some of the Regulars. The King's vaunted army, the world's most powerful land force did not like this new way of fighting, a fluid moving battle with no drawn-out lines.

Every Colonial holding his own musket, was looking down the barrel of his gun, his target wore a red coat. They were nameless, faceless targets of opportunity, the order of the day was fire and maneuver, fire and maneuver. The next place the British were trapped was by *Brook's Hill*.

About one mile east of *Meriam's Corner* was the second trap set for Smith's lumbering column. After the firing at the small bridge at *Meriam's Corner,* flankers were again sent out on either side of the column that was stuck to the center of the road. A large group of Colonials got to the hill on the south side of the road and occupied the high ground.

On the North side was Brook's Tavern, and other ambushers set up there. Nearly five hundred well placed Colonials held the high ground on one side and were concealed on the other side. The British moved down the road toward Lexington and suddenly they were under fire from the Colonials on the high ground.

The British assaulted the hill, and were repulsed, the Colonials held a vastly superior position, and had very large numbers working for them. Next, the fire came from the north side of the road near the tavern. After shooting, the Colonials just vanished into the thicket and woods, their job not yet completed, they instinctively moved down the line toward Lexington.

Continuing easterly, the British column again sent out their flankers. Further down the road it takes a sharp left turn, and then it takes a very sharp right turn. The British, slowed by actions at *Meriam's Corner* and *Brooks Hill,* were completely blind to the drastic bend in the road. This blindness was caused by the slope of the road as it gently but progressively rises.

The Colonials had time to select a perfect point in the road where the lumbering British column would be forced to slow even more. They had the time to find concealment around the natural landscape of trees, bushes, stones, and brush. Hundreds of Militiamen and Minutemen waited for their embattled prey.

Like the ambush at *Brook's Hill* the Colonials fired from both sides of the road. They fired fast and fired without caution, killing and wounding more of Colonel Smith's Column. Here, the British flankers had some success as they went out to surround the ambushers, avoiding a face-to-face engagement.

The flankers got behind some of the Colonials and shot them down immediately. Remembered as the *Bloody Angle*, the carnage was devastating to the British physically and it delivered a near devastating blow to British morale. With spirits broken, bodies shattered, and hope long since faded some began to run. The mighty British army was retreating, exchanging its orderly march for a disorderly retreat on an old country road.

Smith and Pitcairn now realized they had to send out more flankers—and farther from the road. They also needed a competent rear guard, as they traveled away from the *Bloody Angle*. But they now had a greater operational problem that could compromise any tactical operation they put into effect.

Smith's column was running low on ammunition, especially the light infantry being used as flankers. Militia companies from all over Middlesex County, Essex County and beyond delivered the unexpected attacks on the confused, retreating Redcoats, fighting a mobile, unrelenting battle that followed an old country road.

The exasperated British were not far from Lexington after they escaped the *Bloody Angle*. The road is more or less straight, lacking extreme bends, and it was mostly flat, albeit for a few minor slopes. But about a mile out of Lexington, there was a bend in the road, with a stream that crossed the road, and a slope with many rock outcroppings. It was there, where you can still see the rocky slope and the bend in the road that Captain John Parker and his Lexington men waited. Waiting to deliver vengeance.

After the deadly encounter with the British on Lexington Green as the sun was rising, the Lexington men had counted their losses and were determined to exact their retribution in British Blood. When Captain Parker's men regrouped and left Lexington for the Concord Road the pipers played, *The White Cockade,* as the Concord men did when they marched to the North Bridge.

The popular marching tune which reminisced about the British victory at Culloden's Moor, filled the pipes and the hearts of Parker's men as they marched toward a vengeful meeting with the British. At Culloden's Moor, the Scotts were offered no quarter from the British guns that annihilated the Highlanders, and now in the New World his Majesty's Regulars would find no quarter on the quiet, haunting road from Concord. The old Scottish Ballard claims,[lx]

"The prince is gone; but he soon will come With trumpet sound and beat of drum; Then up with shout and out with blade,
Hurrah for the Right and the White Cockade!"[lxi]
An Cnota Ban (The White Cockade)

Parker's men included some of the wounded from the one-sided exchange on the Green that morning. And amongst those marching, one man carried the old sword of his Scottish forbearers. Old Jedediah Munroe had been wounded on Lexington Green that morning, and that afternoon, he marched with Parker's vengeful warriors carrying his ancestral sword from Scotland.

As his Majesty's Regulars approached a slight bend in the road where an old bridge narrowed to cross the stream, the slow-moving column was slowed once more. The British were moving slowly after over 16 hours of marching, fighting and dying.

The hungry, thirsty, low on ammunition, weary Regulars carried many wounded soldiers which only slowed the slow-moving column. With the Regulars moving toward the choke point at the bridge, the patient Parker waited until his prey was well within the kill zone.

The injured and healthy Lexington men took their positions in the woods. Gone was the fear that filled them that morning on the cold dawn as the sun rose over the Green. Fear was replaced by a determination to bring justice to those British Soldiers who had shot and stabbed their family and friends.

Parker's men readied themselves, steadied themselves to deliver an earned execution of those who had mercilessly killed the innocent just hours earlier. Eyes which were filled with tears of grievous loss became focused on their hunted targets.

From a raised outcropping of boulders, from behind old buildings, gathered stones, and trees came the full deliverance of their reprisal. It was now well after 1:00 and the Lexington men were on a slight ridge, the perfect place to dispatch their chaos.

FIRE!

The results were breathtaking, as for a brief moment, the death of family and friends was avenged, the earlier losses swept away in the smoke, noise and killing delivered by the Lexington muskets. Lt. Colonel Smith was hit in the leg and lost his mount as the horse bolted, further injuring him as he fell.

Major Pitcairn had lost his horse earlier and he too was on foot, making both officers as vulnerable as their desperate troops. Without their mounts, the British Officers could not quickly control the Regulars, yet the well-disciplined British soldiers managed to respond with a barrage aimed at where the Lexington men were a few moments earlier.

Others attacked Parker's men by advancing to the hilltop with the same bayonets that had been so effective just hours ago. The Lexington men had prearranged exits to carry them out of danger from the attacking Regulars who amazingly advanced up the hill. The Lexington men did not retreat, they just repositioned themselves further down *Battle Road*, and prepared to ambush their prey again.

The fighting continued and the disorderly British soldiers bolted for nearby Lexington. There was no more honor to be found dying in this wild land. The Regulars became a fleeing mob before the Colonial Militiamen. The officers knew any hope of further command evaporated as Parker and his men had their revenge, fear was suddenly the order of the day for the British army running from Concord.

Those who were without ammunition and were losing the thoughts of surviving the assaults broke into a full gallop. They exhausted their last measures of energy grasping for the promise of salvation or surrender that was to be found in Lexington.

Ensign Henry De Berniere was with Lieutenant Colonel Smith's column that fateful day. Ensign De Berniere, and Captain John Brown volunteered to diagram and map out the routes from Boston to Concord.

De Berniere knew the roads better than anyone in Smith's Column. Just a few months before the expedition set out of Boston, De Berniere created maps for General Gage to use in choosing the best route to Concord.

Writing his remembrances, just a few months after the battles at Lexington, Concord, and running battle on the road, British Ensign Henry De Berniere recalled:

"...all the hills on each side of us were covered with rebels...they kept the road always lined and a very hot fire...but when we arrived within a mile of Lexington, our ammunition began to fail, and the light companies were so fatigued with flanking they were scarce able to act...a number of officers were also wounded, so that we began to run rather than retreat in order..."[lxii]

The Redcoats rushed down the road toward Lexington. It was no longer a retreat it was a sprint. Men with terrified looks on their faces, arms flailing about, legs moving as fast as exhausted legs could move. They were running on adrenaline. They were running for their lives. Every man for himself. As they ran down the Concord Road it took a bend as it neared Lexington Green, around the bend was the Lexington Green, where all their troubles seemed to have begun.

The street was empty as they ran, no more spectators, just the sounds of the muskets following and still firing. Theirs was a specter of disenfranchised hopelessness. Their mighty power had been exchanged on an old country road as they were blindly lead, marched into unseen deadly dangers by an inferior, unimaginative officer.

They traded their noble presence to phantom soldiers who they had believed to be mobs of pitchfork wielding Militiamen. They were running from their enemy and running into that enemy's home.

Without weapons they were at a full dash approaching the Lexington Green, prepared to embrace life or death. The road bends around the west end of the Green, then straightens out just as the Green is on your left. The running red coats saw images just ahead, the images they saw were not green but red. They ran faster hoping that the images they saw would materialize as men in red coats.

Getting closer they could hear themselves gasping for air, their throats burning and dry from breathing so hard. Their hearts pounding ready to burst in their heaving chests trying to keep blood in their lungs and muscles. They were running for their lives with heads full of ghastly images of Colonial horrors.

Freshly seared into their mind's eye was of their scalped comrade at Concord, and their dying friends shot to pieces, from all sides on a bloody country road. They barely stayed ahead of the killers chasing them, filling minutes and seconds with a lifetime of fear and panic.

Sprinting toward the line of discernible red coated soldiers at the east end of the Green, they detected their very salvation. Then they heard the cannons. Boom! Boom!

Two 6-pound cannons fired at the Militiamen chasing the British soldiers. In a day of firsts, another first burst upon the old Concord Road, as General Percy's cannons suddenly changed the dynamic of Lt. Colonel Smith's doomed column. Explosions rang out, crashing into houses and down the suddenly empty road.

The Colonials scattered off the road to save their lives. Percy had placed his artillery perfectly, on elevated positions aimed down the Concord Road.

He had also dispersed his fresh troops into menacing red battle lines defending the road back to Boston.

As the running Red Coats crossed the British lines, their comrades were aghast at what they saw, and what they were hearing. Suddenly a group of Percy's troops broke their lines and charged toward the Colonials.

Like the order that Smith and Pitcairn had lost, Percy felt his grip of command loosen for an uncomfortable moment. He demanded they return and hold their positions. Percy was not going to have his troops devolve into a disorderly mob.

The Colonials had not faced artillery all day. It was the major advantage the British had and the Colonials did not. The cannons were the supreme force on a 18th century battlefield, like the powerful tanks that dominated the battlefields of World War II. The cannons made the greater impression on the Colonials.

The Game had changed.

Part 2
Percy and Lexington

"Whoever looks upon them as an irregular mob will find himself much mistaken."

General Lord Hugh Percy, 2nd Duke of Northumberland (1742–1817)
20 April 1775

It was 2:00–2:30 PM, and the British soldiers had been on the road for 16 hours. They were tired, hungry, frustrated, frightened and many out of ammunition. Before they reached the Green, they were devoid of hope and for many deprived of valor. Lt. Colonel Smith and his Regulars reached the safety of Lexington, protected by the reinforcements sent out of Boston earlier in the day.

The British survivors of the running battles on the old country road complained bitterly about the method employed by the *America's First Soldiers*. Lieutenant John Barker fighting his way down *Battle Road* said:

"...the Rebels did not fail to take advantage...they kept an incessant fire upon us...they were so concealed there was [sic] *hardly any seeing them...their numbers increasing from all parts, while ours was reducing by death, wounds, and fatigue...we were totally surrounded with such an incessant fire as its impossible to conceive; our ammunition was likewise near expended..."*[lxiii]

For their part, the Colonials had lost the opportunity to destroy the British column. By the time the British returned to Lexington they were vastly outnumbered, vastly outgunned, yet managed to survive. Why?

The Colonial Militia companies were independent small units, quick to move, quick to act, but not under a central command. Many Colonial Militia companies were very independent, and naturally resistant to a centralized control.

That made the difference as they mobilized quickly, and found targets of opportunity. But most remained small independent groups committed to their own strategies. They were able to inflict damage but not permanently stop or destroy the column.

Their successful attacks on the column unnerved the British but never stopped them because they failed to surround the British. But in Lexington they too would find a new commander and a determined new strategy. *The Game had changed.*

For the British, gone were horse-mounted officers, drummers, directions, and order. They were introduced to the privation of battle at its most elementary form. They had been shot at by ghosts of men who were nowhere and everywhere at the same time. When the Regulars stopped, they were ordered into a formation, making them easier to wound or kill. They were trust into a new type of warfare, one that offered disorder and chaos to their previously ordered parade ground world.

In Colonial America, the British faced fluid dynamic warfare. British troops were overwhelmed by the superior numbers of the Colonials, and their ability to move and find concealment. The British Officers were flabbergasted at the thought they could be routed by these rustics.

From the site of Parker's Revenge to the Lexington Green the British had run for their lives. And it was General Lord Percy's relief column that saved what was nearly a total disaster for the British army. Had Percy not arrived, it is safe to conclude that Lt. Colonel Smith and his force could have been totally surrounded in Lexington by over a thousand Colonial Militiamen and forced into an unconditional surrender.

General Lord Hugh Percy, 2nd Duke of Northumberland was an heir to a great British fortune. Percy was very thin, appearing sickly to some, with his receding hairline, and gaunt face he seemed much older than his thirty-two years. He was well connected, educated, aristocratic, wealthy, professional soldier. He was also a charming, generous and very cultured man.

While serving in his Majesty's Army, Lord Percy was also a Member of Parliament. He was a nineteen-year-old Lieutenant Colonel, and at twenty-three, he served as an aid to King George III. He had fought on the European continent where he gained his considerable battle experience and served with distinction.

Arriving in Boston in 1774, he was a Brigadier General in command of the *5th Regiment a Foot.* Percy's Regiment was also known as the *Royal Northumberland Fusiliers,* and was already 100 years old when they disembarked in Boston.

Raised in 1674 to fight in England's, *Glorious Revolution,* the Royal Northumberland Fusiliers would make history for nearly three centuries fighting from Lexington, Concord and Bunker Hill, to battle Napoleon, land at Gallipoli and die at the Somme during World War I.

They would be evacuated at Dunkirk, and fight Rommel in North Africa in World War II. Saving the remains of Smith's 700-man column in Lexington was just another historical marker for this historical British regiment.

Percy, like many British officers, did not want to be in America fighting with the Colonials. He was ordered to Colonial America, as were all the top British Generals who were posted there. And he, as many officers who were also members of Parliament, believed that the British policy in the American Colonies was the problem.

He disagreed with many of the policies that seemed to move the Colonials into a state of rebellion. That was his view when he was far from the British American Colonies. After experiencing life in Colonial Massachusetts and just a few months living amongst the rebellious Boston residents, the educated, aristocratic Lord Percy had a clear change of mind.

In letters he wrote back to England, he illustrated his drastic change of heart.

"Our affairs here are in the most critical situation imaginable; Nothing less than the total loss or conquest of the colonies must be the end of it...I really begin now to think it will come to blows...they are most amazingly encouraged by our having done nothing...nothing can secure the Colonies to the mother country but the conquest of them...The people here are the most designing Artful Villains in the World. They have not the least idea of either Religion or Morality... "[lxiv]

Lord Percy and his acidic views of Colonial Americans found himself headquartered for the moment in an old tavern on the east side of Lexington

Green. There, he listened to the disgruntled and frustrated Smith and Pitcairn explain the events of the day. Most disturbing to Percy were the attacks along Battle Road. Colonel Smith whined:

"They did not make one gallant attempt." [lxv]

After patiently listening to the stories Brigadier General Hugh Percy quipped:

"They [The Colonials] *knew too well what was proper to do"* [lxvi].

Percy fully understood that his enemies were pressing their advantages. Percy was everything Lieutenant Colonel Francis Smith was not, and planned his exit from Lexington methodically. He hoped his return to Boston would fare better than his faulty departure had, just hours earlier. Percy's journey out of Boston was beset with remarkable errors beginning at General Gage's headquarters.

Before Lieutenant Colonel Smith and his men left Boston at 10:00PM on April 18, General Gage had informed General Percy that his brigade should be prepared to move out of Boston by 4:00AM the next morning—April 19. Gage told Percy he would send his written orders over shortly. Gage's written orders were directed to one of Percy's staff officers, Captain Thomas Moncrieff, who was not at his quarters.

The orders were left for the captain, who upon coming home, did not see them and went to bed. By 5:30 in the morning, the messenger Smith had sent from Lexington after the first skirmish arrived in Boston, and General Gage was rudely awoken to find Percy's brigade had not mustered to march. He was livid. Not concerned as to why they were not ready to march, Gage demanded that they assemble and prepare to march immediately.

General Gage's worst fear was his troops being shot at and attacked in the countryside. And as he was sleeping, that exact fear had materialized. At panic speed, the soldiers of Percy's brigade assembled and as they completed their assembly, they noticed they were missing one of the assigned units.

The 4th, 23rd and 47th army regiments had appeared, but the marines were not yet assembling. Not a single Marine was present. To assemble the Marines, a note was sent to Major John Pitcairn, commander to the Marines in Boston.

The same Major Pitcairn who was fighting for his life in Lexington. The mistake was finally recognized but more precious time had been drained. Just before 9:00AM the Marines and the army units were ready to march in relief of Smith's beleaguered column—5 hours late. By 9:00AM, Percy's troops should have been with Smith's column in Concord. The failure of the British to assemble and leave Boston at 4:00 AM would have disastrous consequences.

Had that occurred, the day would have been remembered as a British victory, as 1,500 plus soldiers would have been in Concord not 700. Such a massive force, with artillery and supply wagons would have paralyzed the efforts of the gathering Colonials. Undoubtedly, the revolution would have ended before it began with the Colonial victory at the Old North Bridge.

Percy's force of 800 men lumbered out of Boston. Along with the army, and Marines was an artillery train of cannons and wagons of supply. Gage meant business, his conciliatory expressions toward the Colonials were vanished hopes. He wanted to meet violence with a more powerful violence. The revolution would end today.

Percy chose not to follow the route of Smith's column. Besides, all the boats that would have landed him in Cambridge by the Charles River were still in Cambridge waiting patiently for Lieutenant Colonel Smith to return. Percy crossed Boston Neck by land, and continued in Roxbury, Brookline and on to Brighton. It was there he had to cross the Charles River at the Great Bridge crossing into Cambridge. The Bridge deck was gone.

The Colonials, believing that either relief forces coming from Boston, or Smith's Column on its return to Boston would use this bridge stripped the decking planks. They removed all the planks and neatly arranged them on the Cambridge side of the bridge.

Percy could not believe what he saw. He demanded the marines cross the stringers that held the planks and rebuild the bridge deck. This certainly cost Percy more time he did not have. As he crossed the wobbly planks, he ordered his rear guard, and supply wagons to remain at the bridge and finish the job properly. Percy advanced into Harvard Square leaving his supply wagons to catch up with him on the road to Lexington.

Percy stopped in Harvard Square to ask where he would find the road to Lexington. After all his delays, and serious disappointments he did not have a map that identified the most important road he would use—the road to

Lexington. Traveling the last leg of his fateful journey to Lexington Percy had one of two last surprises.

He heard an eerie silence and observed houses shuttered, farms idle, people missing from the streets, people missing from everywhere. He knew then that this would not be a relief mission, but an extraction of a friendly force in a very unfriendly place. He knew he had traveled behind his enemies' lines. As he entered Lexington, he first encountered his wounded countrymen.

They described the harrowing fateful day they endured. And as he approached the Lexington Green, they heard the distinct sound of musket fire. He stopped and set up his headquarters east of the Green, soon he realized his last surprise of the journey to Lexington, the supply wagons were not with him.

His wagons had been captured by a group of horse-mounted, gray-haired old Militiamen. Old School types—men who had fought in the French and Indian War and were deemed too old to fight with the younger foot soldiers of the Minutemen and Militiamen rampaging across the countryside. But these old men were not the types to stay home and knew they could help somehow—somewhere.

The old men found Percy's slow-moving wagons and told the British drivers to stop. The British soldiers paid no heed to the old men. Ignoring the steely, gray-haired old men on horseback was the last thing they ever did. The old men shot the lead horses, shot the two drivers, and the officer in charge. The other British soldiers threw down their weapons and ran for their lives.

Percy's wagons were in Colonial possession. Percy now had limited supplies of ammunition for his soldiers and cannons. He also had none to reinforce Smith's men who had exhausted their ammunition on the road from Concord to Lexington. Another error in judgement, committed by British officers trained not to make such glaring mistakes.

Therefore, the British force was more substantial in numbers, but not proportionally larger in firepower. Percy had some small cannons but what he needed was armed men out on his exposed flanks, armed men in the rear, and armed men in the vanguard.

Having men with little ammunition created a more vulnerable force to protect on the dangerous road lined with Colonial ambushers. The British had made another mistake, a gross miscalculation on this historic day of underestimating Colonial Militiamen from Massachusetts.

This was a major mistake on a day of inexcusable mistakes. First, the Regulars seemingly directed by their officers, fired on and unleashed a bayonet charge at Lexington Green. Such malicious cruelty issued by the British bayonets on their fellow countrymen was unforgivable and gratuitously unnecessary.

Second, the British Regulars had burned the wooden gun carriages in Concord at two different sites. The sight of smoke over the town of Concord led to the conclusion that the British soldiers were burning down the town. Next Lieutenant Colonel Smith sat around Concord for at least two additional hours, allowing his enemy to grow stronger.

Smith also was limited to being reactive on his entire expedition, but particularly when traveling from Concord to Lexington. He never took full use of his grenadiers as he kept them on the road. He did not use scouting parties to understand the terrain he was walking into.

Lastly, the British reinforcements that arrived to relieve Lt. Colonel Smith's beleaguered troops did not have ammunition for those soldiers who had been fighting all day and were low or out of ammunition. The relief column had only enough ammunition for themselves. The Colonists would exact a damming price for such a rudimentary mistake.

Lord Percy sat in Munroe's Tavern and developed his plan. He knew he was being surrounded on three sides: right, left, and rear. His only option was the road that carried him to Lexington. The eerily silent road, with boarded up houses, idle farms, and no people on the streets.

Percy's plan was to travel the fastest road back to Boston and he would travel slowly as to not advance unprepared into an ambush. He positioned a powerful force of five companies of the very tough and battle-hardened 4th Regiment, *The King's own* on his right, or the south side of the road.

That powerful force would keep the Colonials away from the columns right side, they would extend out beyond the effective range of the Colonial muskets. On his left side, the north side of the road, Percy extended many companies of the 47th regiment out beyond musket range.

As his rear guard, he would use a rotating group from the Royal Welsh Fusiliers. The Royal Welsh companies would rotate fresh troops every few miles ensuring that there were always soldiers with plenty of ammunition in the rear—where he was most vulnerable.

Near the rear, he positioned his cannons to deliver a deadly punch if the Colonials attacked the rear in force. The center of his column contained his vaunted Marines with Major Pitcairn. The Marines were deployed to advance in any direction they were needed, this reserve element gave him stronger and faster punching power to deliver a counterattack. At the lead of his column, he placed a contingent of about fifty light infantry soldiers to scout ahead as a vanguard for the column behind them.

They would find the traps before the entire column was ambushed. Percy wanted to locate ambushers and attack them fast and hard from his column. He placed grenadiers just behind the forward elements of the light infantry and he dispersed captured Colonials amongst the column, hoping that the Americans would not fire at their own men.

Lastly, Percy told his flankers that if they encountered snipers or prepared ambushes to attack and kill the Colonials. He also ordered them to clear any property used to conceal Colonial Soldiers.

Percy was not the only General making plans. About the time Percy was preparing his exit strategy for Lexington, General William Heath a well-respected Colonial Militia commander, and Dr. Joseph Warren arrived to take charge in Lexington.

General Heath organized many of the fractured companies into regiments. He was turning the fiercely independent groups into larger organized units that could cause much more damage. Heath was a well-liked, thirty-eight-year-old farmer from Roxbury. His ancestors had been in Boston for over 100 years as he took command in Lexington. He had studied military tactics, and battles his entire life.

Heath believed that the Massachusetts Militiamen were better at hit and run, mobile warfare than parade ground formations. He would put all his knowledge to the test on the road from Lexington to Boston. Although he was not an experienced field commander, he was a very good tactical thinker and understood the weaknesses of Percy's situation.

Heath wanted to establish a perimeter around Percy's column. But this perimeter would be outside the flankers, and it would extend all round Percy from side to side and front to back. In a word, Heath wanted to surround Percy's column. Heath knew that the terrain favored the Colonials and wanted to take full advantage of hit and run, fast mobile attacks against the British.

And he wanted those attacks carried out on four sides including the front of the column. In addition, Heath wanted his *circle of skirmishers* to rotate after each attack. He wanted Percy's column surrounded by a ring of hot, focused, planned fire. He wanted to bring chaos from all sides to Percy's perceived orderly world.

Heath even hoped he could trap Percy's entire force as it tried to cross the Great Bridge between Cambridge and Brighton. Heath had ordered the deck removed; the same deck Percy earlier had to replace. And Heath had dispatched couriers while he was in Lexington to alert the gathering Colonial companies and regiments of his intentions.

The couriers asked that the normally independent Militiamen and Minutemen groups band together to set larger and more deadly traps for Percy and his Column. Lastly, Heath found resupply for the men who had been in the field expending ammunition.

Although some men went home after the British got to Lexington, many more stayed. The ones that left were tired and had in some cases expended all the ammunition they could afford to lose. General Heath knew that and resupply occurred in limited quantities, but the effort was made to have the greatest, most enduring, rotating firepower he could place in the field.

The Colonials were no longer a mob. They had a commanding General, the first general to lead US troops into battle. They had become an effective fighting force, anyone who doubted that would do so now at their own peril. They were led into battle from the front with the strategic goal of destroying Lord Percy's column.

They had instituted tactical plans to locate and attack targets of opportunity where terrain favored the Colonials. And they had operational planning of resupply, communication, and levels of command. They were *America's First Soldiers.*

The Game had Changed.

Percy understood time was against him. The sun was going to set early on that spring day, and darkness only added to his enemies' advantages. Leaving Lexington, the British ranks had doubled, in its size. Over 1500 men prepared to leave Lexington.

So vast was the column that the first British soldiers of the vanguard—the forward elements departed Lexington about 3:00PM. The last British Soldier to leave Lexington departed at 3:30PM, it took thirty minutes to move the massive column.

On Wednesday afternoon, 19 April as Percy's Column exited Lexington it contained over one third of all the British forces under General Gage's command in Boston. Another glaring mistake made by Gage. Gage waited in Boston realizing that he no longer had enough forces to control Boston if an organized uprising was to occur at that point. Gage had put himself in a potentially untenable situation.

Just before Percy and his column exited Lexington, they fired their cannons at the local meeting house. Not content with that level of destruction Percy ordered the burning of some of the houses lining the green. It was a preemptive action to warn his enemy that snipers firing from houses would sacrifice the catastrophic loss of personal property.

Intended to frighten his enemy, it had the opposite effect. The needless destruction just as they were leaving Lexington Green illustrated two more mistakes in a day of mistakes. Such wanton and unbridled destruction of personal property filled every Colonial heart with the spirit of untamable vengeance.

Just a few months earlier, Percy had written his harsh judgements against the Colonials. He, like so many of his countrymen, underestimated the Colonials:

"The people here are a set of sly, artful, hypocritical rascals cruel and cowards…I cannot but despise them completely…"[lxvii]

As Percy departed Lexington, confident of his abilities to command his well conceived plan I wonder if he thought of something he had written just a few months earlier. In September of 1774, in a letter back to England Percy wrote:

"Things here are now drawing to a crisis every day…They have taken up arms in almost every part of this Province…In short, this country is now in as open a state of rebellion as Scotland was in the year '45…"[lxviii]

Before he marched to Lexington, Lord Percy understood the mood of the people of Massachusetts, but he did not understand the history that was surrounding him. He asserts that Boston, and Massachusetts were like Scotland was in 1745, and he understands where he is and why he is there. But his aristocratic sensibilities cannot understand the difference between the two worlds he sees as being the same.

The differences are profound, and well-illustrated on 19 April 1775 in Lexington as the defiant Colonials stand before the great British Army. The British win the field in Lexington but the Colonials defy the mighty British Army, this time in Concord and win the battle of the North Bridge.

Then, the fearsome British Army is routed on the old country road between Concord and Lexington something that never happened in Scotland. These are not to be excused as the vagaries of war, these are cataclysmic events like the events in Scotland in 1745–6, where on a dreary, cold damp April morning, the British destroyed the Scots at Culloden's Moor.

Because it was a battlefield that favored the British guns, soldiers and artillery. But on the road from Lexington to Boston, the battlefield favored the Colonials, some of them of Scottish ancestry, and nearly all of a Celtic origin.

Here in Massachusetts the tables were turned, and as each side began the last act of the historic day it was understood, like on Culloden's Moor no quarter was to be given.

Author David Hackett Fischer framed it best:

"On April 19, 1775, the American education of Lord Percy was about to begin."

Paul Revere's Ride
David Hackett Fisher
Page 238.

The Game had changed.

Part 3
Back to Boston

"We retired for 15 miles under an incessant fire,
which like a moving circle surrounded
and followed us wherever we went"

Lord Hugh Percy
Letter dated 20 April 1775

The Game had changed for all the participants on April 19 1775. The road between Lexington and Boston was nearly 12 miles long and it went through Menotomy, present day Arlington. Menotomy was an old, peaceful, village nestled beside busy Cambridge. It was named by the local Indians long before the European settlers arrived, its name meaning *running water*.

The town changed its name in 1867, in honor of the Civil War dead at Arlington House, Virginia, site of present-day Arlington National Cemetery. On 19 April 1775 *American First Soldiers* gathered along the streets, hid in and near houses, behind barns, stones, trees, and walls, in Lexington, Menotomy and Cambridge. This would be the final act of the deadly drama that unfolded early in the morning in Lexington.

The road from Lexington to Boston was far different than the wild country between Concord and Lexington. There were still some farms and open fields, but for the most part the road was more developed, containing more houses and buildings, shops and barns, intersecting streets and stone walls, and some bridges.

It was a terrain that offered much greater cover for the Colonials. Percy knew that and that is why he loaded up his flankers with many companies, and kept a vanguard or forward scouting party. His slow travel speed was designed to keep him out of trouble, but it also allowed the Colonials greater time to gather, select attack zones, and occupy the advantages offered by terrain.

Not far from his starting point in Lexington, Percy's education began in earnest. The ground was flat, and all British eyes were keenly focused on the certain dangers lurking in front of the column. With nearly all eyes forward, suddenly came the clash of muskets from behind.

The rear of the column was hit fast and hard as the Colonials closed to very close quarters. Called on the attack by General Heath himself, they fearlessly hit the rear guard of the Royal Welch Fusiliers. The Colonials moved in very close, exposing themselves to British fire.

But at close range, their shots would be deadly, and this was a personal fight where no quarter was issued. The Fusiliers tried to march backward as the Colonials kept coming on.

The Royal Welch Fusiliers were raised to fight in the Glorious Revolution in England. The Regiment was nearly 100 years when it landed in Boston. They had been deployed on the European continent fighting the French, Spanish and Prussians.

They served in Scotland in 1745, clearing the Highlanders out of Scotland. Now on the country road in Colonial America they faced some of the descendants of their murderous days in Scotland. The Colonel of the Royal Welch regiment fell dead, as ever-increasing numbers of Colonial skirmishers joined in the attack.

The Royal Welch were overwhelmed by the unbridled violence of the unrelenting rear attacks, before long they had taken enough casualties that they were relieved by a fresh continent of Marines. While still in Lexington General Percy had to move his reserves from the center to the rear of the column that badly needed relief.

The first attack of Percy's column demonstrates one critical component that was absent on the road from Concord to Lexington and from Lexington back to Boston. Despite his planning and execution General Heath never created a road block. If a road block, even a temporary one was used, it would have forced the British to use greater supplies of ammunition, as they would be stationary, and able to reload.

In a frenzied state of being attacked from many sides, it is safe to conclude that ammunition would have been rapidly consumed, creating a potentially catastrophic situation for Lord Percy. Like the many attacks on Battle Road earlier in the day, the results were pleasing for the Colonials, but they could have destroyed Percy, not just damaged him.

With the Marines in place, the column continued. Just as quickly as the Colonials had attacked the rear, they came in from the left British flank. Here again, Heath was present, and encouraged the time and place of the flanking attack. Heath was operating his ring of skimmers exactly as he had planned. And like the attack at the rear just moments ago, the Colonials slammed into the British.

They moved from north to south, got close and made full use of their ammunition. Speed and maneuver, combined with firing from concealed positions was taking an exacting toll from the British. None exempt as all the Regulars understood their vulnerability.

Those not hit with bullets were hit with fear and apprehension, inflicting a paralyzing effect on unit cohesion and contributing to morale breakdown. And like the earlier march from Concord the road was filling with Colonials, the were unprepared, and at times overwhelmed for the sheer numbers of Colonial fighters.

With the passage of time, Percy's power was decreasing as he absorbed more wounded men, and other men fired their finite supply of ammunition. Percy's decreased firepower was offset by the ever-increasing numbers of Colonial companies reaching the road from Lexington to Boston.

Companies from all over Middlesex County had been carrying the fight from Concord to Lexington. Now, as time had passed, companies from Essex County and Suffolk County were all in as the British moved into Menotomy. Men from as far away and Danvers and Lynn would find men from Roxbury, Dedham, Needham, Brookline and Dorchester.

Like the ambushes earlier on the Concord Road, the British soldiers were beginning to fall apart. They were completely exposed to an enemy who would not stand and fight; an enemy that had no fear of them, was well motivated, and very well led. British Lieutenant John Barker included in his diary the action in Lexington. Barker wrote:

"Before we had gone a 1/2 mile, we were fired on from all sides, but mostly from the rear, where people hid themselves in houses until we had passed and then fired...the Rebels did not fail to take advantage of [the terrain]...*the people kept an incessant fire upon us."*[lxix]

Heath's imaginative tactics offered no cover or sanctuary for the British. The main column was still vulnerable as it traveled the lonely roadway between Lexington and Boston. Percy's defense was ineffective at this point on the road back to Boston, the results were unyielding as there was no safe place in the British formation which was subject to fire from three sides— right, left, and rear.

This is where the training of the Colonial Militiamen paid off. They were small, flexible, organized groups with their own operational command. They gathered and drilled in their town and villages. They were related to each other, or were longtime friends. They could depend and trust each other. They were perfectly suited for a running battle on their home field.

As the British put Lexington behind them, they were unaware that the deadliest part of their day was yet to come. The man who had sent them out on their ill-fated mission to Concord was in Boston awaiting any news that would find him. Lieutenant General Thomas Gage had feared what had happened, but had no idea of what was going to happen. Weeks earlier, he had assessed the Colonial fighters writing to London:

"The most natural and eligible mode of attack on the part of the people is that of detached parties of Bushman... [I am] *firmly persuaded that there is not a man amongst* [them] *capable of taking command or directing the motions of an Army"*[lxx]

Gage could not have been more wrong about his enemies. Yes, they did attack at first as detached parties, but they were anything but *Bushman.* The Colonials attacking and killing his vaunted Regulars were not wild savages— like the Highlanders of Scotland, or the Gaelic speaking savages in Ireland.

These were the descendants of those savages, standing as land owning free Englishmen. Men armed with muskets, not swords and shields. And most importantly men who had received an English education in the American Colonies.

Gage, like his predecessors and successors, was grossly wrong about leadership. Possibly, Gage was remembering the chaos at Culloden's Moor 29 years earlier as he participated in the last pitch battle on British soil. But this was not Scotland, yet the Scottish filled many of the Colonial ranks. As Gage sat in Boston, surrounded by the accoutrements of a Royal Governor, his army was in the field marching into a most deadly place.

Menotomy has a section today called Arlington Heights. The Heights are on the south side of the road. Today they consist of steep hills with roads and they are covered with houses. In the 18th century, they were wild hills, untamed by today's suburban encroachment. Steep hills with rocks and trees, the perfect place to hide an attacking force, giving it an excellent view of what was moving easterly on the roadway beneath them.

Before long, the Colonials on the British right flank began their assault. Moving south to north they fired on the British flankers. Like the continuing assaults on the rear and left side, this new attack experienced great success. The Colonials descended the hills rapidly with cold hearts and hot lead. They slammed into Percy's vaunted 4th regiment on his right.

The King's Own took the brunt of the assault. They wavered, and so furious was the fighting that Percy's column stopped. Once stopped, Percy wheeled his artillery around to cover his right flank. His artillery that had a dwindling supply of ammunition. Percy did not want to stop, he had to keep moving. Darkness was not far away as Percy's column marched into the destruction that was Menotomy.

Darkness was only going to befriend the Colonials, adding to the advantage that the surprise attackers already had. Heath's revolving circle of skirmishers was working very well, and in Menotomy had its greatest effect. The artillery was enough to slow the attackers on the right. The artillery was placed in formation and the column began to move.

Percy knew he was vulnerable on three sides, he started moving in the only direction he had not encountered resistance—straight ahead.

As the beleaguered column started to move, the heights on the British right flank started to drop down and eventually gave way to a flatter landscape. And in that landscape was an intersection of some major roads. Menotomy was surrounded by Cambridge, Lexington, Woburn, Medford, Somerville and Waltham.

Menotomy was a cross roads town and the British approached that dominating intersection they experienced something they never expected, an assault on the front of the column. General Heath's circle of fire was complete.

Mounted Militiamen appeared at the front of the column. They rode before the column, dismounted and fired. They then remounted their horses and rode out of range.

They did not fight like a standard *Cavalry* unit, they dismounted to fight, rather than remain an easy target on horseback. The British lead elements were light infantry, foot soldiers without any *Cavalry* to help. These mounted Militiamen were older, and experienced fighters perfect for the frontal assaults.

But with their advanced age, they could not keep up with the faster moving younger men on the ground. Like the older men who captured Percy's wagons on his march to Lexington, these were seasoned fighters, adept with muskets, and the conscience to use them most effectively. The British saw these mounted old men many times as they marched on through Menotomy and into Cambridge.

Each time they arrived quickly, dismounted and fired deadly accurate shots, from their hunting muskets. They brought death to the front of Percy's column, something that was unthinkable as Percy planned his march down *Death's Road* to Boston. Lieutenant Frederick Mackenzie, of the Royal Welch Fusiliers recalled in his diary:

"...the firing as from...all directions, numbers of armed men on foot and on horseback, were continually coming from all parts...we were fired at from all quarters...at the head of the column...the firing was nearly severe as the rear...the Rebels kept an incessant irregular fire from all points at the column..."[lxxi]

Another Lieutenant, John Barker of the 4th Regiment, *The Kings Own* understood and perhaps feared for their existence. One of the men Percy chose to protect his right flank stated in his diary:

"When we got to Menotomy there was a very heavy fire"[lxxii]

With every step they took, the fire around them increased. Like a strong wind driven rain, the bullets flew from all directions. British officers on horseback were targeted, as was any non-commissioned officer barking out instructions. In all the days fighting, no place was as deadly as Menotomy. General Heath, with the fearless Dr. Joseph Warren beside him, moved from place to place.

They always turned up where the greatest opportunities were waiting. The fighting was everything Heath imaged and hoped it would be and it was everything Lord Percy had feared.

To his credit, many British soldiers said Percy was always where his calm manner and military experience was needed. He did not shelter himself, but kept himself as exposed as his men were. Percy knew he needed a game changer, and with his artillery pieces having limited ammunition, and his flankers and rear guard using more ammunition than they could afford to lose he unleashed the British bayonets.

Like the day had begun on Lexington Green, Percy's men were going to make this very personal, very bloody, very unforgiving. The flankers were ordered to assault the houses and shoot and or bayonet anyone they found. All the Colonials were now considered enemies: men, women, young, old, sick, dying, none exempt. General Percy instructed his flanking parties to enter and clear houses.

One house, where the fighting got very personal was the Jason Russell House. Jason Russell was nearly 60 years old on 19 April 1775. He was like so many in Massachusetts a multi-generational, colonial resident. He was a farmer, and believed his house and private property should be defended from the advancing British Regulars.

Russell's house and his orchard were chosen by Militiamen arriving ahead of the British as a perfect spot for an ambush. The newly arrived Colonials from, Danvers, and Lynn amongst other locations, were unaware of General Percy's use of flanking forces in the areas parallel to and out of site of the Road. Other Colonials warned them they were too close to the road, and chose to ignore that caution.

Just before the British main column arrived at the Russell House, the Colonials were overwhelmingly attacked in the rear by the British flanking troops. Many of the Militiamen were shot where they stood, others scattered, with some running into Russell's house.

The retreating Colonials filled the house and the cellar below it. The British violently burst into the house shooting and bayoneting anyone they could find. In the exchange at Russell's house, 12 Colonials were killed, including old man Russell who was shot, and bayoneted multiple times.

The angry British soldiers also burst into the Cooper Tavern, they killed two patrons. They bayoneted the customers and helped themselves to some rum.

As the battle wore on, the enraged British soldiers lost control. Once Percy released the restrictions of a civilized warfare on his men, they became frenzied mobs of killers and robbers. Lieutenant Mackenzie, of the Royal Welch Fusiliers noted in his diary:

"Many of them were killed in the houses on the road side from whence they fired; In some of them, 7 or 8 men were destroyed. If we had time to set fire to those houses, many Rebels must have perished in them... "[lxxiii]

British Lieutenant John Barker, of *The King's Own* recalled:

"We were now obliged to force nearly every house in the road, for the rebels had possession of them...for all that we found in the houses were put to death... "[lxxiv]

Percy had lost control of his bewildered troops. When they were unleashed to attack the houses and buildings along the road they killed, maimed, drank and stole anything they could carry. Percy deemed the attacking of the houses was a military necessity, and that can be defended up to a point, but not the killing and looting. As the intensity of the battle on the road increased, so did the barbarity in the houses.

"The plundering was shameful...The British soldiers even stole the church's communion silver...They smashed and destroyed much of what they could not carry, set fire to buildings, and killed livestock in a saturnalia of savagery. "[lxxv]

It was nearly 6:00PM as Percy's Column arrived at the bridge over a small stream today called, *Alewife Brook*. In 1775, this stream was called the Menotomy River and was the bound between Menotomy and Cambridge. At the bridge the British were attacked for the last time in Menotomy.

Many Minutemen rushed the rear guard and fired. The fire was fast and deadly enough for Percy to stop and wheel his cannons to the rear of the column.

"The minute-men hovered dangerously near his rear guard... [Percy] paused long enough to wheel his two six-pounders about..."[lxxvi]

Remarkably, no one on the Colonial side thought to disable the old bridge over the Alewife Brook. Here, we see Heath's most glaring mistake, for if he had disabled or destroyed the bridge, the damage inflicted on the British would have been unprecedented on a day of unprecedented destruction. Heath would have Percy surrounded and contained by a natural barrier.

The British would have exhausted their ammunition and scattered like they did in Lexington after Parker's Revenge. This was Heath's most extreme error. Perhaps his mind was on the Great Bridge over the Charles River where Heath planned to stop Percy.

In the action in Menotomy, Percy had a button shot off his jacket. And Dr. Warren had a pin shot out of his hair. That is how intense the musket fire was from the warring groups. The exchange rate for the march down that old road in Menotomy was the highest price paid in blood all day.

The toll for marching through Menotomy for the British was breathtaking as 40 British soldiers fell dead, another 80 wounded on the road between Lexington and Cambridge.

Nowhere in all the day of fighting was it as deadly for the British. On this unprecedented day of death, on a quiet country road, in a rural Massachusetts village, whose name is all but lost to history the British suffered nearly 50% of the day's casualties.

If anyplace represented the gross miscalculation of General Gage, his staff in Boston, and superiors in London, it is the short stretch of road between Lexington and Cambridge the *Road to Damnation* in Menotomy.

As his vanguard crossed the bridge over the Alewife, they entered Cambridge, and were half way to safety in Boston. There would be no respite in Cambridge. Blood and death followed his Majesty's Regulars, as every house, barn, wall, tree, and street corner of their perilous journey offered no hope, only more death and destruction.

The Militia groups were pouring into Cambridge from all sides. Percy understood he was vastly outnumbered and was losing the sunlight of this spring day in New England, and his very survival was in question.

Cambridge offered Percy his perceived deadliest obstacles of the day. It was the most urban area he would pass all day. It was full of buildings and houses on both sides of the main road he was passing upon. It had many cross streets, these intersections offered angles of approach for attacking forces.

Cambridge offered infinite places for small deadly ambushes, and infinite places for the Colonials to retreat to. The urban area slowed the flankers as they had to get around buildings and houses. In doing that, those flankers were now more exposed to unseen dangers.

Instead of the large areas he experienced in Menotomy and Lexington, Cambridge offered a death by a million cuts. And the urban areas also offered protection from the cannons that Percy had thus far, so skillfully used.

In Cambridge, he was halfway home, and his attackers knew that. Time and now distance were Percy's enemies. As his distance to safety shortened, he understood the Colonials would become more aggressive as their opportunities were fading away. Time was Percy's other enemy as darkness gave the Colonials a blanket to hide under.

Percy was running very low on ammunition for his riflemen, and his vaunted cannons. He had also lost control of his men, as they understood the vulnerabilities as well as he did. He had loosened control in Menotomy and it was not coming back anytime soon. His men were desperate.

Lastly, Percy was on the wrong side of the Charles River. He would have to cross the *Great Bridge* from Cambridge to Brighton. Earlier as he passed from Boston to Lexington the *Great Bridge* had been partially dismantled.

He knew that would be the case as he arrived at the bridge to get to safety. The bridge represented the best place to stop and annihilate his command. Percy knew the bridge was the key for the Colonials. Cambridge was going to be hell. Percy needed a miracle.

The Game had Changed.

For their part General Heath and the Colonials had problems as the fight entered Cambridge. Gone were the opportunities for the large-scale assaults the open fields in Menotomy allowed. In Cambridge, the firing would be more limited as the buildings and houses offered concealment but occupied greater areas.

Very large numbers of Militiamen were pouring into Cambridge and these new arrivals were not familiar with the circle of skirmishers that General Heath has maintained to great success. This lack of a centralized control meant that targets of opportunity would be engaged by small arriving units, sacrificing a more deadly organized large-scale assault.

Cambridge was an area that had many roads, and Percy saw them as avenues of attack for the Colonials. Heath saw them as avenues of escape for Percy's besieged column. One road in Cambridge led to the Great Bridge, and it was there, General Heath planned his *Coup-de-Grâce*. At the bridge, Percy would not find escape, he would find destruction. That was how Heath planned it.

Earlier in the day, General Heath had ordered the bridge over the Charles River to be dismantled. That was his trap. The Colonials would push the British before the bare bridge and capture or destroy them. It was a bold and imaginary plan that offered more than Percy's end. It potentially offered Gage's end, for Percy had at least one third of Gage's army in Boston.

The loss of such a force would cripple Gage's ability to perform offensive and defensive actions in Boston. Perhaps, such a grievous loss would cause Gage to capitulate rather than face an attack from a massive Colonial army. Cambridge was going to be hell. Heath had to keep Percy on the road to the Great Bridge.

The road in Cambridge offered no salvation for Percy's column. The Colonials were still firing on all sides of the British marchers. The British flankers found a small ambush party at a place called Watson's Corner.

They overtook the Colonials, killing Major Isaac Gardner of Brookline, and three Cambridge men. The Colonials kept firing from between the houses, as *America's First Soldiers* took full advantage of the urban area. British Lieutenant Mackenzie described the action in Cambridge:

"In the field the provincials were seldom visible, from the houses they were scarcely to be seen at all... [In]Cambridge the number and fire of the rebels increased."[lxxvii]

Percy was a mile into his march through Cambridge and things were only getting worse for his column. They had departed Lexington three hours earlier and they were running low on ammunition. Desperation was falling on the British. In his diary, Lieutenant Mackenzie recorded the events of the first mile in Cambridge.

"...our men threw away their fire very inconsiderately, and without being certain of its effect this emboldened them, and induced them to draw nearer...our regiment expended a great deal of ammunition..." [lxxviii]

Percy's Column was in jeopardy of a complete breakdown. Just beyond the one-mile mark into Cambridge, Percy hoped he had found his miracle. On his left was a road that went away from the dangers surrounding him. It veered away from the road he was on in Cambridge and traveled away from the crippling fire surrounding him.

As he glanced down the road, he saw Militiamen standing on the roadway to block his travel. It was the first time General Heath had deployed his Colonial forces in the open all day. Percy instantly felt he was being denied the new road and encouraged to stay on the road his column was traveling.

Fearing the slaughter that awaited at the Great Bridge, Percy realized he was being steered toward his destruction. He nearly was out of options, had been surrounded and attacked all day, now was the time for something unexpected. Percy played what he thought was his only recourse, the miracle he needed was a left turn.

With all the calm of a well-trained British officer, Percy suddenly ordered his cannons to be wheeled around and aimed at the defiant Colonials blocking the road on his left.

"They dispersed on a cannon shot being fired at them" [lxxix] Percy wrote. The Militiamen had no cannons and could only try to find cover. To the surprise of the Colonials, Percy next did the unexpected, and that meant the difference between annihilation and survival.

Percy ordered his column to turn to the road on the left where the cannons cleared away the Militiamen who had blocked it a moment ago. Percy was going toward Charlestown, not Boston.

Everyone, even his own men were shocked by the sudden turn. Was it a maneuver to exit the road of damnation he had been traveling since leaving Lexington? Or was it something else?

It was very doubtful Percy saw the Great Bridge, he just turned off the road to preserve his forces and avoid the potential of being trapped at the Great Bridge. Lieutenant Barker near the front of the column wrote after the running battle on the road:

"...the Rebels thinking we should endeavor to return by Cambridge had broken down the Bridge and had a great number of Men [sic] to line the road to receive us there; however we threw them and went to Charlestown without any great interruption."[lxxx]

Percy masterly steered his troops away from certain destruction, down a mysterious road. With swift suddenness the British were now headed away from the main body of the Colonial Militia forces. He veered off the road in Cambridge not fully knowing what was ahead on the road to Charlestown.

He correctly guessed his chances were better on a new road than the road of damnation he had been traveling. He turned away from the abyss of the known to the hoped emptiness of the unknown.

General Heath could do little but watch Percy's column turn away from his planned destruction of them at the Great Bridge. General Heath had with his plan of encircling Percy's column administered damage to the British Army they could ill conceive before the April day.

But suddenly, Heath's circle was broken, his plans shattered. But not all hope was lost, as he followed Percy down the road to Charlestown. Heath hoped he had one more card to play as the game was nearing its ending. Heath needed that last piece to be there and did not know if it was in place.

Like being dealt that last card in a full house hand playing poker. That last card that gives you a nearly unbeatable hand, that last card that pulls you into the thrill of going all in and beating the table, being the best player at that moment.

Heath was so close to completing a task no one thought possible. If others could block the isthmus to Charlestown Neck, Heath and the thousands of inspired Colonials could finish of Lord Percy within sight on the British Headquarters in Boston.

It was hoped the militiamen from Essex County positioned themselves near Charlestown Neck blocking the narrow road. Like the peninsular of Boston, the peninsular of Charlestown had a narrow isthmus linking it to the mainland.

The British had warships that could cover the Charlestown Neck, but with darkness descending the ships would be of a limited effect. And if Percy was stopped on the road to the Neck, the warships would not be much of a mitigating force. The commander of the men from Essex County was Colonel

Timothy Pickering, and Heath hoped Pickering and his Essex County men would be waiting for Percy and his desperate soldiers.

Percy's column traveled directly down the old road toward Charlestown. The road would first take him to modern day Somerville, a part of Charleston in 1775. Following the mysterious road Percy could see high ground ahead of him as he approached Somerville's Prospect Hill. He could see he was potentially marching into another ambush, and he knew there were Colonials on the hill.

The men on Prospect Hill were not Pickering's troops, but scattered formations trying to catch up to Percy after he made his surprise turn in Cambridge. With darkness falling, Percy had no time to waste. He ordered his cannons wheeled around and fired on the hill.

With those shots, Percy had fired all his cannon shot. The Militiamen scattered for their lives. His cannons were out of ammunition. His most powerful weapons were now just parade pieces carrying the wounded and weak in his column as they marched on toward their salvation in Charlestown.

If the Colonials on Prospect Hill were not the fresh armed regiment from Essex County, commanded by Colonel Timothy Pickering, then where was the Essex Country Regiment and their commander Timothy Pickering?

Colonel Timothy Pickering Jr. was thirty years old on 19 April 1775. He was born and raised in Salem Massachusetts, he was a graduate of Harvard College, a lawyer, a politician, the son of a loyalist, and the leader of the Essex County Militiamen. Captain Pickering should have been able to cut off Percy's troops before they got to Charlestown Neck.

So, where was the young Colonel Pickering as Percy was marching into a trap he never suspected? Percy was past the high ground in Somerville and keenly focused on getting to narrow Charlestown Neck, which offered him the protection of the large British Royal Navy ships in Boston Harbor. And once across the neck the easily defendable high ground on Bunker Hill.

Percy strived toward salvation, and Heath prayed Pickering would deliver the fatal blow to the column nearly out of ammunition.

Where was Pickering?

Pickering's story is well documented. It stands in stark contrast to the remarkable courage, commitment, and sacrifice of *America's First Soldiers* on 19 April 1775. Pickering failed to march his men into Charlestown in a timely manner. Pickering and his regiment were not where they had ample time to have been.

Colonel Timothy Pickering was in Somerville on a hilltop watching Percy's escape unfold in front of him. General Heath would not get that last card to fill out his hand and win the game.

From a distant hilltop, Timothy Pickering watched what should have been the final act of a day-long drama written in the Blood of *America's First Soldiers.*

Why was Pickering where he was?

Pickering's April 19, began in Salem and was interrupted early as he was informed that the British were marching toward Concord, and had fired on the Militiamen on Lexington Green. Pickering had a junior officer depart Salem immediately with a company of men mostly from Danvers. The same men who would attack Percy in Menotomy and pay dearly as they were killed at Jason Russell's farm and orchard.

After watching others leave in his stead, Pickering ordered a meeting be held by the town fathers in Salem. Pickering lost much time as he queried his town council on how to proceed. Yes, a Colonel in the Massachusetts Militia was asking his town council what he should do—after he had already dispatched others to the fight.

The citizens of Salem demanded action, and Colonel Pickering departed with the balance of his regiment. After they were finally assembled the Colonel led his troops out of Salem to a spot where they could have refreshments.

Pickering believed his men needed refreshments and stopped at a local tavern. Yes, he stopped after marching a short distance. He got moving only when prodded by the members of his command. He marched on and decided to stop again to seek refreshments.

Again, it was his own soldiers promoting him to march on toward Boston. Pickering's delays are very hard to comprehend on this historic day, at this historic time. Pickering finally reached the Somerville part of Charlestown. Pickering choose to stop for a rest in Somerville, on the high ground known as Winter Hill.

There, he claimed to have sent a runner to find General Heath and ask for his orders. No better description of Colonel Timothy Pickering can be found than that of Nathaniel Philbrick who wrote on Page 160 of *Bunker Hill* a description of Colonel Pickering's malaise:

"[Pickering]Lingered on Winter Hill...where he stood at the head of his men and looked toward Charlestown...Playing across the lenses of his glasses that evening on Winter Hill were muzzle flashes of British and provincial muskets. [He] *saw not a war to be won but a reason to talk."*

Just as Pickering's purposeful delays have been well-documented, so have the reactions. George Washington, when informed of the events wrote:

"If the retreat had been as precipitated as it was—and God knows it could not well have been more so—the ministerial troops must have been [sic] *surrendered or have been* [sic] *totally cut off. For they had not arrived in Charlestown half an hour before a powerful body of men from Marblehead and Salem was at their heels and must, if they happened one hour sooner, inevitably intercepted their retreat to Charlestown."*[lxxxi]

Timothy Pickering was no soldier. He should have never been at the head of a regiment. Pickering was a vacillating politician who delayed his march and sabotaged its timely arrival to spare himself the dangers and consequences of fighting the British in Boston.

With a loyalist father to influence him, some believe he held back attacking the British in hopes of finding a peaceful resolution to the revolutionary, reactionary events of the day. He could have done that by trapping Percy and encouraging the British who were nearly out of ammunition to surrender. Colonel Timothy Pickering was a calculated, weak, wavering, arrogant, coward of a man.

Regardless of the shame he displayed on Winter Hill in 1775, he would become President Washington's *Secretary of War* (Jan 1795–Dec 1795). He would also serve as *Secretary of State* (Dec 1795–May 1800) for both Presidents Washington and Adams and serve as a US Senator from Massachusetts (1803–11).

Despite his political achievements, he is remembered for shrinking when the challenge of combat leadership effectively paralyzed him. While on a cold New England hilltop, on a dark and dangerous evening in April 1775 he watched others die for his freedom. He watched *America's First Soldiers* vanquish an invading army, define the true meaning of sacrifice and dedication to country and fellow soldiers.

Percy's men found the road to Charleston and safety nearly unopposed. General Percy discovered more than refuge on the high ground of Charlestown he found his survival. On Bunker Hill, the British Regulars held the high ground and the fight ended there as the Regulars took up defense positions for the first time all day on 19 April 1775.

In less than two months, the safety that was Bunker Hill would be the very place many of them would find destruction not salvation. Lieutenant John Barker wrote:

"We got there between 7 and 8 o'clock at night, took possession of the hill...the rebels did not choose to follow us to the hill..."[lxxxii]

The last British soldiers who crossed the narrow neck were the beleaguered members of the rear guard. They had been attacked without let up since leaving Lexington. Fittingly, these last men were the British Marines, commanded by the venerable, fearless Major John Pitcairn.

An army of rebels—Militiamen, and Minutemen a group the British labeled *"an army of rabble"*[lxxxiii], had bested the world's most powerful military land force. The impact of Lexington, Concord and Battle Road was profound on the British military authorities in Boston. General Lord Percy framed the events well when he said:

"They have men amongst them who know very well what they are about..."[lxxxiv]

The British army not only yielded the field and retreated in Concord, they retreated through a running battle from Concord to Boston. The cost to Gage's army was overwhelming as 273 British soldiers fell to the rebels. And most of the 73 dead Regulars fell dead on Battle Road, between Concord and Boston.

Over 50% of those British Regulars killed died on the short stretch of road in Menotomy. If Percy's column plus Smith's column added to 1,500 soldiers, then 20% of those men were casualties on 19 April 1775. One in five lay dead, dying, wounded, or missing on the road from Concord to Boston, a 20-mile corridor of human destruction, the road to damnation.

The burden borne by the Massachusetts Patriots was 95 casualties in the day's deadly events, including 49 killed by British soldiers. *America's First Soldiers* who fell that day called 23 different Massachusetts towns home. It was Lexington that bore the greatest burden supporting the Patriots of 19 April 1775.

Twenty men from Lexington were killed, wounded or missing. that is about 20% of her militia company. One in five men from Lexington fell on the Green, or on the road from Concord to Boston. An astounding price paid in blood by a single town on, on a single day – 19 April 1775.

The grievous death and wounding of 95 Patriots was all the fodder, all the human suffering needed to seal the fate of General Gage, and to drive the British into Boston. They were isolated, locked onto a peninsula that stuck into Boston Harbor. The siege of Boston had begun.

The British had just participated in the fight of their lives. Their commander called it a strategic withdrawal. *America's First Soldiers* who had fought the British in Lexington, Concord, and back to Boston, called it a retreat.

The British, for their part, retreated onto what was then the peninsula of Boston. They secured the neck of the peninsula, effectively bottling themselves up in Boston. Now, the only access to the town was via the sea. The colonists surrounded the land areas of the peninsula.

Throughout the day of 19 April 1775, we have followed the diarist Lieutenant John Barker, quoting him often as he journaled his personal experiences.

Barker was a career British army officer who retired from active duty a Lieutenant Colonel. As a young Lieutenant, Barker reflected on the day in its entirety. He ended with the feelings of a man wounded, who watched many of his comrades be killed and wounded at Lexington, Concord and Battle Road.

"Thus ended this Expedition, which from beginning to end was ill plan'd [sic] and ill executed as it was possible to be…had we not idled away three hours on Cambridge Marsh waiting for provisions that were not wanted, we should have had no interruption in Lexington…we should have reached Concord soon after daybreak before they could have heard us…we might also have got easier [sic] back and not been so much harassed as they would have had no time to assembled so many people…Thus for a few trifling Stores the Grenadiers and Light Infantry had a march of about 50 miles through and Enemy Country [sic] and in all human probability every Man have been cut

off...for when the Brigade joined us there were very few men had any ammunition left... "[lxxxv]

The successes of that April day were more than a military victory, they were a political windfall for the men who had wanted revolution. And it was a disaster for the men who wanted to stop the revolution, both British and Colonial.

The next bloody act began with the British occupation and containment in the small city of Boston. A self-imposed exile, with limited resources, on an isolated peninsular. In just 58 days, it would end on a small hill, separated from the besieged city by a meandering river named for a British King.

Chapter V
Siege of Boston

April 20–June 17, 1775

Part 1
Besieged

"Let the die be cast"
Julius Caesar (100BCE–44BCE)
Crossing the Rubicon River in Italy
10 January 49 BC

On a January day in Northern Italy over 2,000 years ago, Julius Caesar crossed the *Rubicon River* effectively beginning a Roman civil war. Caesar's bold military aggression eliminated the Roman Republic and altered the history of the Western World.

On 19 April 1775 in Massachusetts a group of dogged, determined, Colonial fighters *Crossed the Rubicon*, and forever changed the history of the world. The result of their actions was a cascading of events that was the creation of the United States of America.

On Wednesday, 19 April 1775 as the sun rose, the British Empire governed the Royal Province of Massachusetts, before the sun set on April 19, 1775, the Royal Province of Massachusetts had no government. All the British officials were besieged on a small peninsular of land that jutted out into Boston Harbor. The *Rubicon* had been crossed and the *die was cast* by *America's First Soldiers*.

Thursday morning 20 April 1775, a country that did not formally exist was at war with the world's greatest military power.

The events that occurred at Lexington, Concord and on Battle Road on 19 April 1775, had broken the bonds of kinship between a mother country and her petulant child—The Province of Massachusetts Bay. Wednesday, 19 April was not a day of words, and protests that had become familiar in Boston for many years previous, it was a day of deliberate, deadly action.

A day that the British Government would have to answer with all the force it could muster in North America. The fires of war were burning brightly. What remained of Lieutenant General Thomas Gage's battered forces were located on one of the three peninsular that jutted off the mainland and into Boston Harbor.

Charlestown, Dorchester, and Boston were alike in that each was a peninsula that stuck into Boston Harbor like one's index, middle, and ring fingers lying flat on a table. They were very close together, with Boston in the center, like a middle finger.

Dorchester was about half a mile south of Boston across a body of water called the Back Bay. It was a marshy area that was filled with water by a rising tide, then drained as that tide receded. In the 19th century it was filled in and today some of Boston's most expensive real estate is in the area still known as, *The Back Bay.*

About a quarter mile north of Boston peninsular, was Charlestown Neck. It too, was a narrow peninsular sticking into Boston Harbor. The mouth of the Charles River separated the peninsulas of Boston and Charlestown.

Charlestown was a village at the tip of the peninsular like your fingernail at the end of your index finger. The rest of the peninsular had good grazing fields, and three small hills. Moulton's Hill was 35 feet high and was at the tip of the land jutting out into the harbor and was more of a mound than a hill.

Moving inland next was Breed's Hill, nearly twice as high as Moulton's it was over 60 feet tall and a gentle rise of a hill that afforded views of Boston Harbor and the old settlement of Charlestown Village on the seashore of the narrow peninsular. And lastly, closest to the mainland was the tallest point on the peninsular, Bunker Hill.

Bunker Hill was over 100 feet tall and like Moulton's Hill and Breed's Hill, had open fields with grazing grass. Short fences and stone walls sometimes separated the pastures, with the grass often growing higher than the barriers.

On the north side of Charlestown Neck was the mouth of the Mystic River. It like the Back Bay had its water levels controlled by the incoming and outgoing tides. And like the Back Bay, as the years passed, land was reclaimed as waterways were filled in to create precious real estate. Charlestown, Boston and Dorchester are no longer peninsulas, as they have all been connected by filled in land.

The siege of Boston began as day light faded into darkness, and 19 April became April 20, 1775. The British Army was chased onto their last piece of defendable, occupied territory the town of Boston. The British barricaded themselves onto their lonely Boston existence in fear of the thousands of Colonial soldiers converging into Massachusetts for War.

The American army that had assembled outside the peninsula of Boston was like no other force the colonials had ever gathered. Angered by the blood the invading British soldiers had spilled in Lexington and Concord, militia units came from all over New England.

United in purpose, the militia units built earthworks at the neck of the peninsula of Boston, where it connected to the mainland to keep the British besieged. Once in Boston, General Gage's back was against the sea. His forces were trapped on the peninsula, and Gage understood he had to regain control of the rebellious, uncontrollable Massachusetts Bay Colony. Quickly.

The mustering Militia forces choose Cambridge as their headquarters. It was very close to Boston and sat beside the Charles River. It was a place where many wealthy loyalists had built beautiful homes, it had open spaces and accessible roads. All of value to the men arriving by the hundreds every day to finish off the mighty British Army in Boston. In 1775, the Province of Massachusetts only had militia forces, not a standing army—that was about to change.

The Massachusetts armed militia forces were nearly as old as America's first permanent settlement in Plymouth, Massachusetts. Already well over 100 years old as they gathered at Cambridge, they were the oldest Colonial forces in the American Colonies. There were two distinct branches of the citizen armed forces, the Militiamen and the Minutemen.

Each formed into local companies, with the better trained, equipped, and physically fit men attached to the Minutemen companies. All other volunteers served in the militia companies from their teenage years to their 60s. Each group had to supply themselves with weapons at their own cost.

They served and drilled as a commitment to their families and communities. They were not paid for their service and sacrifices, but they were respected and thanked by the local communities they defended.

The gathering forces around Boston were estimated at over 10,000 Militiamen in a matter of a few days. They were arriving not just from Massachusetts but all-over New England.

To maintain his position on the peninsula of Boston, Gage depended on the ships of the Royal Navy. Those Royal Navy ships were commanded by Admiral Samuel Graves. Irish born Samuel Graves was from a nautical family and had many relatives in the Royal Navy.

After he was promoted to Vice-Admiral, Graves became senior and commanding Royal Navy Officer in North America. In 1774, he was sent to Boston to enforce the closure of the Port, where he made his headquarters. He was also there to assist the Army of Occupation in Boston commanded by General Gage, but he was not under the authority of an Army officer.

On April 20, 1775 Admiral Graves found the British situation in Boston, unacceptable and wanted his sizable fleet of warships in Boston Harbor to open fire with all their guns onto Roxbury and Charlestown. Graves envisioned setting the colonial strong holds ablaze, with destruction delivered by his formidable naval artillery. General Gage did not agree and asked Admiral Graves to stand down.

Gage did not want any military action in the hours and days that followed the military disaster of April 19. Had Admiral Graves fired on and destroyed parts of Dorchester, Roxbury, Charlestown or Cambridge, the British position in Boston would have been overrun by thousands of uncontrollable rampaging Colonial Militiamen.

General Gage needed calm in Boston on April 20, 1775, not an escalation he could not support. Gage, better than most British officials, understood that the colonials, in just a few short hours, went from countrymen to enemies. And he may have had the words of Lord Percy in his head as he tried to bring reason to the unreasonable.

On April 20, the day after the battles, General Percy wrote the following reflection of the efforts of his relief column. Percy, wrote to General Gage:

"During the whole affair, the rebels attacked us in a very scattered, irregular manner, but with perseverance and resolution, nor did they ever dare to form into a regular body. Indeed they knew too well what was proper, to do so.

Whoever looks upon them as an irregular mob, will find himself very much mistaken. They have men amongst them who know very well what they are about...nor are several of their men void of a spirit of enthusiasm...for many of them advanced to 10 yards to fire at me and other officers...[knowing]they were morally certain to be put to death in an instant"[lxxxvi]

General Percy captured his enemies' intentions and actions. His reflections were accurate and contained an aspect of admiration for an enemy many of his peers considered unworthy.

"They have men amongst them who know very well what they are about...nor are several of their men void of a spirit of enthusiasm...for many of them advanced to 10 yards to fire... "[lxxxvii]

Percy who had direct contact with the Colonials in combat delivers a dynamic compliment concerning the battlefield courage and tactics of the Militiamen. Perhaps, his cautionary warning to the cautious General Gage pacified Gage to inaction and to halt the naval bombardment proposed by Admiral Graves.

Meanwhile on April 20, across the blockaded neck of the Boston Peninsular, Dr. Joseph Warren and some of members of the Massachusetts Committee of Safety met to discuss the recent past and recent future of Boston. Dr. Warren voiced his expectations, and ultimately drafted a letter which was no less than a call to arms for the surrounding communities and beyond. Dr. Warren wrote:

"Gentlemen—The barbarous murders committed on our innocent brethren, on Wednesday the 19th instant, have made it absolutely, necessary that we immediately raise an army to defend our wives and our children from the butchering hands of an inhuman soldiery, who, incensed at the obstacles they met with in their bloody progress, and enraged at being repulsed from the

121

field of slaughter, will, without the least doubt, take the first opportunity in their power to ravage this devoted country with fire and sword. "[lxxxviii]

Warren's words are direct in a-fixing blame for all the death and destruction of April 19, on the British soldiers. Labeling the day's events as, *"barbarous murder"*, his choice of words sure to inflame his countrymen's feelings at that very hour.

Warren labelled his new enemy as, *"butchering, inhuman soldiery..."* Warren's description would be read by many more than had participated, and he himself had limited participation as he joined the fighters on Battle Road.

Warren continued:

"We conjure you, therefore, by all that is dear, by all that is sacred, that you give all assistance possible in forming an army. Our all is at stake. Death and devastation are the instant consequences of delay. Every moment is infinitely precious. An hour lost may deluge your country in blood, and entail perpetual slavery upon the few of your posterity who may survive the carnage." [lxxxix]

Warren challenged the spirit, courage, and devotion of his fellow Colonials, not just to his cause, but to defend their families and very existence. He equated an *"hour"* to a *"deluge of blood,"* and the imposing immediate Armageddon of *"Death and devastation are instant consequences."* Warren concluded as an inspired preacher would finish his weekly address to an enraptured congregation. His conclusion began with each reader standing before the Almighty himself as Warren invokes the wrath of God.

"...as you will answer to God himself, that you will hasten and encourage by all possible means the enlistment of men to form the army, and send them forward to headquarters, at Cambridge, with that expedition which the vast importance and instant urgency of the affair demand." [xc]

Warren impugned his fellow citizens establishing a link between the Godly support of the rebellion, and damnation for inaction. As in so many military and political conflicts, the embattled are here accountable to a just God that supports *Their* cause. Many of Warren's fellow citizens answered the call of the Patriots.

The growing Colonial Militia forces gathering along the Charles River in Cambridge, created the largest military encampment the area has ever known. By early June, militiamen from all four New England colonies had gathered outside of Boston. *(Note: In 1775, Vermont was still a contested area between New Hampshire and New York and Maine was still part of Massachusetts.)*

Estimates vary, but it is believed that as many as 10,000 determined men had surrounded the British in Boston. Many of them were raw recruits, few understood war and all its deprivations, and all would eventually learn of the irreversible, permanent consequences of war. The gathering militia around Boston was truly a mix of the residents of Colonial Massachusetts.

Lacking a professional standing army, the local villages and towns organized, staffed, trained, and equipped a militia. Amongst the groups of citizens that were allowed to participate were freed African Americans. Blackman Crispus Attucks fell dead at the Boston Massacre, and Prince Estabrook was counted amongst those who stood at Lexington with the Patriots on 19 April 1775. Estabrook would fall wounded on that day in Lexington. Freed black men were part of the community of Colonial Boston, while enslaved black men were not allowed to serve in the Continental Army.

Often lost or overlooked in historical accounts is that many families in Boston did own slaves at the dawn of the American Revolution. How hollow the words spoken and written by Boston's Patriot leaders must have been to enslaved human beings with no hope of embracing liberty.

How crass and hypocritical the cries of British oppression must have been to those black men, women and children whose very existence was the living embodiment of tyranny.

Boston had many enslaved black people in 1775. According to Nathaniel Philbrick:

"For the citizens of Boston, whose love of liberty didn't prevent one in five families from owning slaves."

Philbrick, Bunker Hill
Page 23

Remarkably, enslaved African American men were denied entry into some of the local militias, but not into His Majesty's Army. With *Dunmore's Proclamation in Virginia in 1775*, enslaved men who served the Crown in North America would be freed after the cession of hostilities. Such a promise of hope to those enslaved attracted many slaves to the British side of the conflict. A promise that required the British to win its war with the American Colonies.

And it was in December of 1775, at a Council of War in Cambridge, Massachusetts newly appointed army commander, General George Washington, *"rejected having slaves in the Continental Army."* [xci] But he ultimately put the question to the Continental Congress, which memorialized the decision made in Cambridge by a revolutionary army fighting for *liberty*.

The Congress that in July of 1776 drafted the Declaration of Independence declared:

"...that all men are created equal, that they are endowed by their Creator with certain unalienable Rights, that among these are Life, Liberty and the pursuit of Happiness."

But as they enshrined their own liberty, the same Congress, the very same men declared six months earlier on January 16, 1776:

"...Congress resolved that free-blacks that had served faithfully in the army at Cambridge could enlist but no others: slaves were excluded from American armies." [xcii]

Why were slaves excluded from service? The answer is as simple as it is disturbing. Slaves were property in the British American Colonies in 1775. And many of those property owners did not want to surrender the economic value that those slaves represented.

Freedom was an elusive term for some in Colonial America, and in Massachusetts. Nearly 100 years later, as Northern Americans fought Southern Americans over issues that included slavery, the Northern, or Union Army was segregated.

It seems incredible to believe that the Armed forces of the United States would not be fully desegregated until July 1948. It took 173 years to integrate the United States Armed Services. Nearly 200 years would have to pass when, not by consensus but by the act of a single man—President Harry Truman signed *Executive Order 9981*[xciii]

With a growing army around Boston, what the Rebels needed was a navy. At Boston in 1775, the gathered colonial forces possessed no naval ships, so it was a relatively easy task for the British Army in Boston to be protected and reinforced utilizing the sea. Easy, but time consuming and very expensive.

The British had the world's most powerful navy—the Royal Navy. Unchallenged in the waters off Massachusetts, the Royal Navy had a very great task to resupply and reinforce Gage's troops in Boston. In the 18th century these were sail powered ships and depended wholly on the speed and direction of the winds.

And England is 3,000 nautical miles from Massachusetts, a very formidable distance. It could take over six weeks in each direction, depending on weather, winds, ship design, etc. So, news, instructions, reinforcements, equipment, as well as supplies moved very slowly.

All General Gage's superiors were in London, so it would take weeks for him to send and receive news or orders. Gage's situation in Boston was difficult and barely tenable, on many levels.

As days became weeks, food supplies for men and horses began to dwindle in Boston. It was not always easy to await resupply by ship, one quick answer for the British was to raid the harbor islands. Boston had many islands in its harbor, and some were home to wild and domesticated herds, as well plentiful hay fields.

The rich bounty on the islands was well known to the residents, who after being persuaded by Patriot leaders burned some hay fields rendering them useless to the British. Meanwhile, the locals were determined to capture the livestock and destroy the crops thus deny the British the sustenance they badly needed.

If it was reduced to a waiting game, the Colonials had the upper hand. Gage needed to secure local food supplies and came up with a plan. The British intended to capture what they needed and sent the armed schooner *Diana*, the armed sloop *Britannia*, and eight barges loaded and 110 Royal Marines to complete the task.

Some of the islands in the harbor were accessible via tidal flats and marshes that were walkable at low tide. Two of them were Hog and Noodle

Island in Chelsea Creek, at present day East Boston where Logan Airport is located. On the afternoon of May 27, 1775, those islands were the targets of the British raids.

Just three weeks before the Battle of Bunker Hill, frustrations again reached breaking point, as Marines and some determined Colonials found each other on a muddy marshland in Boston Harbor. The Colonials as ever had their spies in Boston, and the British plan to invade and secure the herds on Hog and Noodle Islands quickly reached the Patriot leaders in Cambridge. Colonel Israel Putnam and over 300 militiamen were determined to drive the remaining livestock off these two islands.

Noodle Island was in Boston Harbor separated from Boston Peninsular by less than two miles of open water. Hog Island is north of Noodle Island and was closer to the mainland and nearly connected to present day East Boston, and was almost connected to Noodle Island. It was from Boston Peninsular that the British attacked Noddle Island first via the sea.

From the moment the British began to exit the barges, a small band of Militiamen on the high ground opened fire. Vastly outnumbered the Militiamen retreated chased by the Royal Marines to the line Colonel Putnam was holding. Putnam was well dug-in and situated higher ground. The Colonials took their aim and opened fire on the startled British.

The American volley was deadly accurate and nearly stopped the British in their tracks. Then Putnam's men did the completely unexpected to the Royal marines, they opened fire with two artillery pieces. Although they were small three-pound canons they opened fire on the Marines and the barges left on the shores of the Island. One barge was hit and damaged.

The two small British warships returned fire with little effect on the confident dug-in colonials. The Royal Marines tried but could not finish off the dug in Colonials. And in a foreshadowing of the battle that was to come on Bunker Hill, the British could not outflank Colonel Putnam's well positioned men. The British abandoned the field and returned to their barges.

But it was not over.

As the sun rose on May 28, 1775, the British Marines attacked again, but this time at Hog Island. Colonel Putnam and his troops were already dug-in on the high ground of Hog Island. Again, the Colonials released a deadly volley of musket and small cannon fire.

The results were just like the day before, as the British lost another barge, and retreated from the Island. After the two days of fighting, the British counted 20 dead and another 50 wounded.[xciv]

The British also suffered the loss of the armed schooner *Diana*. The ship went into waters the British had not surveyed, and grounded. The currents pushed her close enough to shore that Putnam's men could fire their muskets at the crew. With night falling, the Royal Navy abandoned the hopelessly grounded *Diana*.

The Colonials did not abandon the Diana as they boarded her and stripped her of anything and everything of value. The Americans next set the hopeless ship ablaze. They watched as it burnt to the shallow water and mud holding on to her, denying the ship the sea that promised her rescue.

The mud and shallow waters of the marshes around Boston harbor were metaphor for the British in Boston. They were mired in the morass they had created in Massachusetts. The Ministers in London, an out of touch Royal Monarch, an overwhelmed, understaffed, bureaucratic, aristocratic General, had incubated the ferment of rebellion with their policies and harassment of the local population.

Shuttering the port of Boston increased the hungry and poor, and fed the ranks of those who wanted everything from political change to armed revolt and independence form their oppressors. The British had mired themselves in a world they demeaned, and little understood. They judged the people of Massachusetts as they had judged the Irish, Scottish, and English poor. They were very wrong.

The people of Massachusetts saw themselves as free Englishmen. In many cases the leaders of the demeaned had secured the empowering difference of an English education. Whereas the Irish, Scottish, and English poor were unable to secure an English education in the 18th century.

John Adams, Samuel Adams, John Hancock, Reverend Jonas Clarke, Eldridge Gerry, Robert Treat Paine, and Dr. Joseph Warren were ALL graduates of Harvard College in Cambridge, Massachusetts. The men who guided the British toward their mental and physical morass in Boston, and created the American Revolution were very well-educated Englishmen.

April 20–June 17, 1775

Part 2
Imagination

What we wish, we readily believe,
and what we ourselves think,
we imagine others think also.

Julius Caesar (100BCE–44BCE)
Roman General and Dictator

Lieutenant General Sir Thomas Gage, commander of all his Majesty's soldiers in North America was still in Boston in the Spring of 1775. He hated Boston and its rebellious inhabitants. General Thomas Gage believed the rebellious Colonial residents inferior to him, to his country, to his King, to his way of life, to his very existence. And Gage believed others held his contempt for the Colonial residents of Boston and Massachusetts, after all he was surround by loyalists, and British soldiers.

He was immersed in a world of sycophants. Men who believed not just their army, but their very existence superior to those they had governed before the events of 19 April 1775 fatally damaged that sovereign authority.

Yet, even in defeat, and besieged, and nearly surrounded they were unyielding in their conceit. They maintained their blissful ignorance, by further believing the Colonials knew the British army was invincible and would again rule over the Royal Province of Massachusetts Bay.

As they had abandoned the Old Bridge in Concord, they were forced to conducted a running retreat through the streets of Lexington, Menotomy, and Cambridge the British retreat from the harbor Islands was an embarrassing disaster. It was another example of the underestimation of the Colonials as an organized fighting force.

General Thomas Gage and his officers had at every encounter, grossly miscalculated their former countrymen. General Gage could not afford the casualties of the battles of Noodle and Hog Islands as he was trying to gather additional British soldiers from all the other colonies. Gage would remove troops stationed in New York, and as far away as Quebec to bolster his besieged garrison at Boston. Gage was desperate.

By the end of May, the British increased the size of the Boston Garrison bringing the total number of forces in British to about 5,000 regular army troops. They also possessed several large, heavily armed, imposing warships surrounding and protecting the tenuous British position on the Boston peninsula.

On May 25, 1775, General Gage got his long-ago requested help to maintain order in Boston. The Ministers in London sent him three fighting generals, and a ship named after a mythical beast from Hell.

The ship that sailed into Boston Harbor with the cargo of three generals was the *HMS Cerberus*. HMS Cerberus was a 28-gun, 500-ton frigate with a full-time crew of about 200 Royal Navy sailors and fighting Marines. HMS Cerberus was named for a Greek mythological creature resembling a large dog. But this dog was very special for it had three heads, a snake for a tail, and was believed to guard the gates of Hell, allowing no one to escape.

All three generals and the ship *HMS Cerberus* would meet their fates, as their individual and collective failures in the New American World would be measured as defining their lasting memory in the service of the British Army.

Fifty-two-year-old Major General John Burgoyne was the oldest of the three. And he was junior in military seniority, or service amongst the three new arrivals. He was a member of the *House of Commons*, and a playwright who had his works published and produced in his lifetime.

Known as *Gentleman Johnny* for his impeccable manners, as a published playwright, successful politician, and British Army General, he was well-liked and had a *je ne sais quoi* in British society. Burgoyne was assigned to garrison duty in Boston and would not command at the Battle of Bunker Hill. He would observe and wrote of the day's events.

Ultimately, by 1777, he did command British forces in America. The results were a historic and political disaster. General Burgoyne's army was surrounded at Saratoga, in upstate New York as he tried to move south from Canada, splitting New England away from New York and the other colonies.

Separating New England from the other colonies was an early strategy used by the British in hopes of isolating New England where the revolution had begun. It was a complete and total catastrophe. Burgoyne was surrounded, and capitulated on October 17, 1777, surrendering his entire British Army to the fledgling Continental Army.

General Burgoyne's surrender to the Americans at Saratoga was unprecedented and was the cataclysmic political event the French needed to support the revolution in the American Colonies. After the surrender, Burgoyne returned to England in disgrace, his army career was ended.

Major General Henry Clinton was forty-four years old when the *Cerberus* docked in Boston Harbor. He, like General Burgoyne, was a career army officer, and a Member of Parliament. At the Battle of Bunker Hill, General Clinton served under General Howe, and was assigned to command the reserve forces.

General Clinton would serve again under General Howe who was promoted to Commander and Chief of British Forces in North America in late 1775, after General Gage returned to England in disgrace. It was General Clinton who tried but failed to rescue General Burgoyne's' trapped army at Saratoga.

In 1778, Clinton replaced Howe when Howe resigned and returned to London to defend his conduct of the war in North America. Particularly, the loss of an entire army, over 6,000 troops under Burgoyne at Saratoga. General Henry Clinton would be the British Commander and Chief on October 18, 1781, when General Lord Cornwallis surrendered at Yorktown effectively ending the fighting in Colonial America's war of independence.

Clinton's name and reputation were compromised more than those of Lord Cornwallis after the surrender to Washington and the French at Yorktown. Clinton was in overall command and the blame rested on the failures of his overall administration of the war in North America.

And finally, on the HMS *Cerberus* was 45-year-old, Major General Sir William Howe, the senior of the three generals. Howe was the most experienced, and interesting of the Generals arriving in Boston. Howe like many of his peers in the British military at that time, was a Member of the *House of Commons*. He served in Parliament for twenty-two years representing Nottingham, the home of the mythical *Robin Hood*, and the legendary *Raleigh* bicycle.

Howe was from an esteemed military family, and one of three high ranking officers who were brothers. Including Admiral Richard Howe, and General George Howe, who was killed in action during the *French and Indian War* in New York in 1758.

In a remarkable irony, William Howe's brother General George Howe died in the arms of Colonial Officer Colonel Israel Putnam as they fought the French together at Fort Ticonderoga. George Howe was described as, *"the best officer in the British Army"*[xcv] by legendary British General Thomas Wolfe. At Bunker Hill, William Howe would face his brother's old friend, Colonial Colonel Israel Putnam.

Major General William Howe was a well-respected fighting general. He had served with the renowned British General Thomas Wolfe in Canada against the French. Wolfe was one of Howe's mentors and a friend. Led by General Wolfe the British were victorious over the French in Canada, securing all of Canada as a British Colony.

So grateful was the local British governor that he named Islands in the St. Lawrence Seaway for Generals Wolfe and Howe. And like General Gage, Howes' mentor was at Culloden's Moor. It was at Culloden then Captain Wolfe earned his fearless reputation, fighting with the Duke of Cumberland against the fabled Highland Warriors.

The victory was not enough for Cumberland, as he ordered wounded Highlanders murdered on the bloody field at Culloden. When Young Captain Wolfe was told by Cumberland to kill a Scottish fighter, lying wounded on the battlefield, he refused. His legend grew from the moment he said no to the Duke of Cumberland, the *Bloody Butcher* on the blood-soaked Battlefield of Culloden in Scotland.

General William Howe commanded the British assault on Bunker Hill, and by some accounts was never the same man after the extraordinary carnage of June 17, 1775. General Howe succeed General Gage as *Commander and Chief British Forces in North America* on October 11, 1775.

Like Gage before him, Howe was doomed to inaction, and remained besieged in Boston until he evacuated the city on March 17, 1776. Doing so after the Americans installed cannons on Dorchester Heights to obliterated the British troops and ships in Boston.

Howe could not break the siege and ultimately evacuated Boston peacefully and he chose to sail to Nova Scotia to regroup his forces.

Howe returned to Colonial America in July of 1776, where he led an invasion of New York. Howe's amphibious invasion was at that time stunningly massive, including hundreds of warships and over 32,000 well-armed British and Hessian soldiers. Howe would push Washington out of New York and into New Jersey, and out of New Jersey and into Pennsylvania.

Howe captured and occupied Philadelphia in September of 1777. Howe had defeated Washington time and time again but could not finish off Washington and the Continental Army. Some believe that it was the accuracy and precision of the American riflemen on Breed's Hill that kept him from closing on Washington and his fear of unbearable British loses at the hands of the Americans.

While quartering in Philadelphia, Howe received word that General Burgoyne had surrendered his entire army at Saratoga in upstate New York. It was a disproportionate disaster in America and forced Howe to resign his command. He returned to England in May of 1778 to defend himself, it was an effort of futility as his reputation never recovered.

Command of the British Forces in North America fell onto Howe's successor and a man who had been with him in Boston, General Henry Clinton. Howe failed to win the war against the Americans, and his standing in Great Britain would never be as it was before he exited the HMS Cerberus in Boston Harbor in May of 1775.

He, like Burgoyne and Clinton suffered career ending failure in Colonial America beginning the moment he stepped off the HMS Cerberus in Boston harbor.

The three overall British commanders of the British forces in North America between 1775–81, Generals Gage, Howe, and Clinton were sent home in disgrace. They all suffered landmark defeats that have come to define the American War of Independence. Despite all the advantages that they had, they failed in America. And they all had one other similarity, they were in Boston and had a voice in the Battle of Bunker Hill.

April 20–June 17, 1775

Part 3
The Proclamation

"The fault, dear Brutus, is not in our stars,
but in ourselves…"

(Julius Caesar, Act I, Scene III, L. 140–1)
William Shakespeare (1565–1616)

In early June of 1775, the British were suffering from the effects of the blockage of land-based supplies entering Boston. One item in short supply for the besieged city was hay. Despite the losses incurred on Hog and Noodle Islands, the British tried again and sent troops to forage the harbor Islands.

On June 8th and 9th expeditions were sent out of Boston to search the harbor islands. Diarist, Lieutenant John Barker makes note of each dangerous trip to the islands. Barker calls the spoils found on June 8th as, *"paltry"* and the pickings for the 9th as, *"very small quantity."* He labels these futile attempts as, *"scarce worth sending out 200 men"*, Barker and his fellow soldiers with the events of Hog and Noodle Islands fresh on their minds saw the risk-reward ratio as not beneficial, whatsoever.[xcvi]

But these foraging parties speak to the growing problems that the siege had caused General Gage. Since the embarrassment and losses of April 19, Gage has been building his manpower up in Boston. That demanded more pressure be put on already dwindling supplies. Gage then looked to a political solution to his mounting problems. He began with a prisoner exchange.

On June sixth, Dr. Warren and General Israel Putnam arrived at Charlestown Neck. General Putnam was a well-known Militia leader from Connecticut.

Putnam had served with the British against the French and was well respected as a soldier and he was well liked by his old British friends. Putnam left his Connecticut home after learning of the actions of 19 April. Putnam arrived and was ready for whatever his fellow Patriots asked of him. Both Warren and Putnam met with two British officers at Charlestown Neck on June 6, 1775.

The British officers arrived by small boat from the nearby anchored HMS Lively. Lively was a fearsome gun ladened ship, positioned to take immediate action if the prisoner exchange suddenly turned into an ambush. Out of the small boat stepped British Major Moncrief, an old friend of General Putnam.

The Colonials handed over six British privates taken on 19 April. They also held three officers that they would not release until the British accepted the privates and presented the Colonial soldiers they were holding.

The British privates were interrogated onboard the HMS Lively. They spoke in glowing terms for their caretakers on the Colonial side. All the privates had been wounded and:

"...expressed in the strongest terms their grateful sense of the tenderness which had been shown them and their miserable situation..."

When the officers returned to the ship they held similar feeling about their Colonial captors:

"The regular officers expressed themselves as highly pleased; [they] *politely acknowledged the genteel, kind treatment they had received from their captors.* [xcvii]

The exchange between the enemies ended as it had been conducted with grace and honor. For their part the British were pleasantly surprised at the mercy shown their soldiers by the Colonials. Here again, the mischaracterization of the Colonial Americans by men like General Thomas Gage is turned upside down before his very eyes. For his part in the coming days, General Gage extends again a hand of tolerance to his rebellious countrymen.

Six days after the cordial prisoner exchange the forgiving General Thomas Gage offers an olive branch to the Massachusetts rebels. Using his supreme authority as Commander and Chief of British forces in North America Gage offered a blanket pardon or amnesty toward those who had taken up arms against his Majesty's troops on 19 April 1775. Author Richard Frothingham described Gage's attempt to sooth feelings and create peace as:

"On the 12th of June General Gage issued his memorable proclamation— arrogant in its tone and grossly insulting to the people."[xcviii]

In his diary Barker refers to Gage's proclamation:

"Yesterday a Proclamation was issued by his Excellency General Gage, offering his Majesty's most gracious pardon to all who shall lay down their Arms, [sic] and return to the duties of peaceful Subjects [sic]. Excepting Samuel Adams and John Hancock"[xcix]

General Gage delivered his proclamation as a military dictator. Gage's political expressions of his Majesty's forgiveness was bombast.

"Whereas the infatuated multitudes, who have long suffered themselves to be conducted by certain well known Incendiaries and Traitors in a fatal progression of crimes against the constitutional authority of the state, have at length proceeded to avowed rebellion; and the good effects which were expected to arise from the patience and leniency of the King's government, have been frustrated, and are now rendered hopeless, by the influence of evil counsels; it only remains for those who are entrusted with supreme rule, as well for the punishment of the guilty, as the protection of the well affected, to prove they do not bear the sword in vain."[c]

Gage begins by insulting the population that he is trying to calm. Addressing the Colonials as, *"infatuated multitudes."* He makes again that fatal mistake of misjudgment. Beyond insulting their intelligence, he next accuses them of, *"crimes against the constitutional authority"*

Here, Gage seems to forget that in Massachusetts, people had been governing themselves since the Mayflower anchored at Plymouth. They have been their own authority for over 150 years. His callous disrespect for Americans is on vivid display, as he reminds the formally governed of his *"supreme"* authority, and benevolent use of force, *"not bear the sword in vain"*

Gage's words continue to dam him in the eyes of Colonial Massachusetts:

The infringements which have been committed upon the most sacred rights of the crown and people of Great Britain are too many to enumerate... All unprejudiced people...will find upon a transient review, marks of premeditation and conspiracy that would justify the fullness of chastisement...The authors of the present unnatural revolt never daring to trust their cause, or their actions to the judgements of an impartial public, or even to the dispassionate reflection of their followers, have uniformly placed their chief confidence in the suppression of truth: And while indefatigable and shameless pains have been taken to obstruct every appeal to the interest of the people of America; the grossest forgeries, calumnies and absurdities that ever insulted human understanding, have been imposed upon their credulity. The press, that distinguished appendage of public liberty...has been invariably prostituted to the most contrary purposes...The name of God has been introduced in the pulpits to excite and justify devastation and massacre..."[ci]

Gage's words conjure the damnation of the pulpits of America, *"name of God has been introduced in the pulpits...to justify devastation and massacre."* He speaks of the *"sacred rights"* of others while excluding the Colonial citizens he is addressing, and he labels the struggles in Massachusetts Colony as an *"unnatural revolt."*

He has clearly ignored that nearly 100 Colonial men were killed or wounded on 19 April and not many people across Boston Neck from his desperate situation believes the acts of 19 April *"unnatural."*

"A number of armed persons, to the amount of many thousands assembled on the 19th of April last and from behind walls, and lurking holes, attacked a detachment of the King's troops, who...unprepared for vengeance, and willing to decline it, made use of their arms only in their own defense. Since that period, the rebels, deriving confidence from impunity, have added insult to outrage; have repeatedly fired upon the King's ships and subjects, with cannon and small arms, have possessed the roads, and other communications by which the town of Boston was supplied with provisions; and with a preposterous parade of military arrangement, they affect to hold the army besieged; while

part of their body make daily and indiscriminate invasions upon private property, and with a wantonness of cruelty every incident to lawless tumult, carry degradation and distress wherever they turn their steps...[cii]

Gage next explains 19 April 1775. "*Many thousands assembled on the 19th of April*" Here he is honest, and I wonder if he read his own proclamation. "*Many thousands*" is a large number in Colonial America. He identifies his own lack of responsibilities when he reveals the willingness of many thousands to fire on armed British Regulars. He then calls them all cowards, "*from behind walls, and lurking holes.*"

He relieves himself and his troops of responsibility declaring, "*...use of their arms only in their own defense.*" He next outlines his own desperateness:

"... [The Rebels] *have possessed the roads, and other communications by which the town of Boston was supplied with provisions...*" and that the Colonial Rebels, "*hold the army besieged.*"

General Gage ends his vulgar document promising pardon to those who have raised arms to his Majesty. He promises them all is forgiven, with the surrender of the siege of his Army, and the surrendering of their firearms. He finishes by stating both Sam Adams and John Hancock are not forgiven and they will be punished.

Gage's myopic view is firmly fixed on the fault of others. His aristocratic roots exempt him and insulate him and his troops from responsibility on the 19th of April. His proclamation inflames the Colonial population. It further divides the divided parties.

Gage also proclaimed marshal law on the Boston peninsular. He disarmed all the Boston civilians ordering them to turn in any firearms. He really did not realize how powerless he had become. He still did not understand his deteriorating situation.

Before his very eyes Gage did not want to see and did not want to accept - *The Game had Changed.*

April 20–June 17, 1775

Part 4
The Plans

"All bad precedents begin as justifiable measures."

Julius Caesar (100BCE–44BCE)
Roman General and Dictator

General Sir Thomas Gage believed his measures now justifiable. He had satisfied his own speculations and offered his unworthy enemies an alternative to complete destruction. Gage wanted to release all the military might that England could unleash in the late 18th century.

He would combine all his land and sea assets, moving very fast, from land and sea, with a complicated plan including amphibious assaults. He would move from different positions, throwing his enemies off, those same enemies holding him hostage in Boston.

Under the direction of General Gage, and with the assistance of Generals Burgoyne, Clinton, and Howe the British planned an aggressive attack aimed to break the siege of Boston. It would be a complicated series of amphibious landings, supported by Naval gunfire, delivering British Regulars to the peninsulas north and south of Boston.

The British Generals planned a two-pronged attack. The southern axis of attack, led by fighting General Howe, was directed at the Dorchester peninsular just south of Boston. After landing amphibiously the Regulars would march aggressively onto the area known as Dorchester Heights.

They would secure the Heights and position artillery to bombard the areas inland of Boston. British artillery would then bombard the Colonial positions at Roxbury, while land forces overwhelmed the defenders. Securing Roxbury would help defend the British position on Dorchester Heights from a land based counterattack by the Colonial forces.

Next the British would march toward the Rebel headquarters in Cambridge, with hopes of overrunning the Rebel headquarters, and destroying the rebellion, and re-establishing British sovereign rule.

Simultaneously the northern axis of attack, led by General Clinton, would be an amphibious landing on the Charlestown peninsular just to the north of Boston. Similar to the assault on Dorchester Heights, the British troops would take the high ground at Charlestown—Bunker Hill. Bunker Hill would be armed with British guns that could reach inland toward the Colonial defensive positions at Charlestown Neck and beyond.

The narrow neck would be assaulted by the regulars with artillery support from the Royal Navy, and the artillery located on the secured heights of Bunker Hill. General Burgoyne was to lead the third amphibious assault near the Charlestown Neck area. That was the final amphibious landing of the British assault plans. Burgoyne and his troops would push across Charlestown Neck and create an opening for Clinton's forces. With amphibious forces led by General Burgoyne and additional troops coming over Bunker Hill led by General Clinton the large force would march toward Cambridge.

It was a classic pincher movement, two forces encircling an enemy while traveling to a common point. It had served many a great general on the battlefield, and it promised to crush the untrained, rustic Colonials. One force arriving from the north in Charlestown and the other from the south in Dorchester, each protected from counterattack with artillery from land and sea.

Although heavily outnumbered, the British would rely on their highly trained and disciplined army, working with the full support of the Royal Navy. The British use of a joint army and navy force, combined with three potential battle sites could overwhelm the Colonial Militia forces and their inexperienced officers.

They would meet in Cambridge and destroy the rebels once and for all. It was a good plan that mixed all the assets available to General Gage in Boston. If executed properly Gage's plan would reinstall his and the Crown's authority in Massachusetts. This bold plan was to begin on Sunday Morning June 18, 1775.

In June of 1775, the British in Boston had instruments of war like the United States of America possessed for the invasion of Normandy in World

War II. The Royal Navy had massive, heavily armed *Ships of the Line* like *HMS Somerset*.

She had 70 guns and was the flagship of Admiral Samuel Graves. So imposing was the ship *HMS Somerset*, that its presence in Boston Harbor was memorialized in a popular poem written 85 years after the Battle of Bunker Hill:

> *"The Somerset, British man-of-war:*
> *A phantom ship, with each mast and spar*
> *Across the moon, like a prison-bar,*
> *And a huge black hulk, that was magnified*
> *By its own reflection in the tide."*

Paul Revere's Ride (1860)
Henry Wadsworth Longfellow (1807–82)

The *HMS Boyne* was also a wicked 70-gun behemoth. Some of her guns fired 32-pound projectiles, capable of destroying whatever they hit. The *HMS Asia* was a 64-gun large, intimidating *Ship of the Line* and was at anchor with the Somerset and Boyne in Boston Harbor.

Then, the British had the fast, easily moveable smaller armed sloops: *Lively, Glasgow, Falcon*, and *Spitfire*. Between the ships and shore-based batteries the Colonial forces were facing about 168 guns.

The British Army in Boston also had artillery that was to be placed on the high ground in Boston to aid in the bombardment of the Colonial positions. The British had well trained officers, led by experienced and respect generals who had tasted victory in North America albeit against the French not British American Colonials.

Lastly, the British soldiers themselves were a rough, tough, well-armed, well-drilled, experienced 18th century fighting force. They were perhaps the best soldiers in the world in 1775. And General Gage had the best of the best in Boston for his planned attack. Some of the finest fighting regiments in the British Army were waiting for Gage's orders to attack.

Amongst the many fabled regiments were some with nearly 100 years of service before arriving at Boston. Some of the regiments made history before Boston, at Boston and long after the guns in Boston fell silent.

One such regiment was the *23rd Regiment*, also known as the *Royal Welsh Fusiliers*. They fought on 19 April along Battle Road and fought at Bunker Hill. They would still be standing when Cornwallis surrendered at Yorktown ending the American War of Independence in 1781. Their pride and professionalism carried onto European battlefields where they helped defeat Napoleon at Waterloo.

Also in Boston was the *4th Regiment*, known as the *King's Own*, they fought at Culloden's Moor, Lexington, Concord, Battle Road, Bunker Hill, Waterloo, and Gallipoli in World War I. They would survive into the 20th century fighting against Rommel in North Africa.

General Gage also had 600 Marines led by their beloved commander Major John Pitcairn in Boston. The Marines had been in service to the Crown since 1664, 110 years before they landed in Boston. They were ship borne light infantry, famous for their ambitious landings wherever needed by the British Crown.

Beyond their time in Boston, they would help defeat Napoleon at sea. In the 20th century they would land at Gallipoli, Tunisia, Sicily, Italy and storm the beaches at Normandy. And they would make a difference at Bunker Hill in Boston on June 17, 1775.

And then there was the 52rd Regiment. The 52nd drew blood at Lexington, and Concord, and shed their blood as they ran the gauntlet on Battle Road. They fought with Cornwallis at Yorktown, still standing when the fighting in America ended.

They were led into battle with the Duke of Wellington, making history as they finished off Napoleon at Waterloo. They fought and died at the Somme and Vimy Ridge in World War I, and 169 years after Bunker Hill they participated in the Allied Invasion of Normandy. Completing one of D-Day's most important and difficult missions.

They were known then as the *Ox & Bucks* and captured the pivotal *Pegasus Bridge* outside Caen, France, which was perhaps the finest moment for this historic regiment. In 1775, as spring was becoming early summer in beautiful, rebellious Boston the 52nd Regiment dearly wanted to atone for the loss at Concord and the rout on Battle Road.

The best the British had were waiting to even the score in Boston in 1775. General Gage had history on his side as he prepared to do battle but not all the history belonged to the British army in Boston.

On June 14, 1775, while the Colonial Militia forces were holding the British in Boston, the *Second Continental Congress* created the *Continental Army*. The next day the Congress unanimously elected a new commander for the new army, George Washington of Virginia.

But all that was a mere formality, for nearly two months earlier the *Massachusetts Provincial Congress* authorized the creation of a standing army in Cambridge, called *The army of Observation*.[ciii] It was the foundation on which the Continental Army was built, and it consisted of mostly Massachusetts Militia companies, and some others from Connecticut and New Hampshire.

The Massachusetts Provincial Congress appointed 48-year-old, Massachusetts native General Artemas Ward as the commander. Artemas Ward was a graduate of Harvard College, served in the Massachusetts Militia, was a veteran of the French and Indian War, and served the *Massachusetts General Court* beside John Hancock and Samuel Adams. He was well respected by soldiers and politicians alike, and a very able and respected militia commander.

The Army of Observation that gathered in Cambridge and bottled up the British in Boston had been an independent fighting force for decades. To this very day, the oldest organized regiments in the United States Army are from Massachusetts and can trace their legacy through Cambridge and some back into service in the 17th century fighting as local militia companies organized when the Colonies were governed by the British Crown.

The *181st Infantry Regiment,* the *182nd Infantry Regiment,* and *101st Field Artillery Regiment* can all trace their ancestry to the very first battles fought by the Massachusetts Bay Colony. In 1775, they were known by the county or town that raised them. Massachusetts would field at least 25 infantry companies through the American Revolutionary War. And when the fighting stopped at Yorktown, thirteen Massachusetts companies were still standing with their Commander and Chief, George Washington.

Throughout the eight years of war with Great Britain the American Colonies raised 39 *Loyalist* companies of volunteers who fought for the British Crown and against the American Patriots. These Loyalist Companies were raised from at least nine of the thirteen colonies during the war.

No Loyalist Companies were raised in Massachusetts and New Hampshire. Before the war ended 1783, it is estimated at least 25,000 loyalist men served with the British Army in Colonial America.[civ]

General Gage's Army in Boston was full of regiments with historic pedigrees behind them and great challenges ahead of them. Waiting for those historic British regiments were *America's First Soldiers*, who were to make their own history in the deadliest battle of the American Revolutionary War for the British Army[cv]

General Gage's historic regiments would assault Breed's Hill finding their own history on a hot, muggy, summer Saturday afternoon on a small rolling Boston hilltop.

The Colonial Americans had *"crossed the Rubicon,* with the events of 19 April 1775 *"the die was cast."* There was no going back. Caesar was right, *"...what we ourselves think, we imagine others think."* and General Gage's imagination, and false impressions were about to meet a deadly reality. Caesar cautioned, *"The fault is in ourselves..."* but Gage could not understand and could not apply that to his autocratic world as a Royal Governor, and Commander and Chief of all military forces.

Gage believed overwhelmingly his forces, following his plan which confidently expended *"justifiable measures"* would crush the rebellion in Massachusetts. General Gage's Colonial education was reaching its climax in Boston.

Chapter VI
Bunker Hill
Part 1
A Boston Sunrise

"What we obtain too cheap, we esteem too lightly: it is dearness only that gives everything its value. Heaven knows how to put a proper price upon its goods; and it would be strange indeed if so celestial an article as freedom should not be highly rated."

The Crisis (1776)
Thomas Paine (1737–1809)

The morning air was heavy, promising a hot, humid day in Boston. Just before sunrise a foreign sound rippled through the warm muggy air. It filled the deserted streets rattling off the hard cobblestones and old stone and granite buildings. It careened down alleys shaking windows and wobbling tables, fraying the nerves of a city near its last nerve. It sounded like bursts of violent summer thunder but was close together at times overlapping and rhythmic.

Like the heat that blanketed Boston the foreign sounds kept booming and the besieged city was shuddered awake. Boston's residents woke to the inconceivable sound of massive and prolonged cannon fire. The stillness was shattered, and with it the unimaginable image of British guns firing their destructive cannons at the residents of Charlestown.

The guns of the HMS Lively were firing on the Colonials on Breed's Hill. Admiral Samuel Graves was aboard his flag ship HMS Somerset, Graves ordered a cease fire. Before long General Gage learned why the big guns had fired on Charlestown, he immediately asked Admiral Graves that all Royal Navy guns unrelentingly open fire on Breed's Hill.

Graves was under the authority of the Royal Navy and was not reportable to General Gage. They had a contentious relationship, as inter-service rivalries seem to produce such jaundiced arrogance from high-ranking officers.

But on this day, Graves agreed, because he despised the Colonials that kept him in Boston more than he resented the noble British General Gage. All the Royal Navy guns that could bombarded Breed's Hill and the American position that had seemed to appear out of nowhere.

Although the guns did little physical damage the psychological damage was impressed not only on the men at Breed's Hill, but the awestruck residents all around Boston.

John Quincy Adams as an eight-year-old boy, stood in disbelief and horror as the British guns fired onto Charlestown. Such an assembly of warships as were positioned in Boston Harbor, when they let their cannons loose on the men and property of Charlestown, released a scorn and bitterness that many held for decades.

Those guns, the beginning of the end of the opening act of a separation that had festered in the hearts and souls of the men and women in and around Boston. Seventy years after the event, an aged former President, and son of a President reminisced to a friend, his words still holding the pain a lifetime could not arrest:

"I saw with my own eyes those fires, and heard Britannia's thunders in the Battle of Bunker's hill [sic] *and witnessed the tears of my mother and mingled with them my own..."*[cvi]

March 1846, Letter to John Sturge
(71 years after the Battle of Bunker Hill)
John Quincy Adams (1767–1848)

Overnight the Boston Rebels had seemingly done the impossible, they had built a fort on Breed's Hill, directly where the British were to attack in 24 hours.

General Gage's day and problems were just beginning. He had no idea it was going to be a long, hot, deadly day in Boston, and he could not conceive that the sun had risen on the last Battle this noble, veteran general would fight.

As the sun was rising on June 17, 1775, the construction on Breed's Hill caught the attention of the British Royal Navy. When the sun went down on June 16, there was just the rolling pastureland that reached the top of a small sixty-foot hill that was behind a smaller hill, and in front of another taller hill.

But by morning, the sailors on the *HMS Lively* could not believe what they saw. Seemingly, out of nowhere, a primitive earth works crowned the sixty-foot hill in Charlestown. The *Lively* was at anchor east of the Charlestown peninsula and delivered the first cannon blows to the Colonial earthworks.

The sailors astutely realized that if the earthworks had cannons, the Royal Navy ships were in grave danger. They fired their guns in hopes of making a difference, and alerting the other ships to the danger they all may be in. The cannons did very little damage, except to remind the Colonials of the incredible power and reach of the British Forces. Although the sailors on the *HMS Lively* were surprised, not everyone in Boston was caught by total surprise.

On Friday night June 16, General William Howe was reviewing the plans for the British attack planned for Sunday June 18th. Howe was one its architects and he knew it was a good plan with a high degree of success expected.

General Howe was a seasoned battlefield commander and knew with proper leadership, and discipline in the ranks of his legendary regiments the British Army would rule the day. Not a thought of over confidence was his, just a steadfast belief in the superiority of the British Army in Colonial America.

A respectful knock at General Howe's door, was followed by the voice of Howe's military aid. The Captain told General Howe he had a visitor, as General Henry Clinton purposely walked through Howe's doorway. General Howe politely offered his peer a drink, and Clinton responded curtly he had no time, as he began to explain to Howe what he had witnessed.

Clinton had been alerted by British sentries on duty at the Boston waterfront that something was happening on the Charlestown Peninsular. Howe's questioning passed by the focused Clinton, as he told General Howe he believed a large force was gathering.

Clinton understood that time was of the essence, and strongly felt a dawn landing in the rear of where he believed the Colonials were entrenching was a proper response. Clinton was familiar with American Colonials as his father was the Governor of New York Province for ten years, and as a young man Henry lived amongst the Colonial residents.

Howe believed the sounds coming from Charlestown posed no concern. Howe was concerned with the planned attack for Sunday the 18th and wanted his troops fresh for that action. Clinton was persuaded by Howe's logic that the Colonials were waiting for the British to attack, and any Colonials in a ditch at Charlestown could be overcome.[cvii]

General Clinton's unease was soothed by the old veteran Howe. The Generals retired as a nightmare was being built just a few hundred yards away. The British could hear the voices and sounds of an earthwork being built exactly where they planned to attack in a matter of hours.

What breathtaking conceit these Generals held for an enemy they disliked, distrusted, and totally mischaracterized as impotent. Like the mistakes of 19 April 1775 on Lexington Green, at Concord, and on Battle Road another mistake had been made and its results would be catastrophic for the British.

As Generals Howe and Clinton slept, they had no idea that not only Boston, but North America held their doom and would break both their careers and reputations. It would all begin on a small Boston hill just a few hundred yards from where they peacefully rested.

On the morning of June 17, the rapid, practical, construction on Breed's Hill was brought to the attention of General Gage at his headquarters in Boston. Spies had alerted the Colonial commanders of Gage's planned attack of June 18, and they promptly installed a roadblock to Gage's success. He would have to defeat an entrenched enemy before his invading troops could carry on toward Cambridge. Gage was furious.

Gage examined the Colonial positions on Breed's Hill with his telescope. He could hardly believe his eyes. Overnight, in a matter of hours the Colonials had built a redoubt where Gage had planned to attack in just 24 hours.

How could it be on the eve of his revenge for all the embarrassment he had suffered in Boston an earthen fort was now directly in his path? An earthen fort full of armed dug in Colonials. The same sort of armed determined men as had ravaged his troops on Battle Road just about two months back.

For all his bluster, all his planning, all his dreams of destroying the Colonials, they were on his preverbal front porch and not willing to leave anytime soon. Gage continued to stare at the fort being built just across the mouth of the Charles River from his headquarters.

To add insult to injury, he noticed a Colonial officer directing the men still working on the redoubt as the Royal Navy ships were bombing the rising American defensive positions. Gage hoped his massive armada would begin what he knew his foot soldiers had to finish, the end of the Colonial forces besieging him in Boston.

But for the moment, the Colonial officer on the redoubt was not only directing his men, but he was also taunting the British guns, and holding General Thomas Gages' complete attention.

A loyalist, Abidjan Willard walked into Gage's office to offer his help with the forthcoming battle. What had held Gage's attention was the daring man who seemed to be in command on the Hill. He was unfazed by the naval bombardment.

He walked carelessly, drawing the attention of the British gunners, daring them to hit him. The Royal Navy tried to hit the man that was so defying them, they missed, and his undaunted courage inspired his troops to keep digging and preparing for the onslaught that surly awaited.

Gage handed his telescope to the loyalist volunteer, with candor and respect to the unknown man he asked Abidjan Willard:

"Do you recognize that tall man walking on the parapet?"

Willard took the glass and observed his rebellious countrymen on Breed's Hill. What he saw surprised General Gage, but it did not surprise Abidjan Willard as he watched the Colonial officer defy the British guns. He focused on the man commanding others from the parapet, mocking the British bombardment. He handed the glass back to its owner, looked directly at the British General and said unflinchingly, *"That is Colonel William Prescott my Brother-in-law."* Gage quickly snapped, *"Will he fight?"*

The answer delivered to the British General has come to define the American embodiment of a soldier. The fierce determination and sacrifices of the many generations that have supported our freedom for nearly 250 years. The words that day spoken by the loyalist, describing Colonel William Prescott have echoed from Bunker Hill to Yorktown, reverberated From Bull Run, Antietam, Gettysburg, and Appomattox, to the Muse-Argonne, Iwo Jima, Okinawa, and to the cold wet shores of Omaha Beach in Normandy. It has reflected from the frozen Chosin Reservoir to the steaming Mekong Delta, and a thousand jungle rice patties, to the streets of Kandahar, and Mosul. With unabashed candor that Gage should have taken as an ominous warning; he did not. The loyalist spoke through the voices of *America's First soldiers* and those who still bravely defended our Nation, "[Col. Prescott] *will fight you to the gates of Hell.*"[cviii]

Alerted by their spies in Boston of the British intention to attack on Sunday June 18, the Colonials decided to fortify Charlestown thus protecting the northern flank. On Charlestown Neck, the Colonials decided to hold the high ground, which consisted of two hills. Bunker Hill more inland, and Breed's Hill standing at 60 feet was east of Bunker Hill, therefore, closer to the coast.

Before they went to work on Breed's Hill the Colonial officers in charge argued about which hill was to be defended. While standing atop Breed's Hill, Colonel William Prescott of Massachusetts argued with Colonel Israel Putnam of Connecticut, who wanted to follow the orders from General Artemis Ward to defend Bunker Hill.

Putnam told Prescott, Bunker Hill was more inland, and had a higher elevation making it the better position to defend against attack. Prescott understood his hill, Breed's Hill was a better place for artillery. From Breed's Hill Colonial cannons could reach Boston across the river, and target British warships sitting in the harbor, and had a direct view of any invader by sea.

It was the perfect high ground to defend an invasion by the British. Ultimately Colonel Prescott did not care what you called the Hill he was on; it was the hill that he wanted to defend against the British invasion. The argument ended as Prescott's men went to work building a fort on Breed's Hill, as a disappointed Putnam worked on Bunker Hill.

Overnight, from June 16–17, the Colonials had created extensive earthworks on Breed's Hill consisting of stone, wood, dirt filled barrels, and mounds of earth all rising five to six feet high. Inside the Colonials stood on planks to ensure they could see over the new earth walls. The high ground gave the Colonials the benefits of a bird's eye view of the British as they landed on the beaches of Charlestown.

With the construction on Breed's Hill General Gage decided to go all-in on an assault on Charlestown. Gage called a council of war and told his three major generals that the planned action for Sunday the 18th was off the table. He then informed his war council; he wanted a powerful force to strike the rebels where they had chosen to defend—Charlestown.

Gage wanted to show the Colonials once and for all British superiority and ordered an all-out combined assault on the new Colonial positions on the Charlestown hill. Dorchester, Roxbury, and Cambridge would have to wait. It was time to even the score for the events in Lexington, Concord, Battle Road, and Hog Island.

In his meeting with his generals, they cautioned Gage about a frontal assault on well placed, dug-in, determined, Colonial forces. Gage was told that an attack from the rear, by landing behind the Colonials would work. Gage with all his wounded self-esteem vetoed any attack offered by his experienced Generals.

He was determined to avenge his losses in the Massachusetts countryside with a resounding, bloody, crushing, assault. A swift devastating blow that would reverse the course of history. He would reinstall his government, crush the rebellion where it had begun, and deliver his own political and military resurrection.

He was without realizing it, giving the Colonials more time to dig and reinforce. With his ego blinding him, Gage demanded action, but his proposed swift assault would take many hours to organize, and more time still to carry out. From the time Gage got to Boston time was never his friend, and on the morning of June 17, 1775, it was again like his ego—his nemesis.

Part 2
The Assault

"...to the persecution and tyranny of his cruel ministry we will not tamely submit... we determine to die or be free."

Dr. Joseph Warren (1741–75)
Massachusetts Provincial Congress
Watertown, Massachusetts. April 26, 1775

Gage did not know and could not conceive of his smug misjudgment. He intended on bringing the *gates of Hell* directly to the men defying him, including the bold leader on Breed's Hill Colonel William Prescott.

William Prescott was a tall man for his times. On June 17th, he was forty-nine years old as he defied the British on top of Breed's Hill. He was a native of Groton, Massachusetts and earned a reputation as an excellent fighter during the *French and Indian War*. So respected was this young Colonial fighter, the British offered Prescott a commission in the British Army.

Prescott refused the commission and returned to Groton to live out his days a country farmer, and local militia commander. Massachusetts Militia Commander General Artemas Ward wisely selected Colonel Prescott to build the earthworks and defend the Charlestown peninsular.

Prescott was a fiery, fearless commander who led by example, and never turned away from danger. He never spared himself and worked as hard as any soldier worked on Breed's Hill. The sturdy, organized, aggressive defense built on Breed's Hill was symbolic of Colonel Prescott the warrior. Remarkably, he would remain on that hill till nearly the end, defending his escaping troops with a sword and a defiant, indomitable will.

You will still find Colonel Prescott on Bunker Hill. The imposing statue in front of the massive obelisk is his likeness. The sculptor captures an utterly fearless, determined, swashbuckling man holding a sword as if he could jump off the monument and start fighting again.

While his other arm stretches behind him as if cautioning his precious fellow soldiers to safely stay back, suggesting an, *I got this* moment. He stands impeccably dressed, as a respectable officer of his time approached battle. At his feet are trenching tools, a reminder of his preparation and hard work before the battle.

His hat is confidently cocked, and he still looks down at the Charlestown shoreline, as if still confidently defying the now British ghosts, a permanent place at the top of the historic hill.

On Saturday, June 17, 1775, Charlestown was surrounded on two sides by heavily armed Royal Navy warships. Across the narrows from Charlestown on a slight mound in Boston, the British positioned a battery of 24-pound cannons in an old cemetery. Copp's Hill was a puritan burial ground in Old Boston, and it gave the British guns the elevation they needed to hit Charlestown. The large stationary guns on Copp's Hill added to the intimidating chorus of doom provided by the dozens of Royal Navy guns that pervaded through the still, warm summer's air as they targeted the Patriots on Breed's Hill.

The attack began with the British guns bombarding the colonial positions, the guns fired for hours. The powerful and frightening sounds echoed through Boston and the surrounding towns. The unyielding barrage was heard by thousands of stunned colonists, inside and outside of Boston.

The Colonial residents innocently had never imagined that such power and destruction would descend upon them. Sitting in Braintree across the bay, Abigail Adams and her children, including the future president John Quincy Adams, watched in disbelief and horror as the British demonstrated their remarkable firepower.

John Quincy Adams remembered that day for his entire life. As a US Ambassador, Cabinet Secretary, Senator, and 6th President of The United States, through fifty years of service to the Republic he would not participate in any public recognition of the Battle of Bunker Hill.

His memories enshrined as vivid sights and ghastly sounds of war descended upon men he knew. He was an eight-year-old boy holding onto his mother as he witnessed the destruction of Charlestown, filling his heart and mind with sights and sounds of horror. He could not, would not forget the wanton destruction delivered by the British Government to Boston.

The British lost the entire morning preparing for the assault on Charlestown. Gone was the chance of attacking the unprepared fortifications, as General Clinton had suggested hours ago. Opportunity was squandered by thoughts of superiority, by devaluing a dangerous enemy.

An enemy who had already demonstrated his determination to defend lives and property. An enemy that had shown courage, and cleverness on Battle Road, driving their opposition into more and more dangerous places. *America's First Soldiers* had already proven they were the match of the British Army, a lesson lost on arrogant British Generals, it would exact a damming price.

During the afternoon of June 17, 1775, just under 2,000 British soldiers landed unopposed on the shores of Charlestown. In comparison, on D-Day, 6 June 1944, the first wave of US Army 4th Infantry Division soldiers that landed at Utah Beach consisted of 600 soldiers [cix]

The British bombed the small village on the end of Charlestown Neck, quickly and intentionally setting it ablaze. The rebels on Breed's Hill watched as the old village became engulfed in roaring flames, its smoke momentarily concealing the next act in this deadly struggle.

Slowly, the smoke drifted out to sea only obscuring Boston Harbor, giving the firing warships a ghostly shroud. The view from the rebel redoubt was clear, and the view to British soldiers was equally clear as they landed on a narrow beach at the tip of Charlestown.

The fortified rebel positions were in sight of the British Forces landing by rowboat. They saw well dug-in, fearless, American riflemen that looked down on the British soldiers with scorn and contempt for invading their homeland. The British soldiers brought war to the shores of Charlestown, the lines and intentions very clear to all present.

The British made another mistake in a campaign already filled with misjudgments. The British believed themselves invincible on the Charlestown shore that afternoon. The British believed their mere presence enough to intimidate the rabble before them.

With their cannons firing, bayonets shinning, drums beating cadence, and flags fluttering in the hot summer sun they communicated to the Colonials that further resistance was futile. *America's First Soldiers* were about to teach the British army a lesson that would resonate for centuries.

The British Army and its officers that formed the day on Bunker Hill had history on their side. British General Oliver Cromwell had used his *New Model Army* to conquer, subjugate, and nearly wipe out the Gaelic Celtics of Ireland. The British Army invaded and conquered Scotland, finishing off Scottish resistance near Inverness, at the Battle of Culloden. And they had been victorious over their mortal enemies the French in the *Seven Years War*.

A victory earned and shared by some of the Colonial men dug in on Breed's Hill. As the British marched into formation at Charlestown they were facing an enemy they had fought with and had never fought against in America. The British experience with rustic provincials limited to fighting in Ireland or Scotland, against men who did not speak English, or own muskets.

On Breed's Hill that day, were Militiamen who had been taught to fight by the British, and Colonial Officers that had been trained by the British Army. They were in a word nearly fighting themselves, like a mirror reflecting an image.

But the men on Breed's Hill saw the British as invaders, an army that had arrived to do what had been done in Ireland and Scotland and it was not to happen again. It was not going to happen here. The British misjudged the Colonials on April 19, and they were set-up to do just that again on June 17.

The violent, destructive, ear shattering naval guns fell silent at 1:00, as the British infantry which was handpicked, landed on the northeast corner of the peninsula at Moulton's Point. The British planned to stay at the base of Breed's Hill and try to move on the Colonial left flank. The purpose was to encircle the hill and attack from the rear.

The British understood it as a common predictable plan, for a most common battle. The British believed history favored their modern Army and Navy, yet, in Boston time and time again they had encountered more than they expected. From the Powder alarm of 1774, through Lexington, Concord, Battle Road, and the rejection of a skewed proclamation, a most fearless spirit and determination lived in Boston; in many cases, deeply ingrained in some Colonials from their experiences in places like Scotland, Ireland, and the destitute villages of England.

On Wednesday morning 16 April 1746, 29 years before the Battle of Bunker Hill, history was made at not much more than a small field, outside the Scottish Highland town of Inverness. Culloden's Moor was more than a battle, it ultimately delivered upon the Scottish people the destruction of a way of life that had lasted centuries. The battle pitched the red-coated forces of England's German born King George II against a prince supported but the Scottish people as their leader. On Culloden's Moor, the British army brought their best equipment, officers, and men.

The Highlanders brought history, family, tradition, and their broad swords. The highlanders charged the British line with a few muskets, rather they carried pikes, shields, swords no match for the British artillery and modern army.

Despite the remarkable courage of the Highlanders, the British artillery and muskets were more than enough to drop the charging Scotsmen. They mostly fell before they reached the British lines.

Some of survivors of the Battle of Culloden, and their descendants found a new life in Colonial America, and perhaps a part of the spirit of the Scottish Highlanders found refuge on a small hilltop on the Charlestown Peninsular.

Culloden's Moor was a cautionary tale of empire building, Bunker Hill was to define the cost of tyranny.

As soon as they landed, five British soldiers deserted to the Rebel lines. Five men who no longer sought to kill in the name of a King and his Empire, risked all as they dashed for the rebel lines. Their attempt at a new life ended as quickly as it began, they were captured, and Major General Sir William Howe arbitrarily ordered two of them hanged.

They were strung up on a nearby tree, their worthless lives set to be an example of British discipline and justice. The vivid display of the two soldiers violently struggling for their last moments of life at the end of an old rope, was just the example Howe desired.

Before all gathered, their contortions abruptly ended as they died wearing their red coats, their abbreviated lives now remembered as men hanging from a tree in Colonial America, just a few hundred yards from freedom. Their hearts devoid of loyalty to a tyranny they could not—would not support.

Although theirs was an inglorious end, the message was clear to any and all who harbored such thoughts. The sight of the hanged men was not lost on the defenders of personal freedom on Breed's Hill. It was a vivid and timely reminder of why they were dug-in and preparing to fight for their own liberties.

General Howe quickly determined his forces were not strong enough for his planned attack. He ordered his men to have lunch, and he sent word back to Boston for immediate additional troops to support his attack. What Howe saw on that hill filled him with disbelief.

How could such a fortification be built in hours? How could these fortifications be unaffected by a massive British bombardment? Howe knew then it would be a difficult day. An hour later Howe's reinforcements arrived, lunch was over, it was time to kill, and be killed. His force was now nearer 2,200 Regulars.

While the British under General Howe were trying to get around the hill, a small force under Colonel Pigot moved to assault Breed's Hill from the east moving west heading straight up, while the southern side of the redoubt near the burning town of Charlestown was not engaged.

Pigot's attack was a faint designed to draw the fire from the Colonials, allowing the British to surround the hill from the north and attack from the west side or from the rear.

As the British regulars tried to turn the corner to get behind Breed's Hill they ran straight into entrenched Colonials. The north side of the redoubt was protected by a rail fence that ran all the way to the beach on the Mystic River side of Charlestown. That was the side of the Charlestown peninsular where the Royal Navy remarkably did not position any warships.

When Admiral Graves was asked to position some warships in the Mystic River, he claimed he could not. He was afraid that the ships might ground and be lost as was the *Diana* earlier that spring at Chelsea Creek. The attack would have to be carried by Howe and his fierce group of handpicked Redcoats.

Howe was leading the best British soldiers in all North America. He had full confidence that these crack troops would overrun the Colonials, sweeping aside all resistance and complete a circling maneuver. Howe was a fearless soldier and led from the front and had no idea he and his elite troops were headed into Hell.

Behind that rail fence were New Hampshire men, with a small group of Connecticut and Massachusetts men as well. All commanded by Colonel John Stark, a New Hampshire legend. Stark's men were as close to Special Forces as the Colonials would get in 1775.

They were frontier woodsmen, excellent shots, experienced fighters, tough men of unbendable courage, and unshakable determination. Earlier as his men found their positions behind the rail fence, stones and dirt piles, Stark walked off about 30–40 yards before them.

Colonel Stark understood the Colonials were short on gun powder, and not a single shot could be wasted. He also understood after a lifetime of war the closer the shot the more accurate the shot. Colonial era muskets were not rifled, they were smooth bore weapons prone to inaccuracy over increased distances.

And lastly, Colonel Stark knew that a British soldier violently shot at close range produced bloody and deadly wounds and could unnerve any one of his comrades. Colonel stark finished walking his 30 or so yards and drove a stake into the ground. Turning around, he looked back at his men, and he issued his deadly order, do not fire until they pass that stick.[cx]

Forty-seven-year-old Colonel John stark was a mythical New England frontiersman. He was born in New Hampshire, to a Scottish father, and an Irish mother. His Scottish roots deeply engrained his fighting abilities, and his Irish roots always directed him toward a good fight. He grew up fighting in New Hampshire which in the first half of the 18th century was still an untamed, wild, frontier.

New Hampshire encompassed a wide open, wild area that bordered New York in 1775. Vermont was never a Colony, it was a state that was admitted to the Union in 1791, and in 1775 most of present-day Vermont was part of New Hampshire. Stark was offered a commission in the British army, while fighting with the British in *French and Indian War.* He refused and served in the storied frontier fighting force *Roger's Rangers.*

Stark became an expert at guerrilla tactics, fast hit and run, fire and maneuver warfare. John stark was once captured by Indians he had been fighting against. Young John Stark had fought so fiercely against them that he was accepted as a warrior into the tribe.

During the Revolutionary War, Stark rose to the rank of Major General in the Continental Army. The New Hampshire state motto, *Live Free or Die* is attributed to John Stark. Colonel John Stark defended the American flank at Bunker Hill, not much more than a rail fence with dirt and stone mounds that ran all the way to the Mystic River shore on Charlestown's north coast. General Howe believed this was the Colonial weak point, he was running directly into the unbendable Colonel John Stark.

At the fence, Stark positioned his men in three rows. One behind the other, each line would fire at a different time. This was how he multiplied his firing power. Three ranks their guns loaded and ready to fire when the British passed Stark's stake in the ground. This three-line formation was the same alignment the British had used so effectively to destroy the *Highland Charge* on Culloden's Moor.

Three ranks of British gunners fired at the broad sword and shield bearing Scottish Highlanders as they charged across the rolling, wet, soggy, grassy, moor.

Now from his perch in Boston, General Gage would witness his finest Regulars under his finest fighting General William Howe, smash headlong into the Americans. He did not wait long. His best soldiers now marched across grassy pastures that flanked the hills and hillsides of Charlestown, Massachusetts, thousands of miles from Scotland.

The unshakeable New Hampshire frontiersmen were all excellent marksmen, they drew their aim and waited as the British marched straight for them. The unflinching British Regulars, with ranks closed for attack, were slowed by the uneven terrain. This was what the British trained for, the parade ground battlefield.

With their closed ranks, pomp and display the British marched abreast toward the rail fence and Stark's men. They continued step by step, just as they trained, getting ever closer to the Colonials. Forms that were indiscernible, just a wall of red colored coats seconds ago emerged as men with black boots, black hats and long brown guns.

Then they drew closer, and faces could be seen, eyes, noses, they were now men not monsters. The British Regulars, soldiers feared on multiple continents, soldiers feared through multiple centuries were no longer faceless foes.

The seconds ground down, the Regulars were not quite at the stake, but they were no longer indiscernible images, they were now seen as individual men. Tick, tick, tick, the seconds passed as endless minutes, breathing became deeper more labored as the Colonials understood that a line of nameless soldiers was closing on them to kill them.

Slowly, the sweat passed over focused eyes, blurring but not removing the target or the deadly appointment with destiny that awaited. The red coated targets were big enough and close enough in the bright, hot summer sun that they were men just like the men who drew aim from behind the rail fence.

Step after the step, they fearlessly closed on the stake, no longer strangers they were now locked in the kinship of battle. General Howe walked with his soldiers encouraging them to close on the Colonial position. Then they reached the stake that John Stark had driven into the ground. With one last step, not questioning their duty, many entered a world they would not exit alive.

Fire!

A devastating volley hit the British line. Not a shot wasted. Not an ounce of precious gunpowder used neglectfully. The killing had begun. Howe had chosen these men for their unwavering discipline, they were stunned, but the British Regulars moved to fill their ranks.

They hastily stepped over their dead and dying comrades and closed ranks. Their red coats and white pants covered by the blood stains of fellow soldiers who fell beside them. They closed ranks and stepped forward. They made perfect targets.

FIRE!

Stark shouted and the second row opened on the British ranks that seemed now to melt away. No less determined, Howe ordered ranks closed and incredibly the disciplined Regulars came together and closed their ranks again. How do men find such nerve, how do they not yield to the expected? Regiments with a lineage that spanned a hundred years followed the predictable orders, on this unpredictable day, from a seemingly desperate general who had underestimated his enemy. They closed and again presented a perfect line of fire.

FIRE!

Stark shouted again. The order was carried out as anticipated releasing a blinding volley of smoke, destruction and death. The handpicked brave British soldiers had had enough; they would not close their ranks again. They turned, stumbled over the dead, dying, wounded, and retreated to Moulton's Point.

They had never faced such accurate, fast, deadly fire as was delivered on that rail fence. The Regulars hurried off the field of battle, as Howe stood there alone and remarkably untouched by the hell around him. A General known for his daring and successful attacks, a General with an extraordinary lineage of commanders in his family, a General personally mentored by British legendary General Thomas Wolfe stood in horrified disbelief.

General William Howe a star-crossed British commanding general, turned and walked back following his retreating soldiers. Behind him a field littered with dead and dying red coated soldiers. Howe's attack was a total failure. His soldier's heart and soul never felt such failure. Stark's men had been badly underestimated.

While Howe ran straight into hell as he attempted to get behind the Colonials, the men who committed to the frontal attack did not fare any better, as they were violently repulsed as well. Climbing the hill on that hot humid day the British line was shot at from the burning village of Charlestown.

With flames engulfing old buildings, and seemingly reaching to the sky as they consumed an old spire the shots fell on Pigot's troops as if they were fired from hell itself. They stayed in line and, closed ranks and continued up the hill toward Prescott and his men.

The British cannons stopped firing directly at Prescott's redoubt as the British started up the hill. Colonel Prescott's men were unwavering as they delivered the full vengeance of colonial might to those that attempted to scale the heights of Breed's Hill.

Prescott had insisted, like Stark, that the shooting wait until the enemy was closing. The Colonial officers needed all shots to be effective, even before the battle began gunpowder was in limited supply on Breed's Hill.

Colonel Prescott, Colonel Putnam and others issued such famous instructions as:

"Aim low boys. Fire at their waistbands" and *"fire when you see the whites of their eyes"*, *"aim at the commanders."* and *"Aim at the handsome red coats."* The volleys fired at Pigot's command were just as destructive as the shooting at Howe's troops.

Not accepting that the frontal assault was intended as a diversion, Colonel Prescott focused his soldiers on the hill climbing Redcoats and unleashed a deadly volley. General Pigot retreated to preserve the remaining attack force.

Howe and Pigot were in disbelief. Not only had they been repulsed, but as the survivors gathered it was obvious that many officers were missing. Unlike the battlefields of Europe officers were not exempt on Breed's Hill. The Colonials knew that to kill the officers was to kill the army.

The British army was trained to obey its officers at all costs. But with officers wounded or dead, the army was paralyzed if only for a brief time. Something extraordinary had happened, and a man like Howe knew it could happen again.

Regrouping on the American left flank, Howe knew he had to attack again. He gathered his still living officers and determined his plan. The second attack featured a stronger force committed to the frontal assault to draw as much fire as possible away from the left flank.

General Howe led the attack on the Colonial left side and found the same results. His forces were easy targets with their beautiful red coats, heavy packs and 15-pound muskets. They were again decimated by the New Hampshire men that held the rail fence down to the edge of the Mystic River. Howe withdrew—again.

By now, Howe's losses had significantly weakened his capabilities, and shattered his confidence. Howe had never experienced what he found at the base of Breed's Hill.

In over 30 years of combat experience, on many continents, he had known victory, he had not encountered such determination and skill as he found on his attack of the organized, well lead defenders of the Charlestown Peninsula on June 17, 1775.

Seemingly, the Battle had just begun when Howe ordered retreat. General Howe committed the same mistake that had occurred on April 19. He had underestimated the dogged Colonial fighters and their fearless officers. The British Army was the World's most powerful land based armed forces, supported by the World's most powerful sea-based forces, The Royal Navy.

On the shores of Charlestown, the British Army and Navy combined to bear all the force they thought required to defeat the Colonial contingent. But they did not bring the imagination, and the creativity war demands. They had not put any warships in the Mystic River opposite Colonel Stark's men at the rail fence.

Therefore, Stark had to only concern himself with a frontal assault. They burned the village of Charlestown on south side of the peninsular, in an act of vengeance that offered no offensive advantage to the British. Rather, the needless destruction of the village only fueled the vengeful heart of the Patriots on Breed's Hill.

It may have felt rewarding to destroy the old town, but by doing that the British denied themselves another avenue of approach. With Howe's force attacking the American left, and Pigot attacking the center, think of the opportunities that may have been exploited on the American right flank, instead of the inferno that engulfed old Charlestown village.

Generals Gage, Howe, and Clinton were the three men who would be in overall command of all British forces in North America during the fighting years of the American Revolutionary War. Thomas Gage served from April 1775–October 1775, William Howe served from October 1775–April 1778, and Henry Clinton served May 1778–82. Boston is the one singular location where all three were involved in the planning and execution of a pitched battle, and where all three underestimated their enemy, and lived to lament every moment they ever spent in Boston fighting *America's First Soldiers.*

The front slope, and the path on the north side of Breed's Hill was littered with the dead and dying of Howe's failed attacks. General Howe retreated to Moulton's Point for a second time, and it was then he realized most of his staff officers were dead or wounded. An inconceivable event, never witnessed in the battle grounds of Europe had unfolded before him. In a barely audible tone, General Howe issued his next orders to men of unshakeable conviction, he told those still with him, *"We will go again Gentlemen."* Such valor, such commitment to defeat one's enemy must be admired even when it is so miscast and inappropriate.

Howe needed more soldiers than he had, he called in his reserves, the Marines. They were commanded by Major John Pitcairn. They were like all the British Regulars that attacked the Colonial left flank, handpicked, aggressive, hard fighting soldiers from regiments that could fancy a 100-year history. Pitcairn was a veteran of two decades in the Royal Marines. He was admired not only by his men, but by the Colonial residents who had come to know him as a fair and responsible British gentleman. Pitcairn and his Marines left Boston for the shores of Charlestown. It would be the last battle Major John Pitcairn would fight.

General Howe did not have many options left at Charlestown. Howe devised a plan that differed slightly on this third attempt. He would send the bulk of his forces straight up Breed's Hill, including the Marines, and this time they were not a diversion.

The small group sent toward the Colonial left against the New Hampshire men was a faint. Howe could not break Colonel Stark's New Hampshire and Connecticut men, so maybe he could distract them. From the Mystic River on the north side of Charlestown, across the entire south side where the town was burning, a wall of red coated soldiers advanced in the sweltering heat toward Breed's Hill.

With the sun still high in the sky, the heat of the day had enveloped both sides taking its toll on invader and defender alike. Neither side had enough water, and the Colonial defenders of Breed's Hill had had very little water for over 18 hours. Tired, thirsty, desperate, and with gun powder and shot running very low the Colonials prepared for a third assault.

In complete defiance of the rebels who had held twice before, the British soldiers moved forward on command. Climbing the hill, they stepped over and around their dead and dying comrades. With hearts filled with an unquenchable desire for vengeance they climbed into range of the Colonial guns. The Red Coats did as ordered and marched again, straight into hell.

The storm of lead fired by the Patriots from behind their earthworks was deadly accurate and ruinous. With the carnage around them, the British officers unwaveringly held the third assault together. As they approached the top of Breeds Hill, close enough to see the intrenched Colonials, the firing slowed, and nearly stopped. They knew something was different. Undeterred by their losses the Red Coats would not yield and continued the attack as it became clear the Americans were running out of ammunition.

Major Pitcairn led the Marines in their charge as the British came over the top of the earthworks. The Colonial muskets were firing nails, rocks, glass, and dirt. After the battle some of the British medical authorities believed that these pseudo-bullets were used to intentionally wound the British.

The Colonials defending their redoubt in the closing moments of the third British attack were extremely desperate. Anything that fit into a musket barrel and could be fired was on the table for those last desperate minutes. The only other option was retreat, and that came soon enough.

The British violently attacked with their cold, steel, bayonets. With their rifles reduced to spears the British soldiers assaulted everyone not in a redcoat, seeking to avenge the unmerciful bloody deaths of their comrades and friends. In a frenzied state, the Red Coats cold-bloodedly bayoneted the dead, dying, wounded, and surrendering.

Most of the Colonial hunting muskets did not hold bayonets, the fight was now close, personal, brutal, unforgiving. The final assault claimed the life of Major Pitcairn, who fell wounded into in his eldest son's arms, four bullets had stuck him as he led his men over the top.

Like his father, David Pitcairn was an elite Marine. Major Pitcairn would yield to his wounds days later in a make-shift hospital in Boston. Pitcairn was that rarest of rare men, he would do his duty without hatred, he was one of the best the British put on the field at Bunker Hill.

So respected was Major John Pitcairn that his falling at the top of Breed's Hill is included in John Trumbull's famous painting, *The Death of General Warren at Bunker Hill June 17, 1775*. [cxi] The artist John Trumbull was a militia captain as the battle raged on Breed's Hill. He witnessed the action firsthand from a safe distance. When he painted Warren's unfortunate death, it was balanced with the death of a respected British soldier—British Marine Major John Pitcairn.

The battle turned against the Americans on the redoubt, and as the body of the Colonial forces sought to escape, a fire covered them from the Mystic River side of the line. Colonel Starks's New Hampshire men provided the covering fire that freed some of the Patriots fleeing from Breed's Hill.

Colonel John Stark was equal to his mythic reputation. He was a fearless patriot, who defied the best the British army had to offer at Bunker Hill. Then he and his men drew some of the last blood covering the Colonials trying to escape.

Amongst those brave patriots who voluntarily remained at the Breed's Hill redoubt to protect the men retreating was Major General Dr. Joseph Warren. Warren was amongst the last Americans to fire their muskets; out of ammunition, their guns were reduced to clubs.

The patriots fought by hand, sometimes ripping the guns and bayonets from the heat exhausted British Regulars. Some of the Colonials killed the British with their own bayonets. Nothing was off limits as the battle reached its bloody climax.

Dr. Warren had been part of the patriot cause for a decade, and was an essential and perhaps the key part of the inner circle of its leadership in Boston. He was part of the men known as the *Sons Of Liberty* and was closely associated with: Paul Revere, Samuel Adams, John Adams, and John Hancock.

On June 14, just three days before the Battle of Breed's Hill, Dr. Warren who had become the President of the Massachusetts Provincial Congress, a member of the Committee of Safety, and the Committee of Correspondence, was appointed a Major General in the Massachusetts Militia. Major General Warren ascended Breed's Hill on the afternoon of June 17, as a volunteer private.

He fought in the line on top of the redoubt with the privates and volunteers he so deeply respected. Accepting no special treatment, he also volunteered to lead the rear guard so most of the Colonials could retreat. As the British entered the redoubt Dr. Warren was shot in the head at close range and probably died instantly. That was not enough for one British officer.

Gazing at the dead Dr. Warren, a British officer recalled who the dead patriot was, and he ordered Warren stripped. Dr. Warren had fashionable clothes, more in the style of a Boston doctor than a Boston Militiaman fighting with his fellow patriots on a blood-soaked battlefield. Not pleased with that, he next ordered Warren's corpse bayoneted until it was unrecognizable. Finally, he ordered Dr. Warren's head smashed.

Warren would be identified later by a partial dental piece made for him by fellow patriot and good friend Paul Revere. It was after such desecration that British Captain Walter Sloane Laurie the incompetent officer in charge of the first British retreat on 19 April 1775 at the Old North Bridge ordered Warren's body stuffed into a shallow grave with another dead patriot.

The British officer who was in command when the British soldiers were ably routed, and retreated at the Old North Bridge in Concord, bragged:

"[I]*stuffed the scoundrel* [Warren] *with another rebel into one hole, and there he and his seditious principles may remain.*"

Thomas Fleming, Bunker Hill, P. 256

At the same time as Captain Walter Sloane Laurie was trying to rehabilitate his reputation by profanely violating the body of the brave and selfless Dr. Joseph Warren, another British officer found his rest on Breed's Hill. He had been fighting all day, and wanted a moment of peace, and perhaps mournful reflection.

The field was quiet, as the full realization of the events on that hill filled the minds of those who survived. The British Lieutenant was disturbed by his orderly who cautioned his commanding officer there were two Colonials approaching.

Like General Gage, General Howe, General Clinton, General Percy, and Lieutenant Colonel Francis Smith, Lieutenant John Dutton ignored the two Colonials claiming they were just two surrendering rustics. It was the last thing the arrogant British Lieutenant ever thought or did.

Two shots rang out shattering the mournfully quiet battlefield. The last two British deaths on Breed's Hill were the pompous Lieutenant Dutton and his concerned orderly. They fell dead, the last British soldiers to die on Breed's Hill.[cxii]

The British still did not understand that the words Dr. Warren spoke were his principles. Such words, and deeds would be the foundation upon which our nations indomitable will was built.

"...to the persecution and tyranny of his cruel ministry we will not tamely submit...we determine to die or be free."

Part 3
Aftermath

"The sad and impressive experience of this murderous day sunk deep into the mind of Sir William Howe. "

Bunker Hill: A City, A Siege, A Revolution
Nathanial Philbrick
Page 230

The commotion of cannon and muskets vanished; rattles of swords and bayonets faded; screams of the retreating and charging dulled; cries of the dying disappeared; moans of the wounded to be dead in minutes, hours, or days carried away the will to live; gun smoke rising and falling on the hot summer winds of this manmade Hell; moments of peace descended upon this unpeaceful place; the living questioning it all but not themselves.

It took less than two hours to complete. In his lust to deliver a crippling blow to the Colonials, General Thomas Gage had delivered a crippling blow to himself.

The full measure of British retribution found *America's First Soldiers* on a bloody hilltop in Boston and the price paid by the British to deliver that retribution was nearly beyond their comprehension. It was measured not just in the dead and maimed, but by the political winds that clearly did not favor the British after Bunker Hill.

In just three months, word arrived in Boston that Gage was relieved, and on October 11, 1775, while his army was still besieged in Boston, Lieutenant General Sir Thomas Gage boarded a ship bound for London. His career was in ruins, his reputation irretrievably damaged.

Upon its conclusion, the Battle of Bunker Hill spawned another dozen smaller battles and skirmishes along the thirteen British colonies. Beginning in a matter of months the Royal Navy was fighting along the coast with Colonial ships and the ports they called home.

From Massachusetts to South Carolina, the angered Colonials and the British exchanged shots and lives for their respective causes. They also experienced another half dozen engagements in Canada at Quebec. The Battle of Bunker Hill had unleashed a power that would never again be tamed by British military might and British politicians.

After the last shots were fired, and the Americans retreated, the British Army was easily bottled up the on the Charlestown peninsula. As far as the Colonials were concerned the British could have the Charlestown peninsular, or what was left of it. The isthmus that connected the peninsular to the mainland was less than120 yards wide, and the Colonials blocked it easily.

So, the British were bottled up on another peninsula in Boston Harbor, except this spit of land came at an astonishing price. The carnage of Bunker Hill gained the British nothing, other than a reason to never fight in Boston again. The words of a slowly dying British officer described what happened at Bunker Hill.

The noble and respected Lieutenant Colonel lay suffering from his wounds. His journey to the top of Bunker Hill had begun decades ago as a young officer in the *1st Regiment of Foot*. He was born in the Scottish Lowlands an area loyal to the British Crown. He had fought on European Battlefields, fought the French and the Indians in North America, and helped suppress the Jacobite Rebellion in Scotland fighting at Culloden's Moor in April of 1746.

At Bunker hill, he had faced some of the descendants of his time fighting in Scotland, his career began at Culloden's Moor, and was ended on a bloody Boston hill. A few days after the fighting at Bunker Hill, the brave Lieutenant Colonel realized he was dying from his wounds.

He was shot while leading a grenadier company up the deadly hill that claimed more British dead than any other battle in the American Revolution. He like so many of his peers thought he would find glory and honor on a hot Saturday afternoon in Boston. He did not.

What he found as he climbed that hill was the unwelcome, unexpected constant companion of violent death and wounding at the hands of the Colonials. With what time he had remaining it was time to tell his story to his old friend.

He wrote to his mentor, General Jeffery Amherst, a controversial British general remembered to this day for giving blankets bearing the Smallpox infection to American Indians in 1763. To his mentor the dying Lieutenant Colonel James Abercrombie wrote:

"The rebels behaved most gallantly."

Next, he offered a foreboding caution to his infamous, old friend. He wanted the General to understand what was waiting for the British army in Colonial America. The dying James Abercrombie wrote:

"a few such victories would ruin the [British] *Army"*[cxiii]. An ominous warning that still resonates across centuries.

It was a *Pyrrhic Victory*, and that is a generous offering. General Thomas Gage should have never attacked a dug-in, fortified position with a frontal assault. He let his ego obliterate any military sense he still had. He could have surrounded and attacked the redoubt from three sides with amphibious landings on the Charlestown peninsular.

And once forces landed, they could also have attacked the redoubt from the rear, where Prescott's men had not dug themselves into safety. The rear was the weak point, as General Howe had correctly surmised. Gage's mistake on June 17, 1775, was more costly than just his losses in officers and men. He gave the Americans courage and filled them with a belief they could defeat the British.

The cost to Britain was much more than the generals had bargained for, suffering 1,054 killed, wounded or missing. Between forty and fifty percent of the British soldiers that landed on Charlestown were casualties, that was unprecedented and unacceptable.

Astonishingly, many of the first soldiers targeted in the battle were British officers. Incredibly, one eighth of all British officers who were killed in action during the entire eight years of the American Revolutionary War were killed at Bunker Hill.

Over 12 percent of all British officers killed in action in the American Colonies were lying dead on Bunker Hill on June 17, 1775. Not a large expansive battlefield but a small rise, just a few hundred yards from the Charlestown seashore, a small hill surrounded by pastureland and cart paths.

A most extraordinary event in the then history of the British Army. British General Howe who led the assault muttered:

"Success here is too dearly bought."[cxiv]

General Howe had every officer on his staff killed or wounded – every officer. Every single one of his officers were a casualty. Over forty percent of the commissioned and non-commissioned officers that attacked the Colonials were killed or wounded. It was clear the target of the Rebels was British authority and those who dared carry it onto a battlefield in rebellious Massachusetts.

British authority was no longer accepted in Massachusetts, rather it was targeted to be violently snuffed out.

So shocking was the successful, intentional targeting and killing of officers, and additionally the breath-taking loss of over a thousand soldiers, one historian made the following assessment of General William Howe, the man who succeeded General Thomas Gage as British Commander and Chief Military Forces North America:

"[Howe's] *memory contained a large repertory of similar battles...* [yet he] *was never the same man again, as when standing on Charlestown Beach...this murderous day sank deep into his mind.* [his talents were] *to fail him at the very moment when they were especially wanted...he was destined to lose more than one opportunity...against an intrenchment with American riflemen..."*

Sir George Trevelyan (1876–1962)
The American Revolution Part 1 1766-1776 Page 178

This was to the British a most extraordinary tactic, which they had never encountered in the parade ground battlefields of Europe. It resulted in the British suffering more casualties at Bunker Hill than any other engagement of the entire eight years of the American Revolutionary War.

For the next eight years, the specter of unparalleled death and destruction on an old Boston Hill followed General Howe and General Clinton. For the British, the battle was at best a Pyrrhic Victory, and it was only after the Battle of Bunker Hill that the British began to understand the savage, determined, nature of the rebellious American Colonists in Massachusetts.

The measure of Bunker Hill filled the hearts and souls of those who realized that the British could be defeated. American Independence was not a hope, but a promise delivered by the nearly four hundred of *America's First Soldiers* who were killed and wounded in Boston on June 17, 1775.

On the Morning of June 18, 1775, the sun rose on a very different world than ever before known in the British-American Colonies. In victory the British Army had seemingly yielded a defeat to the world they had known. Despite taking breathtaking losses in men on a near useless bloody hill in Boston, they remained besieged. They had gained a narrow spit of land called Charlestown, and there they were besieged - again.

For all their power, they were powerless.

June 18, 1775, was different for the men of Massachusetts as well. They had done the impossible as through their determined defeat, again, they besieged the world's most powerful army.

While still grieving the dead, tending the wounded, and believing in the dream of independence, the successes in Massachusetts were handed off to a Virginian Militia officer. He was impressive in his stature and bearing and he was the politician offered command of America's First Army.

Conclusion
The Game Had Changed
Part 1
Washington in Cambridge

"I feel great distress, from a consciousness that my abilities and military experience may not be equal to the extensive and important Trust... I, this day, declare with the utmost sincerity, I do not think myself equal to the Command I am honored with."

George Washington (1732–99) Address to the Continental Congress in Philadelphia as the new Commander of the Continental Army June 16, 1775

The British were not done in Boston or Massachusetts. Before long they would have a new commander, who would demand more men, more equipment, more supplies and get nearly all he asked for. London complied, as the King and his ministers went all in on taming the wild Massachusetts Rebels. King George III addressing Parliament on October 26, 1775, decried:

My people in America...openly avow their revolt, hostility, and rebellion...Their ultimate desire an independent empire [which would] *he warned be crushed by decisive exertions of the British army and navy...if the Colonists deceived themselves into thinking that the British forces would be insufficient...the British military had received the most friendly offer of military assistance...from Russia and Germany..."* cxv

The King backed up what he said. The British started to reinforce the Boston peninsular with ever increasing armaments, supplies, ships, and soldiers.

Whatever the new commander asked for, it seems he got. The British would not repeat the mistakes made by General Gage. The long specter of failure was to be resurrected in the blood of the Colonials still holding the British on Boston peninsular, and as well the Charlestown peninsula. For the new commander, it was a matter of time until he could avail himself and his country.

Commanding General William Howe was determined to come out from behind Gage's shadow in Boston. Although he was still bottled up in Boston and Charlestown, Howe's ever-increasing power made it a matter of time and place for a decisive attack and victory.

Howe's chance to end the rebellion in Massachusetts once and for all was like a ticking time bomb. The Colonials waited and anticipated what they knew was coming. They did not know the time or place, but they did know that the British with all their fury were coming.

General William Howe was living in the same house of cards that defined the other British generals in Boston, a place where British superiority and Colonial inferiority lived in a symbiotic predetermined existence. Author David McCullough captures this loathsome spirit:

"To the British and those Loyalists who had taken refuge in Boston, they were simply "the rebels," or "the country people," undeserving the words "American" or "army." General John Burgoyne disdainfully dubbed them "a preposterous parade," labeling them, *"rabble in arms."*

1776
David McCullough
Page 25

They were such slow learners and completely miscast to their responsibilities in Boston. Howe and his sycophants would make the same mistakes Gage and his sycophants made. They constantly broke one of the cardinal rules of warfare—do not underestimate your opponent. In the 6th century BC, Chinese warrior Sun Tzu cautioned all warriors—*Know your enemy*. General William Howe knew war in Europe, at Bunker Hill, he experienced war in America. Still, he did not understand the men he was fighting against.

As summer was fading and the autumn winds began to blow in Boston, General Howe secured his strength by the sea, increased his fire power and formed his plans. He had little idea what was happening across the river in Cambridge, he was busy looking for the right place and the right time to attack the dug-in Colonials. He understood his options were limited; he was, after all, besieged on a peninsula. With haunting memories of Bunker Hill fresh in his mind, he knew he did not want to attack a Colonial position that was dug in.

Yet, his delays afforded the Colonials the opportunities they needed to entrench themselves in fortresses of earth on elevated positions. Howe wanted his revenge on the Massachusetts Colonials and understood there was another way.

He and his army and navy could leave Boston and attack New York, master the Hudson River and sever New England from the other Colonies. But the aristocratic Howe was content to quarter in Boston for the winter 1775–1776.

European armies did not like to fight winter campaigns, they rested, regrouped, and resupplied. He was their problem he reckoned, and had the luxury of time to decide the next step.

On the Colonial side of the Charles River there was no doubt the *Rubicon* had been crossed; any chance of peace was buried with the valiant dead of Bunker Hill. There was no going back from either side now the *die was cast*. It was all just a matter of time and General Howe was not the only general making plans, the Colonials had a new general.

Just a few weeks after the carnage of Bunker Hill, the Colonials Militia forces got a new commanding General. On July 2, 1775, George Washington arrived to take command of the army now in Cambridge. With his presence, the *Massachusetts Army of Observation*, became the *Continental Army*. Estimates vary but Washington was now in command of perhaps ten or fifteen thousand Militiamen.

Those men who made up Washington's army had been under the command of Massachusetts General Artemis Ward. And they had been inspired by men like Lexington's John Parker, and Groton's Colonel Prescott the commander of Bunker Hill.

The Massachusetts army had its soul ripped out when Dr. Joseph Warren, their true leader, and the leader of the rebellion in Boston was killed on Bunker Hill. The loss created a giant vacuum in which Virginian George Washington entered.

In July, just after he arrived in Cambridge, a Plymouth, Massachusetts doctor saw an elegant, well-appointed gentleman on horseback. Writing in his journal, he recorded his sighting of the man who would lead the continental Army to victory, and a group of British colonies into becoming a new nation.

"I have been much gratified this day with a view of General Washington. His Excellency was on horseback, in company with several military gentleman. It was not difficult to distinguish him from all others; his personal appearance was truly noble and majestic... "[cxvi]

George Washington was a wealthy Virginia plantation owner, he owned thousands of acres of land, hundreds of human beings, and was a member of the Continental Congress. When he was 22 years old, he was appointed a Lieutenant Colonel in the Virginia Militia and charged with negotiating with the Indians on the western frontier of Virginia.

He encountered a small French patrol, in present day Pennsylvania where his militia forces fought and defeated the French. Unfortunately, the leader of French soldiers was carrying diplomatic messages for the English. It was a grave mistake and one of the sparks that ignited the flames of the French and Indian War.

Next, Washington was part of a multi-colonial force that surrendered a fort to the French. Released after his surrendered Washington then served with British General Braddock, as he attacked the French Fort Duquesne, in modern day Pittsburg, Pennsylvania. While serving under General Braddock Washington met a young British Lieutenant Colonel Thomas Gage.

And it was then that Washington met Scotsman Hugh Mercer who like Washington was a Colonial Militia colonel. They established a lifelong friendship. Hugh Mercer was a very experienced soldier, who began his career fighting the English for the Independence of Scotland.

Hugh Mercer had very little in common with George Washington. Washington admired British officers, and desperately wanted to receive a British commission. Washington believed his status as a Colonial Militia officer was far beneath the status of a commissioned British officer.

He imitated the British officers in his appearance and bearing, understanding them to be the consummate in gentlemanly behavior and fearless soldiery. Hugh Mercer did not share Washington's undying respect for

British officers. Mercer had seen the measure of British officers on April 16, 1746 at Culloden's Moor. He witnessed first-hand British brutality on and off the battlefield.

Mercer survived the slaughter of Culloden and as a Jacobite soldier he was wanted for treason against the British Crown. He was on the run in Scotland and continued to run until he found passage to the Colony of Pennsylvania in North America in late 1747. There, he practiced medicine, he was after all, a university-trained doctor before the Jacobite revolution.

Washington resigned halfway through the French and Indian War and returned home. After the war Hugh Mercer moved to Virginia from Pennsylvania to be closer to his countrymen. He settled into life, married, and opened his medical practice near Fredericksburg, Virginia. His old friend George Washington gladly sold him a piece of land along the Rappahannock River which had been Washington's boyhood home and family farm before moving to Mount Vernon. Hugh Mercer would raise five children of his own and find the peace he had once known in Scotland. That peace would not last long as he was needed to defend his new home from an old foe.

Hugh Mercer put aside his family and business interests and like George Washington accepted a commission in the new Continental Army. Mercer was by 1775 one of George Washington's closest friends, they even belonged to the same Masonic Lodge.

That friendship graced their common efforts to defeat the British as General Hugh Mercer was a close and trusted advisor of Washington. Mercer stood beside Washington when the darkest hours of the war were at hand in New York, and New Jersey.

It was the Scotsman General Mercer who was one of the principal motivators to push Washington back across the Delaware River and attack the British on December 25–26, 1775. The Colonials crossed the river and swept in on the unsuspecting Hessians and British. The victory was exactly what Washington and his faltering army needed. It gave the sagging fortunes of Washington and his army a great morale boost.

A week later, Washington decided to attack the British, and confront Lord Cornwallis, perhaps the best British field commander of the war. Washington assigned General Mercer to lead his column. While out on the road toward Princeton, Mercer was surprised by British forces. They shot his horse, and they then surrounded him. Hugh Mercer drew his sword; he was not going to surrender to the British soldiers that surrounded him.

Mercer was hopelessly outnumbered. Still, with that fighting spirt of a Scotsman he defended himself, until his enemy overwhelmed him and inflicted several mortal blows. His men fled back toward the American lines, where they were stopped by Washington himself, who led them back to the fight and the defeat of the British.

Hugh Mercer died on the snow-covered cold road to Princeton, New Jersey. He had given his last breath for his new country, trying to vanquish the enemy of his old country—Scotland. General Hugh Mercer would have a remarkable legacy as an American soldier. His great grandson would fight as a Colonel in the Confederate forces during the Civil War. Colonel George S. Patton Sr. was killed in battle, as was his brother. They died defending their homeland of Virginia.

George S Patton Sr. would have a grandson who would wage war across the European battlefields of World War II. His grandson, George S. Patton Jr. would lead the American 3rd Army from Normandy to Germany, finishing off Hitler and his tyrannical Nazis.

George Washington's limited military experience gave him the knowledge of working with and knowing British officers, and a deep appreciation of the devotion of men like Hugh Mercer. Although his military career was not very successful, Washington did acquire the skills of a good leader and became a most adapt administrator.

Those attributes transferred to his business and political life. Washington married a wealthy young widow, Martha Custis and raised her two children as his own. Martha Cutis Washington had a great grand daughter, Mary Anna Randolph Custis, in 1831 she married another noted Virginian, the son of Revolutionary War Major General Henry *"Light Horse Harry"* Lee, Robert E. Lee commander of the Confederate Army of Northern Virginia.

With his property and that which he acquired by marriage to Martha, George Washington became one of Virginia's wealthiest men. He owned thousands of acres of valuable farmland, was a tall, dominating, cultured man, and excellent horseman. With his wealth and culture, he became a dynamic political force.

While attending the Second Continental Congress, Colonel George Washington was unanimously elected as Commander and Chief of the new

Continental Army on June 16, 1775. He was also granted the commission of a Major General and provided with a staff of experienced Militia commanders. It was a political appointment, although in the end it was the best choice the Continental Congress could have made.

Washington arrived in Cambridge and rejected the house chosen as his headquarters. It was too small for his staff, family, and servants. He was satisfied by occupying the largest most prestigious house in all of Cambridge. Today we know it as the *Longfellow House*. It was large, imposing, grand, and commanded a sweeping view of the Charles River. It was the best there was, and he got it. But having a residence fit for royalty did not endear him to the citizen soldiers suffering all over Cambridge, Roxbury, Somerville, and Dorchester.

America's First Soldiers were common men of uncommon bravery and determination. Proud and satisfied, they held the British Army captive in Boston. Humble men of little means, they slept in tents, built common latrines, and bathed in the Charles River.

Washington was out of place, with people he disliked, and he was not malleable to changing anytime soon. So, he set out to change them. Washington was determined to build his rag-tag lot into a real 18th century army. The slave owning, aristocratic Washington was out of place in Cambridge, and Massachusetts. He was amongst people he understood to be simple and selfish.

He did not like them, because they offended the nobleman who was always obeyed on his slave-holding hierarchy plantation in Virginia. Washington disliked nearly all New Englanders, or Yankees as he cast them disparagingly.

"Washington found them to be men of a decidedly different sort than he had expected, and he was not at all pleased." [cxvii]

Washington's problems were not limited to the differences between Virginian Southern and Boston Northern. From where he stood in Cambridge there was no government to aid him. Since 19 April 1775 Massachusetts had cobbled together group of patriots who managed to hold the population somewhat together.

Gage had abolished the legal Massachusetts government, and there was barely a shadow government in Massachusetts for Washington. The Continental Congress had their own problems of divided colonial sensitivities, they were not yet a solid determined group. Most were still in fear of the overwhelming British retribution they were sure would arrive. They would not be united until July of 1776 when together they signed the Declaration of Independence.

But in July of 1775, George Washington was in command of an ill-tempered, unfunded, poorly disciplined group of thousands of mostly New England men—Yankees, men George Washington despised:

"...with increasing losses from disease, desertions, and absences in one sort or another his army was in serious decline...There were still too few tents, still a shortage of blankets and clothing...In truth the situation was far worse than they realized and no one perceived this more clearly than Washington...He knew how little money was at hand...[Washington] *struggles with his mounting contempt for New Englanders...he railed against the Yankees as, "exceedingly dirty and nasty" nothing like he had expected. He had only contempt for "These People" he confided in a letter to congressman Richard H Lee...The heart of the problem was an "unaccountable kind of stupidity" in the lower classes of these people.*[cxviii]

Washington easily and often showed his contempt for the residents of New England. Like his British counterparts Washington's ego blinded him from the history they made without him. George Washington wanted to be recognized as a great soldier, and in New England he forgot how great the Yankee soldiers were before he got there.

The events that took place between April 19, 1775 and June 17, 1775, are the foundation of Washington's command. The Yankee army that had beaten the British, endured a powerful British assault and kept the British Army effectively besieged was the army that was to be built upon.

Yet, he seemed blinded to those facts as he pursued victory and eternal glory at the head of a liberating, revolutionary army. Washington was very much like his friend across the Charles River, British Lieutenant General Thomas Gage.

Washington, like Gage, had no respect for his Colonial Militiamen. Washington callously held his British enemy in a higher esteem socially and morally than those he had labeled in a disparagingly, contemptible, gratuitous nature.

Washington was the embodiment of southern aristocratic pride and prejudice; he was cast in the beginning unequally in the Revolutionary War for a part, he could have played nearly a century later in the American Civil War. As a Virginian general, defending his seceded homeland. He was in a few words, very much out of place in Massachusetts.

In a letter written on January 14, 1776, the Commander of the Continental Army, Virginian George Washington seems to reveal his distress. Words written six months after he had taken command also reveal his coming to terms with the herculean task before him.

As Washington lamented his army of rebellion languished only a few hundred yards from the British, yet they are fighting only a cold New England winter. The army and its commander appear to be disabled; his forlorn hopelessness captured in a few pragmatic words. From his comfortable quarters in Cambridge, Massachusetts General Washington wrote:

"The reflection upon my situation and that of this army produces many an uneasy hour...Few people know the predicament we are in..."[cxix]

The man chosen to lead had questioned his *Yankee* soldiers, and now he questioned himself, *"I have often thought how much happier I should have been if, instead of accepting of a command under such circumstances, I had taken musket upon my shoulders and entered the ranks..."*[cxx]

Washington watched and could feel as his army slowly disintegrated, and his ability to lead them, perhaps, fatally fractured. He was torn between the British evacuating Boston at any time, and his belief that he had let slip, perhaps, the only opportunity to deliver a deadly blow to an enemy trapped on two peninsulas in lonely Boston Harbor.

He felt time slipping from his grasp, and spring inching closer, allowing the British easy escape from their forced Boston lodgings. The relatively open sea lanes, navigated by the world's most powerful navy could easily evacuate Boston. And the Royal Navy could land those evacuated from Boston unopposed on any Colonial American seashore. The walls were closing in on Washington.

Washington acknowledged his *difficulties but* did not acknowledge his inability to unify his command, rather he reminded the reader, he had been victimized by *a backwardness.* He labelled his predominantly Yankee army as, *old soldiers.* His words codify not his inabilities, but the stark reality that leading a New England army was not his fault, but the fault of that army—those *backward old soldiers.*

If failure was to follow the events in Lexington, Concord, Battle Road and Bunker Hill it would not be his burden to carry, he writes for posterity, the lines that assuage his guilt, *"Could I have foreseen the difficulties which have come upon us, could I have known such a backwardness would have been discovered in the old soldiers to the service, all the generals upon earth should not have convinced me of the propriety of delaying an attack upon Boston..."*[cxxi]

Beyond all his challenges, opinions, and lamentations what Washington needed most in Cambridge was help. That help arrived from the most unlikely of places, it arrived in the form of three remarkable men. All three men would become indispensable to Washington and the Revolution.

Two of them became Washington's most trusted advisors, dependable generals, and loyal friends. They had been in Cambridge before Washington got there, and were well known, and respected men who understood the situation in Cambridge, and they were all Yankees.

The first vital Yankee was a Nathaniel Greene a quaker from Warwick, Rhode Island. Greene rose to the rank of General, and served in Massachusetts, New York, New Jersey and Pennsylvania. Greene was the General that Washington assigned to fight Cornwallis in the southern theater of the war.

Greene was masterful as he forced Lord Cornwallis to chase him and thereby forcing Cornwallis to sacrifice his only advantage, the size of his army. General Greene fought the British in Georgia and the Carolinas. Nathaniel Greene was with Washington when Cornwallis's trapped, undersupplied army surrendered at Yorktown, Virginia.

The second essential Yankee was John Glover. A fearless sea faring merchant from Marblehead, Massachusetts. Glover would also raise to the rank of general, and it was Glover's Marblehead men that got Washington out of New York and into the safety of New Jersey. Then Glover got him out of New Jersey to the safety of Pennsylvania waiting across the icy near frozen Delaware River.

And it was Glover's men that ferried Washington's beleaguered army back across the frozen, nearly unnavigable Delaware River to attack the Hessians and British, perhaps saving the revolution as Washington and his army had faced defeat after defeat since leaving Massachusetts.

The nearly impossible task of crossing the ice ladened, nearly frozen Delaware River delivering Washington in a blinding snowstorm was the virtually impossible task that fell upon Glover. That allowed the victories Washington so badly needed in late 1776. General Glover provided Washington with the only thing that would keep his army unified—a victory.

The victories at Trenton and Princeton inspired the Colonies to believe that the British Army could be defeated in the field, and the Revolution still could be won.

Washington's last Yankee was of the utmost importance. He was indispensable and exactly what Washington needed, at exactly the right times, throughout the entire War of Independence. He was the son of Scot immigrants, a Boston-born, book-loving, street-fighting, gregarious Yankee. He was George Washington's Babe Ruth.

Part 2
Washington's Yankee

"...there is no man in the United States with whom I have been in habits of greater intimacy; no one whom I have loved more sincerely, nor any of whom I have had a greater friendship."
Letter to John Adams
July 4, 1798
George Washington

Like Babe Ruth, he was a big man in a small man's world. Like Ruth, he towered over some men at six foot two inches, and just like Ruth he had a large head, big strong arms and a barrel of a chest that produced a booming voice.

Like Ruth, when he entered a room, he filled it with size and spirit, and like Babe Ruth, he was a game changer. He would give Washington hope in Washington's hopeless hours in Cambridge.

Like Babe Ruth's ability to deliver power hitting game changing home runs, he was the man who time and again appeared at the right time, the right place, with the right stuff. He was Washington's Babe Ruth, and he was a Boston Yankee.

He arrived in Cambridge a few days following the events of 19 April 1775. He had to escape from Boston where he lived with his new young wife, the daughter of loyalists. He had tended his failing *London Bookstore*, because General Gage closed the port of Boston from all importations, including books from London.

He snuck out of Boston and brought his wife to safety far inland. He then proceeded to the new, *Camp of Liberty* as the growing military assembly in Cambridge was called. Like George Washington, who would arrive seventy-five days later, he found the camp disorderly and dysfunctional.

But he understood he was amongst citizen soldiers who were sacrificing their time, and livelihoods to remain in Cambridge to hold General Gage's forces in Boston. He was with men of little training, but of enormous accomplishment, humble men who had tasted tyranny and met it equally on the battlefield. He was with his own kind, *America's First Soldiers*—New England Men.

This New Englander was first noticeable by his size, he was a large man, who carried 250 pounds on his six feet two-inch frame. He had a friendly, engaging personality and an endearing manner that people liked to be around. When he was a teenager, he was in a Boston street gang and often got into fist fights, most of which he won.

He loved to read and taught himself Greek, Latin, and French. And he was only one of a handful of men in camp who understood military engineering, preparing fortifications, and the emerging and rapidly expanding science of artillery.

This Yankee would give Washington what he needed to deny General Howe a sweeping decisive victory in Boston. Forcing General Howe to evacuate Boston on March 17, 1776. It was the Americans who embraced a sweeping and decisive victory in Boston thanks to what he brought to George Washington. After Boston, he followed Washington through the defeats in New York, New Jersey and into Pennsylvania in the early dark days of the war.

When Washington desperately crossed the Delaware River December 25, 1776, he brought Washington a Christmas present, the artillery that insured victory over the Hessians and British at Trenton and Princeton. He was with Washington when he nearly lost his army at Valley Forge in the winter of 1777–8 to disease, malnutrition, and the bitter cold.

He stood with Washington at the Battle of Brandywine in September of 1777, where Washington made an error that nearly cost him his entire army and could have ended the war with a British victory. In 1781, he stood by Washington when troops from Pennsylvania and New Jersey mutinied for better pay and conditions.

He was with Washington in New York when the General learned of the betrayal of Benedict Arnold. And most importantly he was with Washington at the end in Yorktown commanding the artillery that shattered the besieged British position forcing Cornwallis to surrender and effectively ended the war.

At Yorktown, the American and French forces laid siege to Cornwallis by land and sea. The French fleet blocked an escape or any resupply efforts by the Royal Navy. Washington prepared for an attack on Cornwallis that attack would have to succeed by November 1, because the French fleet was to leave Chesapeake Bay and return to the Caribbean.

It was already October 7, when the attack began, Washington had three weeks to finish off Cornwallis, he turned to his Yankee master of artillery. By October 9, the Colonial guns began to punish Cornwallis, in just eight days the American artillery had crippled the British, and on October 17, they asked to surrender.

The British had 214 guns to defend their position at Yorktown, Washington's Yankee silenced them all. A French general expressed the defeated British opinion of the American artillery:

"The English marveled no less at the extraordinary process of the American artillery, and the capacity and instructions of its officers."[cxxii]

Lord Cornwallis wrote after the battle, *"The fire continued incessantly from heavy cannons…mortars…howitzers…until all our guns were silenced, our work much damaged, and our loss of men considerable."*[cxxiii]

With the fighting at an end General George Washington asked Congress to promote his Yankee to Major General. On 4 December 1783, Washington called together his staff to tell them he was to resign his commission to Congress, he then appointed his Yankee, his successor as Continental Army Commander.

On 19 April 1775, he was a Boston bookseller, on December 4, 1783, he was a Major General and George Washington's handpicked successor. Washington's Yankee was Boston born and a New Englander to his core. His name was Henry Knox.

Henry Knox was born in Boston in 1750 to Scottish immigrant parents, Mary Campbell and William Knox. He was one of ten children, but only one of four that survived to adulthood. His father was a successful Boston ship builder. His mother and father were both of Scottish heritage who immigrated to Massachusetts from Northern Ireland.

Henry's father William found success in Boston and began his own business. They lived in a stately home on Boston's waterfront beside his ship building business. Henry went to the prestigious Boston Latin School. A primer for Harvard College. Life for the Knox family of Boston, and the bright young Henry could not have been more promising.

In 1759, the ideal life of Henry Knox was shattered, as a nine-year-old boy had to become a young man. Henry's father abandoned the family after his business failed. Nine-year-old Henry Knox, his mother Mary, and younger brother William were suddenly on their own.

Henry was forced to quit school while he was young boy and started to work in the Boston book bindery and bookstore, *Wharton & Bowes, Booksellers.*

Young Henry read constantly, and he was allowed to read anything on the bookstore shelves. Knox from a young age was fascinated with all things military and read any military book he could find. When young Henry was only twenty-one years old, he opened his own bookstore in Boston, *London Bookstore.*

The citizens of Boston loved his small bookshop and bindery where he could sell you a book from London or mend a book and build blank books.

Whenever a British officer would enter, Henry would seek as much information from the soldiers' experiences as possible. He was always hoping to learn something new or be schooled on an important lesson from a distant battlefield.

Henry Knox loved artillery and read every book he could find on the subject. He also read extensively on mathematics, after all artillery is a science and distances and angles are mathematical calculations.

Remarkably, Henry Knox was nearly everywhere history was made in Boston. On the night of 5 March 1770, while he was walking down a Boston street, he was a witness to the Boston Massacre. He saw the Colonials taunting the British sentry and warned the sentry not to shoot at the rude, brazen Bostonians sneering, insulting and jeering the sentry to fire his weapon. He urged the sentry to not react to these provocations. When the firing started, he had a bird's eye view, and later testified in the infamous event.

He also witnessed the Boston Tea party on 16 December 1773. He had joined the Massachusetts Militia the year before and was assigned as a guard of the three ships full of British tea. When the ships were attacked by *Mohawk*

Indians, the Colonial guards were told to stand down. Henry Knox was just twenty-three years old as he watched hundreds of chests of tea thrown into Boston Harbor.

On the morning of 19 April 1775, Henry Knox watched as Lord Percy passed by him on his way to rescue Lieutenant Colonel Smith in Lexington. He was very impressed as the powerful column marched out of Boston. Henry could not conceive the battle they would fight on Battle Road in just a few short hours.

Seven years earlier on 1 October 1768, young Henry Knox was on the Boston waterfront when two British regiments arrived in Boston. He always remembered the splendid formations, the syncopated march with drums and fifes. He saw the resplendent officers in their finest uniforms with their rattling swords. He watched as the enlisted men passed and each one looked as menacing as the other.

Same uniform, same boots, same kit and cartridge boxes, and each had their own brown musket, and long deadly bayonet. As these men marched, he saw in Boston Harbor the magnificent warships that carried the soldiers to his very doorstep. He harbored no illusions as to the power and might of the British Army in Boston.

In 1775, George Washington was only in Cambridge two days when he accidentally encountered Henry Knox. Washington told the young man he was going to inspect the Roxbury defensive works. Roxbury was, after all, one of the logical places for General Howe to attack.

Knox had overseen the building of the earthworks at Roxbury and was very confident they could withstand a British cannonade. When Washington saw what Knox had built, he was overwhelmed. He realized that this young Yankee was something special, a man who understood military science.

Soon Washington became smitten with the tall, large young man, with the booming voice, that everyone seemed to know and like. And his Yankee took an instant liking to his new father figure, the cultured, aristocratic, Virginian General George Washington.

When he could, Washington dined with Knox. In their constant exchanges they found within each other a kindred soul who completely understood the frailties and dangers the Colonials were facing from the locked-up British in Boston.

They each grasped and shared their persistent understanding that they needed artillery to shell the British Army in Boston. Those guns would wear the British down enough for an opportunity to attack, and they could fire at those deadly Royal Navy warships bristling with powerful cannons.

Washington and Knox knew they only had so much time, for sooner or later General Howe was going to bring hell to Washington's doorstep. With time running out they knew artillery was needed.

Washington was given permission by the Continental Congress to bring the guns at Fort Ticonderoga to Boston. An impossible task as they were 300 miles away. George Washington needed a home run from his Babe Ruth— Henry Knox.

Part 3
The Guns

"...that he will put on, or rather he will not put off the true character of a
man, and generously enlarge his views beyond the present day...
The sun never shined on a cause of greater worth"

Common Sense 1776
Thomas Paine

On January 24, 1776, the big man walked into the headquarters of George Washington in Cambridge, Massachusetts. He had been gone for fifty-six days and he was twenty-four days late.

When he departed Cambridge as ordered by Washington, he was a citizen on a secret mission. When he returned, he was promoted to full colonel and the man in charge of General Washington's artillery. He was indispensable to George Washington from that day forward until the war ended in victory.

Twenty-five-year old Henry Knox had completed the impossible task of transporting the captured French and British guns at Fort Ticonderoga in New York and delivering them to Cambridge, Massachusetts. He pulled, pushed, and muscled fifty-eight cannons and mortars weighting thousands of pounds, with men and oxen. He worked and traveled in snow, rain, ice and sleet storms through nearly impassable woods, up and down hills, over frozen lakes and rivers.

Three hundred miles of endless challenges had been mastered by Washington's pragmatic Yankee.

Henry Knox was issued Washington's orders on November 16, 1775. Knox reassured the desperate Washington he would return with the guns of Ticonderoga. Everyone else told Washington Henry Knox would fail.

Before he traveled to Fort Ticonderoga he rode with his brother William to New York City, and then to Albany. Washington wanted and trusted Knox to accumulate a full accounting of what other guns and ammunition were in the New York. George Washington had requested the Continental Congress commission Henry Knox a full colonel. When Knox left Cambridge that commission had not arrived.

Knox had letters of introduction from General Washington for wherever he went, but he departed Cambridge a private citizen, on a secret and critical mission for the war effort.

In New York, Henry Knox met Colonel Alexander McDougal. Forty-three-year-old Alexander McDougal was a Scot immigrant to New York Colony. He was born in the Scottish Highlands and was not fond of His Majesty's red coated soldiers.

When Knox asked for his artillery to use in Boston, McDougal only allowed the small guns to move, he kept the big ones on hand to defend New York.

Next Henry traveled up the Hudson River toward Ticonderoga. He was halted a few days later, before he could reach Ticonderoga at Fort George. A heavy snow was falling, and he was still at least one day south of his destination when he put up for the night. Room was scarce so he was offered room in a cabin being occupied by a captured British officer.

Sitting before the fireplace Henry and the British officer began a pleasant conversation. Each man was well-read, cultured, and respectful of the other. Henry enjoyed the company of such an educated man, regardless of his stature as a young British officer.

Remarkably that British officer was John Andre, the British spy who accepted Benedict Arnold's offer to change sides and join the British Army in September of 1779. Arnold escaped, but his British handler was captured by American sentries. Henry Knox would meet John Andre again.

In 1780, Henry Knox was chosen by General Washington to be on the *Board of Senior Officers*, who would decide if John Andre should hang as a spy. Along with his favorite Yankee, Washington also choose two other Yankees to judge suspected spy John Andre, Generals Nathanial Green, and John Glover were also appointed to the board. John Andre was hanged on October 2, 1780.

Very early on the morning of December 5, 1775, Henry Knox departed his new British friend and traveled to Ticonderoga. Fort Ticonderoga was a state-of-the-art block walled fort built by the French. It was captured by the British during the French and Indian War. On May 10, 1775, American Colonial forces led by Ethan Allen and Benedict Arnold captured the fort with no loss of life.

Henry arrived and immediately went to work choosing the guns he needed in Boston. Once the guns were selected, they were dismantled and loaded onto the wooden sleds he had made. Sources vary and accounts list either 58, 59, or 60 as the number of guns he chose for Boston.

On December 17, 1775, Henry Knox and over 100,000 pounds of cannons, gun carriages, and ammunition on 42 sleds pulled by over 150 oxen, began a journey of over 300 miles. Henry Knox scheduled a grueling journey back to Boston. He believed he could be back in Cambridge by January 1, 1776. He was wrong.

Knox needed snow to speed the pulling of the sleds. At first none came, then on Christmas morning 1775 Henry Knox got a Christmas present of a fresh snow fall. Two feet of snow had fallen and with that the *Noble Train of Artillery* was off to Cambridge. Word started to spread that Knox was moving the cannons from Ticonderoga to Boston.

Henry Knox's secret mission was no longer a secret. Seems everyone but the British knew that the big guns were headed to Boston. Over five thousand people turned out to watch the *Noble Train* pass in Albany. Next, he crossed the Hudson River, and he was on his way to the hills and valleys at the border between New York and Massachusetts.

He passed over the Berkshire Mountains in western Massachusetts barely getting the sleds over the hills and facing a greater challenge as they slowly descended those mountains. Holding back the sleds that weighted well over five thousand pounds each was very difficult and very dangerous.

Knox would need over three thousand feet of three-inch rope to handle the sleds. After the Berkshires things got easier.

His *Noble Train* was greeted from Springfield, Massachusetts all the way to Cambridge. His men were offered food and drink and cheered as heroes as they pushed along the guns that would finish off the British in Boston.

While the guns were still in Framingham, twelve miles from Cambridge Henry Knox walked into Washington's headquarters. He had managed to do what other said could not be done.

General George Washington whose hopes had been faltering for weeks was elated. He knew those guns could make a difference. The euphoric Washington told Henry Knox his commission had arrived, he was a colonel in the Continental Army, and Washington's Chief of Artillery.

Washington had not found a way to finish off the British bottled up in Boston. He had wasted away the autumn months and now the winter months were slipping from his grasp. Rumors circulated from London to Boston, from Philadelphia to Cambridge, that the British would shortly reinforce Boston with hundreds of Artillery pieces, more Regulars, and plentiful ammunition.

The already overcrowded Boston Harbor was to be further overcrowded with more Royal navy ships and their powerful naval cannons. Henry Knox and his dedicated men had delivered to General Washington the tools that would end the siege of Boston and write the final chapter of the historical events that had begun on 19 April 1775. Next, Knox would position the guns where they could do the most damage.

The Continental Army camped outside Boston, was composed of ninety percent New Englanders – Yankees. It was time for Washington and his *Yankee* army to finish off what was begun just ten months earlier on 19 April 1775. The twenty-five-year-old, large, street fighting Boston bookseller told Washington he would bring the guns back to Cambridge. Like Babe Ruth hitting a game winning home run, Henry Knox gave Washington what he needed to find his victory, and salvation in Boston.

Part 4
Boston is Free

"I know you will not turn your faces from our foes... press forward until tyranny is trodden under foot, and you have fixed your adored goddess Liberty... on the American throne."

Dr. Major General Joseph Warren (1741–75)
Address 5 March 1775
Anniversary of the Boston Massacre
Old South Church, Boston

Since 2 October 1768, British troops were stationed and quartered in Boston. They had been the military arm of the tyrannical British government that closed the Port of Boston. The presence of British soldiers living in and amongst formerly free Englishmen in Boston inflamed the agitated patriots, impressed the uncommitted, cauterizing a conversation into a cause.

It was the presence of British troops in Boston that was the most egregious of all the mistakes the King and his Ministers made. They created the opportunities for armed conflict with the New England men who did not fear armed men. They were armed men too, and they began the American Revolution in Lexington, Concord, along Battle Road and at Bunker Hill.

And it is fitting that the British were driven out of Boston not by an aristocratic Virginian in command of a rag-tag army. But by the pragmatic Boston genius who dragged 60 cannons, over 300 miles, positioned them in the defensive installations he built, and aimed and fired them at a vulnerable British General besieged on the lonely peninsular of Boston.

On February 16, 1776, General George Washington convened a council of war at his headquarters in Cambridge. Washington who had watched as time and opportunities had escaped him knew he now had what he needed to strike a devastating blow against General Howe's army nearly surrounded in Boston.

Washington said:

"that a stroke well aimed at this critical juncture might put a final end to the war and restore peace..."[cxxiv]

Colonel Henry Knox was already busy positioning his cannons and mortars to bombard Boston. His crowning achievement was to place some of the most powerful guns on Dorchester Heights overlooking Boston, and all the war ships in the harbor.

By February 26, 1776, Colonel Knox had already placed his guns in Cambridge, Roxbury, and Dorchester but not yet on the Dorchester Heights. His guns faced the city of Boston from three sides, and he was prepared to exact a terrible price on the British Army occupying his beloved Boston.

Beginning March 2, Knox's guns fired on Boston providing an immediate impact. The historic event was recorded by a witness in Boston. A witness who had been at Lexington, Concord, Battle Road and Bunker Hill. Stuck in Boston with the rest of General Howe's army British Lieutenant John Barker wrote in his diary:

"1776, March 2, At about 11:00 at night...the Rebels began to bombard the Town of Boston...They continued throwing in shot and shells until daybreak...the same was returned to them...Our shells [sic] very bad, most of them bursting in the air or not at all..."[cxxv]

The next day the British veteran again recorded in his diary Henry Knox's bombardment of Boston. And he keenly noted that a mortar had been moved closer to Boston from its initial position in Somerville. And recorded how little effect the British guns had on the rebel positions.

"3rd, At 10:00 this night the Rebels began again and a warmer fire was kept up by both sides 'til [sic] daybreak...the Rebels had moved the Mortar from Phipps Farm to Cobble Hill...most of their shot and shell fell in Town...Our artillery a little mended a few [sic], of our shells answering."

The next day, Monday March fourth Colonel Knox and his artillery unleashed an enormous bombardment on Boston. It was the third night in a row Knox's guns unleashed their hell on the confined British army. And it was the most violent bombardment of the three days as Barker records the increase in Colonial firepower, calling it, *very hot.* John Barker and his regiment were in the middle of it. Barker again enters into his diary what was happening to him and the Town of Boston and for the first time mentions casualties:

"4th March. The firing began at 7:00 at night continued very hot till daybreak...seven men of the 22nd regiment [sic] wounded..."

It was a diversion.

On the fourth of March under the cover of darkness four hundred oxen and over two thousand men all under the command of Henry Knox placed the biggest guns from Fort Ticonderoga guns atop Dorchester Heights. Overnight Knox and his men had created earthworks and installed the mighty guns in position to hit Boston and the British ships in the Harbor.

On Tuesday, March 5, Knox opened fire on his former hometown. He was not destroying Boston as much as those in it, the British. General Howe realized those guns must be silenced.

Howe ordered his forces to cross the Back Bay and attack Dorchester. They could not. Miraculously, his men could not row across the wind driven waters of the Back Bay and land in Dorchester. The wind was blowing furiously offshore pushing General Howe's boats back to the Boston side of the bay.

The howling winds continued to blow the next day, further denying Howe his Boston victory. Howe's forces were stuck in Boston and being bombarded by Knox's deadly accurate cannon fire. Again, we investigate the diary of British Lieutenant John Barker in Boston.

"March 5 This morning works were perceived to be thrown up on Dorchester Heights, very strong ones tho' [sic] only the labor of one night: 5 regiment embarked...the Men were not to load [their guns] but fixed bayonets: in the night it came on to blow such a gale the—boat could not possibly land which stopped the expedition, and gave the Rebels [time to complete their] Works [sic] and make them too strong to be taken without Men [sic] than we [could not] spare."

Washington reinforced Dorchester and the Heights, presenting to Howe a force he knew he could not beat. The horrors of Bunker Hill surely must have been reflected in the mind of General William Howe. He fully understood he could no longer assault Dorchester; it was just too strong a dug-in position. That lesson, he had learned on Breed's Hill, nine months ago never left him. One last glimpse into Barker's diary vividly illustrates the hopeless British position.

"March 6 It was determined by a Council of War to quit the Town. Orders [were given] *to get ready with all expedition* [to leave Boston] *... "*

Overnight the most powerful military position in all Colonial America was erected just a short distance from the British in Boston. Just like the night before the Battle of Bunker Hill the Colonial forces had built fortifications on a hilltop. But the fortifications at Dorchester Heights contained massive destructive guns, and just the right man to command them, *Washington's Yankee Henry Knox.*

Overwhelmed with the speed the earthworks had been erected one British officer remarked:

"They were all raised during the night." General Howe was heard to lament, *"...that he did not know what to do what he should do...the Provincials had done more work in one night than his whole army would have done in six months... "*[cxxvi]

Before it was over the streets and hillsides in Roxbury and Dorchester were full of those who observed the history unfolding in front of them. Many of them had seen the British bombardment of Charlestown, now they witnessed a sight never thought imaginable. The Americans were bombarding the British into submission.

The British agreed to evacuate Boston and if granted safe passage they would not burn Boston to the ground. Not lost to history, Boston still celebrates March 17 as Evacuation Day, a local holiday.

Boston was Washington's first military victory. It is hard to overstate the importance of the victory in Boston, and impossible to overstate the contributions of Henry Knox. The movement of the guns from Ticonderoga to Cambridge was an astonishing feat of engineering and the key to Washington's victory as Knox positioned and fired the guns that broke the British ability to remain in Boston.

The Revolution would take Knox from volunteer to Major General. It would lead to Knox being Washington's handpicked successor and the second Commander and Chief of the Continental Army, and President Washington's first Secretary of War.

The victory in Boston kept the cause alive and emboldened the unifying American Colonies. The mighty British had been defeated, and it fostered a renewed spirit of independence. Indeed, after the victory in Boston the Continental Congress adopts, *The unanimous Declaration of the thirteen united States of America.* Remembered as, The Declaration of Independence, the most important document in the history of the United States of America.

In its opening, you can hear, and feel the victories in Massachusetts granting the capability of common men to dissolve the power of the King and raise themselves up to form a free government.

When in the Course of human events, it becomes necessary for one people to dissolve the political bands which have connected them with another, and to assume among the powers of the earth, the separate and equal station to which the Laws of Nature and of Nature's God entitle them...

In London the news of the disaster in Boston was received as one would expect, with shock. In the highest seat of British Government, The House of Lords the sides were split defending the Crown and his ministers for their action in Massachusetts.

These are the words of a man who rose and stated plainly what he understood had happened three thousand miles away. The Duke of Manchester disappointed at the events in Boston, Massachusetts plainly stated:

"The mode of the retreat may, do to the general [Howe] infinite honor, but it does dishonor to the British nation. Let this transaction be dressed in what garb you please, the fact remains that the army which was sent to reduce the province of Massachusetts bay has been driven from the capital, and that the standard of the provincial army now waves in triumph over the walls of Boston. The army of Britain equipped with every possible essential of war; a chosen army with chosen officers, backed by the power of a mighty fleet...sent to assert

British authority; has for many months, been imprisoned within that town by the provincial army...and British Generals whose names have never met a blot of dishonor, are forced to quit that town which was the first object of the war, the immediate cause of the hostilities... "[cxxvii]

The British had killed just a handful of *America's First Soldiers* on Lexington Green on 19 April 1775. They would pay an unimaginable, extraordinary price over the next eight years, as they lost all the American Colonies. Soon the events that had begun on a flat green field in the quaint New England town of Lexington, Massachusetts would find their partial conclusion as the British left Boston as they had arrived, by sea.

Time and opportunity had slipped away from General William Howe, replacing his needed victory with a legacy of British failure in Boston.

The British would never return to Massachusetts to fight again. General William Howe realized too late that—*The Game had Changed.*

Epilogue

"We hold these truths to be self-evident,
that all men are created equal,
that they are endowed by their
Creator with certain unalienable Rights,
that among these are
Life, Liberty and the pursuit of Happiness"

The red *Raleigh* bicycle rested gracefully on its kick stand. The shiny red paint, slightly worn brown leather seat, shinning aluminum rims caught your eyes as they moved to the glistening chrome handlebars. And that distinctive emblem on the frame, the proud red R above the word Raleigh and Nottingham, England where she was built.

Reading Nottingham my imagination always wandered to Robin Hood and his glorious deeds. Sitting in the old garage it called out every day of summer to be ridden.

Burlington, Massachusetts was a short bicycle ride from nearby Lexington. The excited rider on a red, 3 speed, Raleigh bicycle goes racing down Lexington Street, and at its end turned left onto the Middlesex Turnpike. The broad turnpike is more of a highway to the young rider, more cars, and modern buildings dot the old turnpike road.

A half-mile beyond the underpass, near the old lumber company the road forks and the rider bears to the right. The busy traffic fades the turnpike is now a modern memory on this nostalgic trip. Suddenly the sound of the antique dark green chain drive dump truck, with its smiling old driver passes the rider and turns into the old sand pit.

The dust from the truck raises up as does the sound of the engine and clacking chains passing over the sprockets. The pace slows slightly as the old

Raleigh 3 speed and its young patient rider climbs the gentle slope on Adams Street. At the top there is the sign—Lexington.

It is all downhill, as Adams Street Burlington becomes Hancock Street Lexington, and momentum guides the sleek Raleigh and its excited rider over the railroad tracks to the Lexington Green. The streets are the very same ones that existed in Colonial times, the roads that Colonial Militiamen traveled as they gathered to become *America's First Soldiers*.

This youthful bike rider enjoying a New England summer's day finds rest as the ride ends in the center of the old town. Large full green trees providing shade, and fresh cool green grass offering rest are a perfect setting to survey the history all around this historic place. Many buildings surrounded the Green, and most were old, white houses with black shutters that looked as if they had been there forever.

A venerable, large white church dominated one end of the Green. It had a large steeple that seemed to pierce the heavens, the white steeple climbing into the perfectly blue summer sky a reminder that God watches over this hallowed place.

There is another building, distinguishable by its chalky yellow exterior, and black faded shutters held open by old steel twisted scrolls. Buckman's Tavern seems a colonial era relic, mostly unchanged from the fateful April morning nearly 200 years ago.

The flag on the Green was unfurled by the warm breeze snapping in a rhythm that seemingly accompanies a walk through the green grass. At the end of this place the young bike rider comes face to face with a huge green man.

Captain John Parker's statue stands behind a rock outcropping with flowers and greenery. His bronze image greened with dulling tarnish, rises above the rocks and he is parallel with the flapping flags. He holds his musket with both hands, it rests on his bended left leg as his fixed gaze reaches from the historic Green onto the road the British used to enter Lexington. He stands like an eternal sentry guarding a place and an ideal still honored nearly two centuries after he defied America's last king.

Standing alone away from other memorials sits an ancient rock, it is gray with black streaks. It rests on this early afternoon covered by the shade of the cool green trees presenting a welcome relief on the summer's day hot sun. It has a flat face and walking closer it has the chiseled likeness of an old musket and powder horn, the old words under the gun indicate the Colonial line of defense was not far from here. Beneath the gun and powder horn, words are deeply chiseled into the rounded rock, like the letters on a weathered gravestone. The youthful bike rider reads those words, but it will take decades to understand:

> *"Stand your ground; don't fire unless fired upon,*
> *but if they mean to have a war, let it begin here."*

Walking the long field at Gettysburg, where Picket's Virginians died for the immortal General Robert E. Lee, falling at the high watermark of the South's, *"Lost Cause"*—Walking the Somme, and Verdun on the western plains of France, each still haunting with names conjuring images of places otherworldly. Places of ghastly death. Being humbled by the massive and moving World War I memorial at Vimy Ridge, outside Arras in Western France. Tracing the name of a long ago fallen, and once forgotten soldier, *M.R. McNutt.* His name carved into the white stone base, memorializing a family's contribution to our collective freedom. Finding Bastogne in the Ardennes Forrest, a place that only wishes to forget its violent past. Sitting in Sainte-Mere Eglise, square at midnight every year, and waiting for the men of the 82nd and 101st Airborne to fall all around me. Watching the Sun rise over Omaha Beach at low tide, at H-Hour when they came ashore—a foreign army invading a foreign country to fight a foreign enemy and liberate a foreign people. On Normandy's shores they made history and saved a world. Walking the bluffs above the old beach, where thousands of Americans find their final resting place, their stunning white gravestones facing west, forever looking back from whence they came. A vivid reminder of the ultimate price some of those we will never know.

Lexington Green is where this writer first understood the price Americans have paid for their freedom. Here a quaint New England town made History when *America's First Soldiers* stared down the repressive guns of tyranny.

Here, first stood America's finest, encouraging my journeys to find far off battlefields. A summer's bike ride decades ago, to a place where a young, inspired student could see and touch History. A place never forgotten as the journey continues and the mission's meaning finds further purpose:

"Learn The Stories – Don't Let Their Glory Fade"

Part 2: The Places: 2021

Boston, Massachusetts
Green Dragon Tavern

11 Marshall Street Boston

Walking toward the Green Dragon you walk down an old Boston cobblestone street. The buildings, and cobblestone streets look like Paul Revere and Sam Adams would be right at home and waiting in the Tavern for us to join them.

There, we would share a pint, and our expectations and plans. If we were one of the trusted Sons of Liberty, we would be welcomed by John Hancock, John Adams, Dr. Joseph Warren, Samuel Adams, or Paul Revere amongst many others.

It would be warm on a cold winter night, and the conversations would be about our common dislike for King George III, General Thomas Gage, any Red Coated British soldier, and of course our most disappointing loyalist citizens of Boston—Tories. Paul Revere said:

"In the fall of 1774, and the winter of 1775, I was one of upward of thirty, chiefly mechanics, who formed ourselves into a committee for the purpose of watching the British soldiers, and gaining every intelligence of the movements of the Tories. We held our meeting at the Green Dragon."

Siege of Boston
Allen French (1870–1946)
Page 176

The current tavern is not the original, but it feels old. Walking into the historic Green Dragon is always a joy and reminds me of the men who gathered there to plan the American Revolution. Stop by, sit surrounded by history and thoughts of our brave *Founding Fathers* raising a pint or two to the dreams they could hardly envision as we live every day in the United States of America.

Exiting the Green Dragon, it will not be difficult to find the Freedom Trail that will take you into Boston's Historic North End via Hanover Street. But before you restart your colonial journey you should realize you are just a few footsteps away from the New England Holocaust Memorial at Union Street Park.

Take a few moments and walk through the unique and informative memorial to the Jewish victims of World War II. Boston's Colonial history will wait for you, as you pass beneath the large glass pillars. Look closely and notice the endless amounts of numbers etched into the glass towers, each number a name, a person, a life. All lost in the Holocaust.

Sit on the benches or walls in the parks and reflect on the roll the United States played in liberating the camps at the end of the War. Your colonial journey will mean even more as you process what a free country like the United States can do to end oppression and suffering all over the world.

Find your way back to the Freedom Trail and walk toward Boston Harbor, you will be walking easterly as you enter Boston's North End.

Old North Church

193 Salem Street

Boston (North End)

Nestled into one of Boston's oldest neighborhoods is one of America's oldest active churches. The large, antique, red brick building is one of the stops on Boston's Freedom Trail in the old neighborhood of Boston's North End. I followed the trail down Hanover Street enjoying a sun filled walk down the restaurant and shop lined old street.

I took left then turn and travel by Paul Revere's statue which is located in Paul Revere Mall. Stroll through Paul Revere Mall and enjoy the tree lined brick and granite walkways. Standing in front of Revere's memorial statue I see the North Church in the background. Striking to see Revere and the Church in a historical alignment. A most fitting placement knowing the connection the church and mounted brass rider share.

Follow the Freedom Trail and enter the rear grounds of the church as you pass the old open brick and black iron fence and gate. Within the grounds of the church is a simple memorial to the soldiers who have fought in America's most recent war in Iraq and Afghanistan.

Stopping for a moment, I feel like I am between two historical bookends as I leave the modern memorial and stroll toward the church. It is a massive brick building that looks like it is from another time. Walking around to the front I gaze up at the steeple and see the windows that were illuminated in America's first and maybe most important secret message.

I smile as I hear the words Longfellow's poem filling my mind:

"One if by land, and two if by sea; And I on the opposite shore will be..."

I continue to stare, and it seems like the steeple pierces the perfect blue sky over Boston this day. Dropping my gaze down the towering steeple I notice a large white stone marker attached to the building reminding visitors of the historic event at the center of the building's life. As you enter the church be mindful it is an active sanctuary still functioning as an Episcopal Church. The interior looks old like the outside of this place, yet the brightly painted white surfaces contrast with the early stained wood that is sparingly used as trim.

Notice the pews are arranged in boxes, and numbers as to identify who sat there so long ago. Where your seat is located, denotes your wealth and standing in the community. Upstairs sits a large, beautiful pipe organ and more traditional pews reserved for Boston's less wealthy pious residents.

Below the church is a cellar that contains crypts. One of those crypts holds the remains of none other than British Major John Pitcairn. He was wounded at Bunker Hill and died a few days later. He rests peacefully in the town he tried to conquer - Boston.

The Old North Church is a very enjoyable place to visit, and a must for the historic traveler. As you exit the church, the Freedom Trail takes you up a gentle hill with a historic cemetery at the top.

Copp's Hill Burial Ground

Hull Street Boston

Walk out of the Old North Church and head straight up the hill. It is not a steep hill, rather a measured slope, and an easy to walk on the marked sidewalks. Look for the familiar red brick markings of the Freedom Trail. You are walking toward Charlestown.

When you near the top you will see a set of stone stairs on the right. The aged stone wall has a black iron fence on the top and attached to that fence is the sign welcoming you to the historic, Copp's Hill Burying Ground. The sign informs us that this burying ground was opened in 1659, over 100 years before our Revolution.

It is loaded with old grave markers, and stone monuments. Some are very interesting, and it is worth your time to walk around and spend some time with Boston's long dead residents. I was there to understand how the British bombarded Bunker Hill and Charlestown from Copp's Hill. Today as you walk toward the Charlestown side of the cemetery—that is highest point of the old burying ground, and where the British put their big cannons.

Standing there, you are looking at an old row house that runs the length of that side of the cemetery. Long gone is the view the British gunners had of the valiant American defense of Charlestown. But with its proximity to the Old North Church, I recommend you walk up the hill and visit this interesting, very old, and historic burying ground, that was for the British army a place filled with cannons to shell the Americans dug in at Bunker Hill.

Leave Copp's hill on the street you traveled away from the Old North Church—Hull Street. Travel toward Charlestown, and away from the Old North Church, and you will descend the hill to Commercial Street. You will turn left onto Commercial Street and walking just a block or so a large garage building will be on your left as you approach Prince Street. That was the Brinks Building, and site of one of the largest robberies in American history.

Brinks, the robbers and the stolen money are long gone, and the historic building is now an innocuous parking garage. As you are walking in front of the garage look to your right for the place the Freedom Trail crosses Commercial Street and directs you over a foot bridge into Charlestown.

Finding the historic obelisk in the Charlestown skyline is not difficult and the trail will lead you to the old bloody hilltop, sight of the Revolutionary War's most deadly battle for the British Army.

Bunker Hill Monument

Monument Square

Charlestown Section-Boston

Bunker Hill is an extraordinary monument. It is in the Charlestown section of Boston, but in Colonial times Charlestown was an independent town. It was a small village at the end of the Charlestown Peninsula.

Today, it is a quintessential old Boston neighborhood. In this case, an old Irish neighborhood. When I visit the strikingly tall obelisk surrounded by the old row houses, I think of the rich irony and how it is proper that an old Irish neighborhood watches over a monument to those that defeated the British Army.

Today the monument stands defiantly looking out to Boston Harbor. It pierces the sky seemingly reaching to the Heavens. It stares out at the water as a deadly reminder of the dangers faced by those who trampled the liberties of 18th century Bostonians. It is a place often crowded. Bunker Hill is the final stop on the Freedom Trail that began on the other side of the Charles River at Boston Common.

The monument stands 221' tall and made of solid gray granite, quarried in nearby Quincy, Massachusetts. It took nearly fourteen years to build and was financed privately.

The obelisk is at the top of Breed's Hill, where the American earthworks were hastily constructed the night before the battle. Beneath your feet the British Regulars fought and died to deny the rights we Americans, especially we in Massachusetts have enjoyed since the battle ended. And where remarkable men—America's First Soldiers fought and died there for us. We are their legacy.

Months after the battle the British Army (retreated) evacuated Boston, never to return to face the Soldiers of Massachusetts. Never.

Find a place where you can reflect. Think of what happened directly where you are standing. The brave and selfless men who died there helped create the freedoms we enjoy as citizens of the United States of America. Remember those who sacrificed and fell in the name of freedom – our Freedom.

Lexington, Massachusetts
Lexington Green

1625 Massachusetts Avenue

Lexington, Massachusetts

This is a most historic place. It has changed little since that April Morning in 1775. It is still a grassy plain in the center of this old New England town. Trees line the Green today offering shade from summer's heat, and in autumn vibrant colors that are quintessential New England.

Monuments line the edge of Green which is surrounded by modern asphalt roads paved with history. Looking east is the road the British used to travel from Cambridge through Arlington (Colonial Menotomy) and into and onto the Lexington Green.

That road forks as it reaches the massive statue of Captain John Parker, with one road going toward Burlington, Woburn or Bedford, and the other the road to Concord. Walk the grassy Green, feel history beneath your feet as you stand with the men watching the massive British force approach and then march onto the green.

If you try you can hear the rolling drums beat their cadence, the clanking of the swords, muskets, cartridge boxes as the men in red coats line up in frightening precision before you. Look toward the houses that surround the Green, see the gathered residents prepared to watch the men and boys they love be shot dead or rammed through with a deadly British bayonet.

Feel your heart race, your throat gets dry, and your trembling hands hold fast to your musket. Close your eyes, and image the voices of the British officers demanding you *Disperse!* And your friends and family do not move, so neither do you.

Together, you are defying what seemed impossible to defy. You are standing in the shadows of real American Heroes, remember them, and don't let their glory fade into just ghostly names.

Walk to each monument, some older than others. Read Captain Parker's orders to his fellow citizen soldiers—to America's First Soldiers:

"Stand your ground; don't fire unless fired upon, but if they mean to have a war, let it begin here."

Parker's orders still define the spirit of the American Soldier. Do not seek or start the battle but do run from the tyranny of the wicked. John Parker issued that command to merely eighty men early on the morning of 19 April 1775, while he was facing an overwhelming large well-armed determined enemy.

And find the stone where he is remembered with a memorial on Lexington Green:

"In Honor of Prince Estabrook—Prince Estabrook was a slave who lived in Lexington. At dawn on 19 April 1775, he was one of the Lexington Minute Men awaiting the arrival of the British Regulars...In the battle which followed, Prince Estabrook was wounded on Lexington Green. Through circumstances and destiny, he thus became the first black soldier to fight in the American Revolution..."

Find the monument that contains the remains of those who died long ago. They sacrificed for their dreams of freedom, our lives of freedom. Read their names and encourage others to recite out loud that short list of names. They were the first to die for us but not the last. Remember them. Leave a penny on the base of the monument as a reminder you were there. It is an old military custom and means you visited their grave. Keep alive their memories and deeds.

Old Burial Ground

Lexington Green, Harrington Road
Lexington, Massachusetts 02420

Just a short walk from the green behind the First Parish Church, is an old historic cemetery. It has graves dating back to the 17th century. It is interesting, like most cemeteries of the Colonial era. I am there to see the memorial to Captain John Parker, commander of the Lexington Militiamen on 19 April 1775.

Captain Parker was a man I learned of as a child in school. I have visited the Lexington Green countless times and always pay my respects at his statue on the Green. His memorial in the cemetery is very humble, and worthy of a visit to think quietly about Captain Parker and his place in our history.

Without his courage to hold his ground on the Green, to express his right to assemble as, at that time a free British subject, we perhaps have no American Revolution. In history there always seems those moments where everything changed. Sometimes those moments are big—like the D-Day invasion in World War II, or the Battle of Gettysburg in our Civil War. And Lexington Green, with the stand of Captain Parker and his troops is for this author as important as place Americans have fought for liberty.

He gathered peacefully, with his fellow citizens, on the public square. Standing together with his fellow citizens he was molested by the British troops as the sun rose on 19 April 1775. He did not run away from the danger, rather, he held his ground. Not easy facing the world's most powerful army.

Go to the Green and walk in Parker's footsteps, then walk to Ye Old Burial ground and pay your respects. I left a stone, and a penny to express my gratitude to one of my heroes – Captain John Parker.

Look up Captain Parker's grandson, Theodore Parker. He led a peaceful and productive life, and some of his quotes have been used by important Americans into the 20th century.

Battle Road-Trail
Parker's Revenge

Minute Man National Historical Park
250 N Great Road
Lincoln, Massachusetts 01773

Just off Massachusetts Route 2A, the modern road between Lexington and Concord, is the Visitor's center on the Lexington end of Minute Man National Park, Visitor's Center. Start your journey there, where you will be in the competent hands of the very qualified Park Rangers.

Perhaps, you will find Patrick, he is a knowledgeable and passionate former teacher filled with all the facts you need to know to walk into history on the Battle Road. You can sit and watch the movie they provide, look at the artifacts they display, and get a guidebook of Battle Road trail.

I was there on a warm early autumn day. The center is perfect for a rest and has clean restrooms. I was able to talk at length with the staff members who are all extremely qualified and full of great stories. Browse the gift shop— they sell a lot of historical books – Maybe this one someday.

Exiting the Visitor's Center, the trail is just a short walk away. It has stone walls on each side, it is brown crunchy soil that speaks with every step you take. I turned onto the trail and traveled toward Concord. I was walking the direction of the Redcoats in the early morning hours of 19 April.

Behind you is Lexington Green, where you and your fellow regulars just killed eight armed Lexington citizens. You are walking west toward Concord and your appointment with history that is remembered as the *"shot heard round the world."* My walk is leisurely, and I am joined by others seeking history, and others who are just out walking.

There is much to see along the trail, and keep in mind this part of Battle Road—was the actual road the British traveled. Enjoy each bend, notice the home sites, some standing others long since reduced to stone foundations. You will also encounter memorials the British soldiers who were killed and buried along this historic route. Stop and pay your respects.

I turn around and head back toward Lexington. Now my footsteps are in the direction of the retreating British soldiers on afternoon of 19 April 1775. I am beyond the first three ambush sites (Meriam's Corner, Brooks Hill, and Bloody Angle) that are in Concord and Lincoln. I am walking away from the last of the ambushes—the Bloody Angle.

The old dirt path is the same road they retreated on after the engagement at the Old North Bridge in Concord. They were desperate to get back to Boston. Their agonizing retreat remembered as a fluid battle that ran for nearly sixteen miles.

They were trying to survive the unbridled wrath of the Americans closing in on each side of the old road, while firing on them from near and far. The British Soldiers on the very path I follow were in desperation as they grasped for the freedom, they had been sent to deny others.

Walking a short distance, the old road crosses a new road. The new road goes to Hansom Airport, a former US Air Force Base. The new road was a creek in Colonial times. Stop before you cross the new road, look around into the woods and can see the area is as it was two centuries ago—a wetland.

I was there after some days of rain, and it was easy to discern the area that was wet. That is important because it would have slowed the British down as they funneled onto what was a narrow bridge. Crossing the street was representative of crossing the long-gone stream.

On the other side of the new street, we make a sweeping bend to the right. Stop there and investigate the woods as the ground gently raises and exposes many small rock outcroppings. Walk into the woods along a wooden boardwalk, and at the end of the boardwalk is an explanation of what happened there on 19 April 1775.

Look up at the slight rise, and the rocks and large trees would have concealed Captain John Parker and his vengeful Militiamen as they ambushed the retreating British column. Where you stand was where the British flankers protecting the main column stood. As they crossed the stream and the narrow bridge erased by time's passage the British were ambushed.

The ambush conducted by the men and the commander of the day's first encounter on Lexington Green. There are no hard facts about the casualties suffered by the British there, but what is well known is that was the last straw as many British soldiers broke ranks and ran toward Lexington center.

The firing was so intense that Colonel Smith and Major Pitcairn were each knocked off their horses. The colonials on the hill had hearts full of vengeance and were determined to exact a damming price from the British Regulars.

Standing, imagining over 100 guns firing at you is a sobering thought. Each bullet over a half inch thick, emerging before a sheet of white smoke and a cacophony of noise just behind the deadly projectile. They were just as they had been at the other ambush sites—easy targets in their red coats, and all grouped together.

Walk up the hill like the Redcoats did after the deadly volley was released by Captain Parker's accurate killers. Imagine what it was like for the Regulars attacking an enemy they could not see. When they reached the top, the Redcoats found most of the Lexington men were gone. Whatever stragglers they found, they killed. They walked back down and followed their frightened, fleeing countrymen toward Lexington.

There would be two more ambushes on Battle Road in Lexington. They are marked as you walk the trail. First was at *The Bluff*, less than a half mile from the Parker's Revenge site. The last was at Fiske's Hill about a half mile down the trail after the Bluff.

Lexington was the darkest time for the Regulars, they were greatly outnumbered, low or out of ammunition, exhausted, hungry, confused, and frightened that their life was the next to be sacrificed for *King and Country*. They broke at Parker's Revenge, they broke at the Bluff, and at Fiske's Hill, some running nearly all the way to Lexington Green.

Before you reach the Bluff, an old home is identified as that of Jacob Whittemore. The house looks as if Mr. Whittemore still lives there. Well preserved, its occupants on 19 April 1775 witnessed history going west and returning later traveling east.

The stone markers that are shaped like an obelisk denote where you are. One side tells you the distance to Boston Harbor and the other to Meriam's Corner where the antique road ends in Concord.

Concord, Massachusetts
Col. James Barrett Farm

448 Barrett's Mill Rd, Concord, MA 01742

The homestead and Farm of Colonel James Barrett still stands. The house is well preserved and sits much closer to the road than it did during the British inspection for cannons and other materials of war. The house looks as if the Barrett's still live there.

It is beautifully maintained and warrants a visit for its offering of excellent example of an 18th century colonial Massachusetts home. Its surroundings are very natural and have not been encroached by the 21st century. It is open only by appointment, or when the announce an open house on the website— http://www.jamesbarrettfarm.org

Across the street is an active farm owned by the Town of Concord. Standing there I can imagine that the view is different from as it was on 19 April 1775, but not strikingly different. It is worth a visit to see this well-preserved gem.

Wright's Tavern

2 Lexington Road, Concord, MA 01742

Walk up to Wright's Tavern in the center of Concord. Its dark red clapboard exterior, with its black trim, hip roof and multiple chimneys let you know you are looking at history. It is still used today, but not as a tavern. It is used for educational purposes and is affiliated with the Church behind it.

Walking up to the old tavern you can see a sign reminding you of its historical significance as a meeting place on 19 April 1775. I can imagine British Lieutenant Colonel Smith exiting Wright's Tavern assembling his forces for what he knew was going to be a most deadly day. From Wright's Tavern, Smith and his forces would travel a road of damnation back to Lexington, four miles and six ambushes away.

It was at Wright's Tavern where Smith, and Major Pitcairn waited for the relief column they vainly hoped would find them. Without the relief column they planned how they would try to get back to Lexington, and eventually Boston without getting annihilated by the growing number of Militiamen and Minutemen gathering outside Concord. They stepped out of Wright's Tavern and into history as they began the running life or death struggle remembered as, Battle Road.

Across from Wight's Tavern is a church and a cemetery on a hill. Old Hill Burying Ground is across from Wright's Tavern, beside the big white church. It includes the graves of many of the men who defended Concord on 19 April 1775, including the family plot of Colonel James Barrett.

The old stones are well worn and at times indiscernible. It is worth the walk to climb to the hilltop and look at the view, and remember those brave soldiers who defied an empire and King to create this great nation of ours.

Sleepy Hollow Cemetery

34A Bedford St. Concord

Not far out of Concord center, you will find Sleepy Hollow Cemetery. It is a very interesting place where some important Americans are buried. The graves I sought out were on *Author's Ridge.* This is accessed from the main street by a gate—*The Author's Ridge Gate.*

I sat on a bench not far from the graves of Mary and Alisha Keyes gathering my reflections from my visits with, Henry David Thoreau, Ralph Waldo Emerson, Louisa May Alcott, and Nathaniel Hawthorne. Many others are there as well, including Daniel Chester French the man who famously carved the minuteman statue at the Old North Bridge, and the massive statue of Abraham Lincoln at the Lincoln Memorial in Washington DC.

Also, one of Concord's best historians and chronicler of the events of 19 April 1775 finds his eternal rest in Sleepy Hollow. Professor Allen French, who wrote an outstanding account of the events of 19 April 1775, *The Day of Concord and Lexington: The Nineteenth of April, 1775* is buried at Sleepy Hollow. Visiting this Cemetery which is still active, is a real treat and a good way to spend an afternoon.

Also, one of the famous, *Band of Brothers* is buried at Sleepy Hollow. Look up the grave of another Concord hero—Frederick 'Moose' Heyliger, he was a captain in Easy Company, 506 PIR 101st Airborne in World War II.

Battle Road Trail – Meriam's Corner

Concord and Lincoln Massachusetts

Leaving Wright's Tavern, you are on Lexington Road. As you leave Concord center it seems history is not done with you. Before you arrive at Meriam's Corner there are places of interest you will pass. Notably you will pass the house of the Alcott family at 399 Lexington Road. Known as, *Orchard House.* This is where Louisa May Alcott wrote the American classic, *Little Women.*

Continuing toward Meriam's Corner you will find *The Wayside.* located at 455 Lexington Road it was originally the home of the Alcott family, it is remembered as the house of Nathaniel Hawthorne author of, *The Scarlett Letter, House of Seven Gables* and other works of classic American literature.

Passing these homes is a reminded of the other history of Concord. Before long you will see the signs for the Meriam's Corner parking lot. There, at the end of a long field you will see the well persevered colonial home. standing at the maker that identifies where you are you read, 'The Battle Begins."

But look away from the house and look at the roads. At Meriam's Corner three roads converge, there are still standing stone walls. It is easy to stand, or crouch behind the walls and look back toward Concord and imagine the oncoming British Regulars marching toward you and a harsh destiny. The area is open with walls, trees and fields.

On the old section of Battle Road is a stream covered by a deck of planks, and you realize that such a bridge, crossing a narrow stream was a major impediment for Colonel Smith and his struggling force. As your mind's eye glances to the British soldiers you can understand the carnage and confusion that emerged from the historic encounter.

Battle Road Trail – Brooks Hill Village

Concord and Lincoln Massachusetts

Leaving Meriam's Corner get back onto Lexington Road heading toward Lexington. Before long you've traveled another mile or so and you are climbing a gentle hill. At the top are some old Colonial Houses – most are yellow. Look for the sign to park in the visitor's lot. It is open, with little modern building.

Farm fields and pastures are all around you. The road has stone walls on each side that would afford excellent coverage for ambushing the British soldiers on the road. Look back toward Meriam's Corner and you notice the incline and understand how the British Regulars were blind to the trap they were walking into.

The old stone walls, tree patches afford cover with deadly views of your red coated prey. The British Army of the 18th century was a fighting force that gathered on a large open field and exchanged shots with its enemy. Here along this road, you can imagine how defenseless they saw themselves as they were ambushed a second time.

Battle Road Trail – The Bloody Angle

Concord and Lincoln Massachusetts

Get back on the road toward Lexington. Travel another mile or so and on your left is a granite marker like all the others that mark Battle Road. It is at the corner of Massachusetts Route 2A, and Old Bedford Road. That is the route the soldiers traveled, and today part of it is a private lane, that is unwelcoming to auto traffic.

So, to get there you must continue on Massachusetts 2A toward Lexington to the next parking lot—Hartwell Tavern. Park your car and walk the lane to Hartwell Tavern. It is a well-preserved Colonial era tavern, and it is worth your time to visit the site and surrounding grounds. When you are there, you are on the road they traveled.

This part of Battle Road is Battle Road. Although at times Battle Road is on the modern roadway—Massachusetts Route 2A, here it is not. Take your time, look at all that surrounds you, it is nearly as it was on 19 April 1775. Progress and civilization have not encroached here. It is quiet and devoid of modern structures, and noise. The birds sing and you can hear your own footsteps.

My footsteps take me past Hartwell Tavern I am on a mission to get to the Bloody Angle. It is to me, like the site of Parker's Revenge a special place. At the Bloody Angle Militiamen and Minutemen from miles away converged onto this hill and intersection.

But approaching it in the opposite direction is not how I want to experience it. I managed to get a friend to drop me off at the corner of Massachusetts Route 2A, and the Old Bedford Road.

Exiting the car, I look back from where the British Regulars traveled on Lexington Road from Concord.

225

I turn and look at the old road and begin my awaited walk into history. I am traveling in the direction they traveled, my vision is as close as you can get to what they saw. The road is paved, but the asphalt is in a state of disrepair, and shortly the asphalt ends, and I hear my footsteps on the old dirt roadway.

The terrain here inspires me, my steps are slow, as theirs were. I look and, in some places, the old road still has the stone walls on each side. At times the stone walls have rail fence above them. I wonder if the rails were there on the fateful April day. Behind the walls look like old farm fields and pastures, no longer needed as nature has seemingly reclaimed them as they as covered in large trees and bushes.

Gone may be the exact view they saw, but with little effort your imagination fires away, looking left and right waiting to hear the crack of a musket, and witness another death or wounding on this road of damnation.

As I continue up the gentle hill it levels out to be near flat and I strain to see that before long I will be at the angle, where the road turns nearly 90 degrees to the right. Walking slowly toward the sharp angle in the road, I notice the stone marker identifying that British Soldiers were buried there.

So far from home back in England, they rest in peace in a peaceful place that is ironically free of their King's tyranny. I pay my respects wondering just how terrible their last full day, or last hours of life passed. Standing and turning around a full circle it is still obvious how such a devastating attack could be delivered to a marching, close quarter column.

The marker provided by the National Park Service headlines, *"Between Two Fires."* It provides a quote from a British Officer, and an explanation of the firing that was so deadly. It begins:

"Some of the most intense fighting on April 19, 1775 happened in this area."

By the time the British reached the hilltop and slowed the massive slow lumbering column, to turn they were in a trap. The British were outnumbered, outthought and outfought. It was a deadly lesson provided to his Majesty's soldiers by his Majesty's armed and unafraid subjects.

Go to the Bloody Angle site, rest, lean or sit on an old stone and just think about the history made all around you. Imagine yourself one of Emerson's *"embattled farmers."* You have been invaded by the mighty British Army, and here where a gentle hill finds an old intersection you are poised to have your vengeance. You are determined to be free; you patiently pull back the hammer of your musket and take aim—at history.

Go to the Bloody Angle site, learn the stories, walk where both oppressed and oppressor walked, fought and died.

My last stop in Concord is always the Old North Bridge. Get back to Concord center and follow the signs to the Minute Man National Historical Park. The Bridge, like Lexington Green, and Bunker Hill is where America's First Soldiers stood up and fearlessly faced the most powerful army on Earth in the 18th century.

The Bridge, the monuments and the path that links them all are a perfect and fitting ending to a Colonial Journey. The Bridge is where the citizen soldiers found their enemy, where the poet found his words, where the sculptor fulfilled his vision and we their descendants come closest to all of them.

Old North Bridge

174 Liberty Street, Concord, Massachusetts

"On this green bank, by this soft stream,
We set today a votive stone;
That memory may their deed redeem,
When, like our sires, our sons are gone."

The Concord Hymn (19 April 1836)
Ralph Waldo Emerson (1803–82)

The old dirt lane guides you toward the Bridge from the east side. It is the very same rustic road they fought and died over. The view of the Bridge is aligned with a memorial at each end. The large gray memorials at each end of the Old Bridge have stood for over 100 years and each holds a different meaning.

Approaching the first memorial on the left are two old stone columns connected by an old chain. The chain bars you from coming any closer to the two British flags flanking and old stone. The flags are the old-style Union Jack, the British flag of 1775.

Unlike the modern version, there are two red stripes missing crossed like the bars of a Confederate Battle Flag from the American Civil War. The missing cross is that of St. Patrick of Ireland, which was not added until the early 19th century.

The flags are the correct representation of 18th century Britain. The stone has an old, gray metal or stone piece attached that reads:

GRAVE OF TWO BRITISH SOLDIERS
"They came three thousand miles and died, to keep the past upon its throne: Unheard, beyond the ocean tide, their English mother made her moan."

19 April 1775

1849

James Russell Lowe (1819–91)

Across from the grave marker of the fallen Regulars is a very old looking monument. It is an obelisk, sitting on a square pedestal, on a small round mound of dirt and grass. Looking at the monument there is no rounded edges, it seems to be cut in ninety-degree angles.

Each corner as sharp and crisp as the day it was cut. It towers into the flawless blue autumn sky, shadows dance on the mound from the slight breeze moving the tall colorful trees that surround us. Standing before it you feel the passion of the stone cutter, and finally my gaze captures the words attached to the obelisk base.

They are black and not deeply cut, on an old white weathered background. The white background is yellowed and cracked; it looks as old as the long-ago battle fought here. It reads as follows:

"HERE
On the 19 of April,
1775,
was made
the first forcible resistance
to British aggression
On the opposite Bank
stood the American Militia
Here stood the Invading Army
and on this spot
the first of the Enemy fell

in the War of that Revolution
which gave
Independence
to these United States
In gratitude to GOD and
In the love of Freedom
this Monument
was erected AD. 1836. "

Turing away from the monument, before I cross the Old Bridge, there is one more order of investigation. From the time the Old Bridge came into sight, I have noticed something I never expected to see in Concord today. First, from the greatest distance it was just something red framed by the sea of green, yellow and faded red leaves hanging from the trees.

As my slow steps brought me closer and the red was very intense, as was the white below it. Closer still, and I was looking at a British Redcoat. He stands like a sentry, not far from the Bridge, on the east side where the British Regulars engaged the Colonial Minutemen on the historic day. It was unexpected, and I was unprepared to meet a Regular, 245 years after the Battle.

Thinking like a proud American, the conclusion is obvious; if any soldier should be here, he should be a Minuteman. Drawing closer his uniform is clean, and his coat a deep red like the discernible coat of an 18th Century British officer. It has wide black lapels and cuffs that his shirtsleeves pass beyond.

On the black lapel and cuffs are bright brass buttons shinning as if he just finished polishing them. His black felt hat falls perfectly aligned on his well-trimmed hair. It has an attached black cockade ribbon marking him as one of King George III loyal supporters. He stands erect with a soldier's bearing, each of his hands attached to his musket which he bears in front of him, at the ready.

Tourists ask to be photographed with him, small family groups surround him and smile. Cell phones, out of place with the soldier's uniform, are the cameras that catch the images. Most do not speak to him, just say hi or node their heads.

He watches from a shady spot at the many travelers, some speaking foreign tongues, in this a foreign place, this foreign soldier occupies. He eyes those that stop at the grave marker for his fallen British comrades, some surprised, and others amused at the poem carved into the old stone. He is finally alone; I cautiously approach the *enemy*.

"*Good Morning Sir,*" I said with an extended hand to complete the greeting. He smiles a friendly smile, shakes hands and returns.

"*Good Morning.*" He has no British accent when one was clearly expected based on his near perfect representation of an 18th century British officer. Surprised at the disconnected appearance and speech, the question must be asked:

"*You are not British?*" He nods, smiles gracefully saying, "*No, I am American, a local re-enactor.*" Still quite surprised and filled with questions, I ask:

"*Why re-enact as a Regular?*" I allow no time for an answer as my mind is racing:

"*Why not a Colonial Militiamen, or Minuteman?*" Still more questions run on as I squint in the bright sunshine. I raise an eyebrow slightly asking:

"*Why not an American Officer?*"

The brief interrogation is not complete as he has not been allowed to answer.

Smiling warmly, he raises his chin slightly and tells me there is so much more to the stories of the American Revolution than most visitors know. He tactfully speaks of the Battle from British side, offering interesting, unknown, pieces in the minds of most tourists.

He takes a few minutes and tells me the stories he likes to repeat. One of which is that the British did not burn or try to burn down Concord on 19 April 1775. He reminds me of the little known and less repeated ending of the burning of the gun carriage in Concord center.

Yes, the British started the fire, but fearing the potential of the fire spreading they formed a bucket brigade and tried mightily to stop the fire. He also reminds me that the Colonials needlessly attacked a dying soldier with a hatchet.

His stories are told with care for the history that surrounds us both. He brings dignity to the stories, and I realize he plays the part of a British Officer near perfectly. Others have gathered for their photo-ops, like he is a prop. He is much more than that. I say thank you, shake his hand and leave him to others who will question and photograph.

The walk is slow approaching the inclined Old Bridge, and nature is on display as much as history. The riverbanks on each side, rich with green foliage, and the trees behind them seem to shading the slow passing river. The water moves making little sound, it is a quiet place as an old battlefield should be.

The old dusty dirt road leads to the wooden deck of the bridge. Not much of a bridge by our modern times, it is a humble structure rebuilt many times since fought over in April 1775. Leaning on the railing I look north to the peaceful river slowing passing, and the view from the south the same as the river travels toward Concord.

There are many people on the Bridge today, and I spy another re-enactor, and he too is in a redcoat and occupied telling the tourists the story of the battle at the Old North Bridge. He stands at the top of the incline looking west and telling his story.

I stop as well at the top of the old bridge, waiting for a moment of quite as the re-enactor and his small audience move off the bridge. I am halfway between each side. I think how short a divide it is from one side to another. But the halfway point is metaphor as I imagine the feelings of each side as they prepared to battle over the bridge.

Every participant, British Regular and Massachusetts Militiaman was at that moment a British subject. Each man a countryman, loyal to the same king and his flag, yet, poised to kill each other. Here, at the North Bridge the lines of battle were drawn, perhaps inspired by other historical encounters between the mother country and her rebellious offspring. The results of years, decades, generations of neglect and abuse.

Looking at each side I continue my journey over the bridge to the American side.

Exiting from the west side of the Bridge is a huge bronze man with a musket and a farm plow. The man has rested his overcoat upon the plow and is walking away from the plow. This all sits atop a massive light-gray granite base with carvings reminding us of the date, the battle, the sacrifice.

It was created for the 100th anniversary of the Battle by a brilliant Concord artist, Daniel Chester French. French carved many famous American sculptures; his masterpiece is the iconic seated Abraham Lincoln in the Lincoln Memorial.

Carved into the base beneath the bronze minuteman are the words of a brilliant Concord writer and philosopher, Ralph Waldo Emerson. Today the base and statue on top are silhouetted by a cloudless perfect blue sky.

Walking from the bridge puts you facing the Minuteman. He does not look down at you, his gaze is fixed toward the Old Bridge, and easterly toward where the British were on Wednesday, 19 April 1775. He holds tightly onto his musket which has the flint raised, in the firing position.

His powder horn slung over his shoulder and looks heavy like it is full of gunpowder, further projecting readiness. Walking behind him his plow seemed to stop by a large rock at his feet, holding it in place. Representing the wish, he will return to his plow when his sacrifice to country, friends, family is completed.

He stands as *America's First Soldier,* but is actually representative of all American Soldiers standing as our valiant defenders have since 1775. It is humbling to see him; he represents the best of us.

From behind the pedestal my view toward the east is positioned with his. I see the arched bridge, and the obelisk aligned in harmony with the imposing bronze Minuteman in front of me.

Each side of the granite base is rough and uncut, a reminder of the rough, uncut Minuteman perched above. On the front of the base etched into the granite are the words of one of Concord's favorite sons.

Ralph Waldo Emerson wrote, *"The Concord Hymn"* for the 1836 dedication of the obelisk across the river from the Minuteman statue. His poem carries the sound of the pulpit a reminder the Emerson's grandfather was a reverend in Concord.

Reverend William Emerson (1743—76) lived close enough to the bridge that he witnessed the battle. The first stanza of Emerson's Concord Hymn is chiseled beneath Daniel Chester French's Minuteman Statue:

> *"By the rude bridge that arched the flood,*
> *Their flag to April's breeze unfurled,*
> *Here once the embattled farmers stood,*
> *And fired the shot heard round the world."*

The Concord Hymn (April 19, 1836)
Ralph Waldo Emerson (1803–82)

It was Emerson who gave us the one sentence that captures that day of Battle in April 1775, finding a perspective that has bridged centuries. Without that, *"...embattled farmer firing the shot heard round the world"* the *Declaration of Independence* in 1776, and the *War of Independence*, the very creation of our nation is questionable.

On this near perfect very late summer's day, walking past the statue, the well-worn path leads through the grass to a slight inclined, inappreciable ridge. Take a minute and remember *they* were there, the *embattled farmer* and his kin, neighbors and friends. Much has changed in the world since they stood there, but this place and its purpose have never been more important than they are today.

Look to the ridge and back toward the bridge, not much of a distance measured feet but an immeasurable distance in accomplishment. Think of them as still up there on the top of the slight hill. The British crossed the bridge, to their perceived safety. They were not safe. Their officers had made a remarkably egregious, historic, error in judgement. They were not safe. They were standing in the way of history.

Looking at where the trees are now is where the Patriots stood. Regular, hardworking men with not a professional soldier amongst them. A rag tag lot in appearance only, not a man stepped back. They stood together, shoulder to shoulder, they stood for each other and with each other.

I have a smile on my lips, and a tear in my eye as I think of them marching down to meet the British. In their ranks I see men in blue and gray, Dough Boys in khaki, GIs in olive drab from Normandy, Okinawa, Korea, Vietnam. And young faces that still fill out army uniforms in Iraq, and Afghanistan. The volunteers who keep us free.

Like all historic adventures through military history, it is the sacrifice made by others that remain alive if you look and listen hard enough. Emerson's words frame the faceless heroes of our country past and present.

"Spirit, that made those heroes dare,
To die, and leave their children free,
Bid Time and Nature gently spare
The shaft we raise to them and thee."

The Concord Hymn (19 April 1836)
Ralph Waldo Emerson (1803–82)

References

Bailyn, Bernard. *Voyagers to the West: A Passage in the Peopling of America on the Eve of the Revolution.* New York: Random House. 1986 Print.

Barker, John. *The Diary of Lieutenant John Barker, Fourth (or The King's Own) Regiment of Foot, From November, 1774, to May, 1776.* (1928). Journal of the Society for Army Historical Research, 7(28), 81-109. Retrieved from http:// www.jstor.org/stable/44232571 November 2019.

Barker, John. *The diary of Lieutenant John Barker.* November, 1774, to May, 1776. Lieutenant in the 4th (or The King's Own) Regiment of Foot, up to 12 January, 1776, and after That Date Captain in the 10th Regiment of Foot. (Continued)." *Journal of the Society for Army Historical Research*, vol. 7, no. 29, 1928, pp. 145—74. *JSTOR*, www.jstor.org/stable/44219393. Retrieved December 2019.

Beeman, Richard. *Our Lives, Our Fortunes and Our sacred Honor: The Forging of American Independence 1774-1776.* New York: Basic Books. Print 2013.

Bell, J.L. *The Road To Concord: How Four Stolen Cannon Ignited the Revolutionary War.* Yardly, PA: Westholme Publishing, LLC. 2016. Print

Borneman, Walter R. *American Spring: Lexington, Concord, and the Road to Revolution.* New York: Little, Brown & Co. 2014 Print.

Brumwell, Stephen. Redcoats: The British Soldier and War in the Americas, 1755-1763. New York: Cambridge University Press. 2006.

Clarke, Rev. Jonas. *The Battle of Lexington: Opening of The war of the Revolution.* Lexington Historical society: Lexington, MA. 1901. Print.

Coburn, Frank Warren. The Battle of April 19, 1775: In Lexington, Concord, Arlington, Cambridge, Somerville, Lincoln, Charlestown, Massachusetts. Project Gutenberg eBook August 20, 2015 [eBook #49742]. https:// www.gutenberg.org/files/49742/49742-h/49742-h.htm

Curtis, Edward E. Ph.D. *The Organization of the British Army in the American Revolution.* New Haven: Yale University Press. Print

Draper, Theodore. *A Struggle for Power: The American Revolution.* New York: Vintage Books. 1997. Print

Emerson, W., Emerson, A. (Forbes). (1972). *Diaries and letters of William Emerson, 1743-1776: minister of the church in Concord, chaplain in the Revolutionary Army.* kouros.info/kouroo/thumbnails/E/ ReverendEmersonPere.pdf

Fischer, David Hackett. Paul Revere's Ride. New York: Oxford University Press. 1995. Print.

Fleming, Thomas J. *Liberty! The American Revolution.* New York: Viking Press. 1997. Print

Fleming, Thomas. *Now We Are Enemies: The Story of Bunker Hill.* American History Press: Staunton Virginia. 2010. Print

Fogleman, Aaron. "Migrations to the Thirteen British North American Colonies, 1700-1775: New Estimates." The Journal of Interdisciplinary History, vol. 22, no. 4, 1992, pp. 691—709. JSTOR, www.jstor.org/stable/205241.

French, Allen. *"The British Expedition to Concord, Massachusetts, in1775."* Journal of the Society for Army Historical Research, vol. 15, no. 57, 1936, pp. 17—31. JSTOR, *www.jstor.org/stable/44227945.* Pp. 19-20 Retrieved November 2019.

French, Allen. *The Day of Concord and Lexington: The Nineteenth of April, 1775. Boston:* Little, Brown & Co. 1925. Print

French, Allen. Professor. *The Siege of Boston.* New York: The Macmillan Company, 1911. Print.

Frothingham, Richard. *History of the Siege of Boston, and of the Battles of Lexington, Concord, and Bunker Hill:* Also an Account of the Bunker Hill Monument. With Illustrative Documents. Boston: C.C. Little & J. Brown. 1849. Google Book. *https://books.google.com/books* Retrieved December 2019.

Frothingham, Richard. *The Life and Times of Joseph Warren*, Boston: Little, Brown, & Co., 1865, Print.

Hakim, Joy. *From Colonies to Country.* New York: Oxford UP, 2005. Print

Henretta, James A, and David Brody. *America A Concise History.* New York: Bedford / St. Martin's, 2010. Print

Hosmer, James Kendall (1834-1927). *Samuel Adams.* Boston: Houghton, Mifflin & Co. 1885.
https://catalog.hathitrust.org/Record/000367068 Retrieved November 2019.

Kostyal, K.M. *Founding Fathers: The Fight for Freedom and the Birth of American Liber*ty. National Geographic Books. 2014. Print

Langguth, A.J. *Patriots: The Men who started The American Revolution.* New York: Simon and Schuster, 2013. Print

Lossing, Benson J. *Life of Washington: A Biography, Personal, Military, and Political, Volume 2.* New York: Virtue & Co. 1860. Print

Louth, Rexford. *God Shed His Grace On Thee: The Christian Foundations of America* WestBow Press: Bloomington, IN. 2014. Print.

McCullough, David. *1776.* New York: Simon & Schuster, 2005. Print

Mackenzie, Frederick Lt. ed. by Allen French. *A British Fusilier in Revolutionary Boston.* Diary of Lt. Frederick Mackenzie, Adj. of the Royal Welch Fusiliers, Jan 5 - April 30, 1775.

Micklos, John. *Why We Won the American Revolution*, Berkeley Heights, NJ: Enslow, 2013. Print

Philbrick, Nathanial. *Bunker Hill: A City, A Siege, A Revolution.* Penguin Group: New York. 2013. Print

Pocock, Tom. *Battle for Empire: The Very First World War 1756—63.*

Michael O'Mara Books. 1998. Print.

Prebble, John. *Culloden.* New York: Penguin Books. 1967. Print

Plus, Mark. *Henry Knox Visionary General of the American Revolution.* New York: Palgrave MacMillan. Print. 2008.

Revere, Paul (1735 -1818) *Letter from Paul Revere to Jeremy Belknap, circa 1798.* Massachusetts Historical Society, Collections on Line. https:// www.masshist.org/database/99

Royle, Trevor. *Culloden; Scotland's Last Battle and the Forging of the British Empire.* Little, Brown: Boston. 2016.

Savas, Theodore, P. & Dameron, J. David. *A Guide to the Battles of the American Revolution.* New York: Savas Beatie, LLC. 2006. Print

Tourtellot, Arthur. *Lexington and Concord: The Beginning of the War of The American Revolution.* New York: W.W. Norton & Company. 2000. Print.

Tourtellot, Arthur Bernon. *William Diamond's drum: The Beginning of the War of the American Revolution.* Doubleday: Garden City, N.Y. 1959. Print.

True, Henry, and Amos Barrett. Journal And Letters of Rev. Henry True of Hampstead, New Hampshire: Who Was Chaplain In the New Hampshire Regiment of the Provincial Army In 1759 And 1762 : Also an Account of the Battle of Concord. Marion, Ohio: Printed for H. True...[by] Star Press, 1900.

Lockhart, Paul. *Bunker Hill: America's Greatest Battle?* Military History Quarterly, May 3, 2011,
http://www.historynet.com/bunker-hill-americas-greatest-battle.htm

Varney, George J. (1836-1901). *The Story of Patriot's Day, Lexington And Concord, April 19, 1775: With Poems Brought Out On the First Observation of the Anniversary Holiday, And the Forms In Which it Was Celebrated.* Boston: Lee & Shepard, 1895. Print. https://www.hathitrust.org retried November 2019.

Volo, James M. and Volo Dorothy D. *Daily Life on the Old Colonial Frontier.*

Westport, CT: Greenwood Publishing Group. 2002.

Webb, James *Born Fighting: How The Scots-Irish Shaped America.* New York: Broadway Books. 2004.

D-Day June 6 1944 *Operation Overlord Landings and the Battle of Normandy.* http://www.6juin1944.com/assaut/utah/en_index.php Retrieved Oct. 2019

Endnotes

[i] Royle, Trevor. Culloden; Scotland's Last Battle and the Forging of the British Empire. Little, Brown: Boston. 2016. Print. Page 17.

[ii] Kostyal, K.M. *Founding Fathers: The Fight for Freedom and the Birth of American Liberty.* Page 18

[iii] Tourtellot, Arthur. *Lexington and Concord: The Beginning of the War of The American Revolution.* New York: W.W. Norton & Company. 2000. Page 21.

[iv] French, Allen Professor. The Siege of Boston. New York: The Macmillan Company, 1911. Print Page 22.

[v] French. *The Siege of Boston.* Page 22

[vi] Tourtellot, Lexington and Concord. Page 23.

[vii] *Ibid.* Page 24.

[viii] Clarke, Jonas. *The importance of military skill, measures for defence and a martial spirit, in a time of peace.* A sermon preached to the Ancient and Honourable Artillery Company in Boston, New-England, June 6. 1768. Evans Early American Imprint Collection. https://quod.lib.umich.edu/e/evans/N08489.0001.001?view=toc

[ix] Louth, Rexford. *God Shed His Grace On Thee: The Christian Foundations of America* WestBow Press: Bloomington, IN WestBow Press 2014. Page 24

[x] Gunn, Robert M. The Highland Clearances: *"the anti-climatic destruction of the great and proud Highland army...The 'pacification' of the Highlanders and the Clearances which followed a generation later, completed the ruin of that once proud and ancient tribal society known as the Highland Clan System."* http://www.scottish-history.com/clearances.shtml. Retrieved September 2019.

[xi] Pettinger, Tejvan. *"Facts about the American Revolution"*, Oxford,

www.biographyonline.net, 21st February 2017. Retrieved September 2019.

[xii] Bailyn, Bernard. *Voyagers to the West: A Passage in the Peopling of America on the Eve of the Revolution.* Pp 7-8

[xiii] Fogleman, Aaron. *"Migrations to the Thirteen British North American Colonies, 1700-1775: New Estimates."* The Journal of Interdisciplinary History, vol. 22, no. 4, 1992, pp. 691—709. JSTOR, www.jstor.org/stable/205241. P.695

[xiv] Volo, James M. and Volo Dorothy D. *Daily Life on the Old Colonial Frontier.*
Westport, CT: Greenwood Publishing Group. 2002. Page 27.

[xv] Gunn, Robert M. The Highland Clearances. Retrieved September 2019.

[xvi] The John Grey Centre. *A brief history of emigration & immigration in Scotland.* Haddington, East Lothian, EH41 3DX Scotland.
https:// www.johngraycentre.org/about/archives/brief-history-emigration-immigration- scotland-research-guide-2/ Retrieved September 2019.

[xvii] Volo, James et al. *Daily Life on the Old Colonial Frontier.* Page 28.

[xviii] Philbrick, Nathaniel. *Bunker Hill: A City, A Siege, A Revolution.* New York: Penguin Group. 2013. Print. Page 28.

[xix] Pocock, Tom. *Battle for Empire: The Very First World War 1756—63.* Michael O'Mara Books. 1998 Page 29

[xx] Revere, Paul (1735-1818) *Letter from Paul Revere to Jeremy Belknap, circa 1798.* Massachusetts Historical Society, Collections On Line.
https:// www.masshist.org/database/99 Retrieved November 2019.

[xxi] National Park Service. website.
https://www.nps.gov/mima/learn/
education/upload/Gen.%20Thomas%20Gage.pdf_retrieved August 17, 2019.

[xxii] Tourtellot, Lexington and Concord. Page 33.

[xxiii] Ruppert, Bob. T*he Earl of Dartmouth: Secretary of State for the Colonies, Third Year: August 1774—November 1775.* Journal of the American Revolution.
https://allthingsliberty.com/2019/01/the-earl-of-dartmouth-secretary-of-state-for-the-colonies-third-year-august-1774-november-1775/
Retrieved November 2019.

[xxiv] French, Allen. *"The British Expedition to Concord, Massachusetts, in1775."* Journal of the Society for Army Historical Research, vol. 15, no. 57, 1936, pp. 17—31. JSTOR, www.jstor.org/stable/44227945. Pp. 19-20 Retrieved November 2019.

[xxv] French, Allen. *The British Expedition...* Page 36.

[xxvi] Hakim, Joy. *From Colonies to Country.* New York: Oxford UP, 2005. P 73.

[xxvii] The Lexington Minutemen. *Captain Parker's Company of Militia, April 19, 1775* https://www.lexingtonminutemen.com/captain-parkers-company-of-militia.html retried august 13, 2019.

[xxviii] Tourtellot, Arthur Bernon. *William Diamond's drum : The Beginning of the War of the American Revolution.* Doubleday: Garden City, N.Y. 1959. Prologue.

[xxix] Tourtellot. Lexington and Concord. Page 41

[xxx] Barker, John. *Diary of Lieutenant John Barker Fourth (or The King's Own) Regiment of Foot, From November, 1774, to May, 1776.* (1928). Journal of the Society for Army Historical Research, 7(28), 81-109. Retrieved from http://www.jstor.org/stable/44232571 Page 98. November 2019.

[xxxi] Barker, John. *Diary of Lieutenant John Barker* Page 43

[xxxii] Clarke, Jonas. *The Battle of Lexington: Opening of The war of the Revolution.* Lexington Historical society: Lexington, MA. 1901 Page 43

[xxxiii] Curtis, Edward E. Ph.D. *The Organization of the British Army in the American Revolution.* New Haven: Yale University Press. 1926. Page 44.

[xxxiv] Curtis, Edward E. Ph.D. *The Organization of the British Army...*Page 44

[xxxv] Fischer, David Hackett. *Paul Revere's Ride.* New York: Oxford University Press. 1995. Page 45.

[xxxvi] Clarke, Jonas. *The Battle of Lexington.* Page 45.

[xxxvii] Hakim, Joy. *From Colonies to Country* P 73

[xxxviii] Barker, Page 46.

[xxxix] Clarke, *The Battle of Lexington...* Page 47.

[xl] Barker, Page 47.

[xli] Pitcarin, John Major. *Major John Pitcarin's Report to General Gage. 26, April, 1775. Boston, Massachusetts.* Digital History.

http:// www.digitalhistory.uh.edu/active_learning/explorations/revolution/ account3_lexington.cfm. Retrieved November 2019.

[xlii] French Allen. *The Siege of Boston.* Pp 55-56.

[xliii] Hosmer, James Kendall (1834-1927). *Samuel Adams.* Boston: Houghton, Mifflin & Co. 1885. Print Pages 330-1. https://catalog.hathitrust.org/ Record/000367068 Retrieved November 2019.

[xliv] Conway, Moncure Daniel. *Emerson at Home and Abroad.* Boston: Osgood, 1882 P. 135

[xlv] Emerson, W., Emerson, A. (Forbes). (1972). *Diaries and letters of William Emerson, 1743-1776: minister of the church in Concord, chaplain in the Revolutionary Army.* *kouros.info/kouroo/thumbnails/E/ ReverendEmersonPere.pdf* Page 52. Retrieved November 2019.

[xlvi] True, Henry (1726-1782) *Journal and letters of Rev. Henry True of Hampstead, New Hampshire: also an account of the Battle of Concord. by Amos Barrett* (1752-1829) Marion, Ohio: Star Press, 1900. *https://catalog.hathitrust.org/Record/100280101* Retrieved November 2019. Page 53.

[xlvii] True, Henry. Journal and letters of Rev. Henry True. Page 53.

[xlviii] *Ibid.* Page 53.

[xlix] French, Allen. *The Day of Concord and Lexington: The Nineteenth of April, 1775.* Boston: Little, Brown. 1925. Page 55.

[l] Borneman, Walter R. *American Spring: Lexington, Concord, and the Road to Revolution.* New York: Little, Brown & Co. 2014 Page 56.

[li] National Park Service. Minute Man National Historical Park. *Colonel James Barrett House.* https://www.nps.gov/mima/learn/historyculture/colonel-james-barrett-house.htm Retrieved September 2019.

[lii] Bill of Rights Institute. Arlington, VA. *The Rights of The Colonists* https:// billofrightsinstitute.org/founding-documents/primary-source-documents/the-rights-of-the-colonists/ Retrieved August 2019.

[liii] French Allen. *The Day of Concord and Lexington.* Page 59.

[liv] Borneman, Walter, R. *American Spring.* Page 59.

[lv] D. Michael Ryan Michael, D. *White Cockade: A Jacobite Air at the North Bridge?* The Lincoln Minute menhttps://www2.bc.edu/donald-hafner/lmm/music-articles/white_cockade_ryan.html retrieved September 2019.

[lvi] Age Of Revolution *An Cnota Ban (The White Cockade)* http:// www.troubadourinteractive.com/born-in-battle-the-american-revolution- online/music/the-white-cockade/ Retrieved September 2019.

[lvii] Tourtellot, Arthur. *Lexington And Concord.* Page 62.

[lviii] True, Henry (1726-1782) *Journal and letters of Rev. Henry True...*Page 69

[lix] French Allen. *The Day of Concord and Lexington.* Page 70.

[lx] D. Michael Ryan *White Cockade...*retrieved September 2019.

[lxi] Age Of Revolution *An Cnota Ban...*Retrieved September 2019.

[lxii] De Berniere, Henry Ensign. *An ACCOUNT of the Transactions of the British troops, from the time they marched out of Boston, on the evening of the 18th, 'till their confused retreat back, on the ever memorable Nineteenth of April 1775.* The Project Gutenberg EBook of Gage's Instructions, by Thomas Gage and Ensign de Berniere. *https://ia802806.us.archive.org/22/items/ gagesinstruction36536gut/36536-8.txt.* Retrieved December 2019.

[lxiii] Barker, John. *Diary of Lieutenant John Barker* Page 75.

[lxiv] Draper, Theodore. *A Struggle for Power: The American Revolution.* New York:Vintage Books. 1997. Page 77.

[lxv] French, Allen. *The British Expedition...* Page 77.

[lxvi] 66 *Ibid*, Page 77.

[lxvii] Draper, Theodore. *A Struggle for Power.* Page 83

[lxviii] *Ibid*, Page 83

[lxix] Borneman, Walter R. *American Spring.* Page 87.

[lxx] Mackenzie, Frederick ed. by Allen French. *A British Fusilier in Revolutionary Boston.* Diary of Lt. Frederick Mackenzie, Adj. of the Royal Welch Fusiliers, Jan 5 - April 30, 1775. Scanned from microform by ND. Published by Harvard University Press, Cambridge MA 1926. https://archive.org/details/A BritishFusilierInRevolutionaryBoston_392/page/n61. Pp.55-57. Retrieved December 2019.

[lxxi] Mackenzie, Frederick ed. by Allen French. *A British Fusilier in Revolutionary Boston.* Page 89

[lxxii] Barker, John. *Diary of Lieutenant John Barker.* Page 90.

[lxxiii] Mackenzie, Frederick. ed. by Allen French. *A British Fusilier in Revolutionary Boston.* Page 91.

[lxxiv] Barker, John. *Diary of Lieutenant John Barker.* Page 91.

[lxxv] Fischer, David Hackett. *Paul Revere's Ride.* Page 91.

[lxxvi] Coburn, Frank Warren. *The Battle of April 19, 1775: In Lexington, Concord, Arlington, Cambridge, Somerville, Lincoln, Charlestown, Massachusetts.* Project Gutenberg ebook August 20, 2015 [EBook #49742]. *https:// www.gutenberg.org/files/49742/49742-h/49742-h.htm#Page_91* Page 91. Retrieved December 2019.

[lxxvii] French, Allen. *The Day of Concord and Lexington.* Pp. 252-254

[lxxviii] Mackenzie, Frederick Lt. ed. by Allen French. *A British Fusilier in Revolutionary Boston.* Page 94.

[lxxix] French, Allen. *The Day of Concord and Lexington.* Page 94.

[lxxx] Barker, John. *Diary of Lieutenant John Barker.* Page 95.

[lxxxi] Tourtellot, Arthur. *Lexington And Concord.* Page 98.

[lxxxii] Barker, John. *Diary of Lieutenant John Barker.* Page 98.

[lxxxiii] Micklos, John. *Why We Won the American Revolution.* Berkeley Heights, NJ: Enslow, 2013. P. 10

[lxxxiv] Crawford, Mary. *Old BostonDays and Ways.* Penguin Group: New York. 2013. Print. page 99.

[lxxxv] Barker, John. *Diary of Lieutenant John Barker.* Page 100.

[lxxxvi] Micklos, John. *Why We Won the American Revolution.* P. 10

[lxxxvii] Ibid. Page 104.

[lxxxviii] Frothingham, Richard. *The Life and Times of Joseph Warren*, Boston: Little, Brown, & Co., 1865, Page 105.

[lxxxix] Frothingham, Richard. *The Life and Times of Joseph Warren* Page 105.

[xc] *Ibid Page 106.*

[xci] Morgan, Kenneth. *George Washington and the Problem of Slavery* Journal of American Studies. Vol. 34, No. 2 (Aug 2000), pp. 279-301 (23 pages) P. 107. https://www.jstor.org/ retrieved August 2019.

^{xcii} Morgan, Kenneth. *George Washington and the Problem of Slavery.* Page 107.

^{xciii} Executive Order 9981: *Desegregation of the Armed Forces* (1948) https://www.ourdocuments.gov/doc. Retrieved August 2019.

^{xciv} Savas, Theodore, P. & Dameron, J. David. *A Guide to the Battles of the American Revolution.* New York: Savas Beatie, LLC. 2006. P. 15.

^{xcv} Philbrick, Nathaniel. *Bunker Hill: A City, A Siege, A Revolution.* New York: Penguin Group. 2013. Print. Page 113.

^{xcvi} Barker, John. *Diary of Lieutenant John Barker.* Page 116-117.

^{xcvii} Frothingham, Richard. *History of the Siege of Boston, and of the Battles of Lexington, Concord, and Bunker Hill:* Also an Account of the Bunker Hill Monument. With Illustrative Documents. Boston: C.C. Little & J. Brown. 1849. Pp 112-113.

^{xcviii} Frothingham, Richard. *History of the Siege of Boston.* Page 117.

^{xcix} Barker, John. *The Diary of John Barker November.* Page 117.

^c Gage, Thomas. *1775 Offer of Amnesty.* Digital History ID 158. *http://www.digitalhistory.uh.edu/disp_textbook.cfm* Retrieved December 2019.

^{ci} Gage, *1775 Offer of Amnesty.*

^{cii} *Ibid.*

^{ciii} Hannum, Patrick H. Lt. Col (Retired) USMC. *America's First Company Commanders.*
https://www.benning.army.mil/infantry/magazine/issues/2013/Oct-Dec/Hannum.html Retrieved November 2019.

^{civ} Savas, Theodore, P. & Dameron, J. David. *A Guide to the Battles of the American Revolution.* PP xli- xl.

^{cv} Savas, *etal. A Guide to the Battles of the American Revolution.* P 136.

^{cvi} Massachusetts Historical Society. *The Battle of Bunker Hill - 10 Accounts* https://www.masshist.org/bh/jqap3text.html retrieved August 2019.

^{cvii} Fleming, Thomas. *Now We Are Enemies: The Story of Bunker Hill.* American History Press: Staunton Virginia. 2010. Pp 128-129.

^{cviii} Fleming, Thomas. *Now We Are Enemies...P. 130.*

^{cix} D-Day June 6 1944 Operation Overlord Landings and the Battle of Normandy. http://www.6juin1944.com/assaut/utah/en_index.php

^{cx} Philbrick. Bunker Hill. Print. Page 137.

[cxi] Trumball, John. *The Death of General Warren at Bunker Hill, June 17, 1775* https://collections.mfa.org/objects/34260. Painting. Retrieved September, 2019.

[cxii] A. J. Langguth. *Patriots: The Men who started The American Revolution.* New York: Simon and Schuster. 2013. Page 145.

[cxiii] Brumwell, Stephen. Redcoats: The British Soldier and War in the Americas, 1755-1763. New York: Cambridge University Press. 2006. Page 147.

[cxiv] Walker, Paul K. *Engineers of Independence.* Washington, DC: Historical Division, Office of Chief Engineers, 1981. P. 148.

[cxv] Beeman, Richard. *Our Lives, Our Fortunes and Our sacred Honor: The Forging of American Independence 1774-1776.* New York: Basic Books. 2013. Page 150.

[cxvi] Philbrick, *Bunker Hill.* Page 152.

[cxvii] McCullough, David. *1776.* New York: Simon & Schuster, 2005. Print 1776 Page 155.

[cxviii] McCullough, David. *1776* Page 156

[cxix] Ibid 1776 Pp 157-158.

[cxx] Ibid Pp 157-158.

[cxxi] Ibid Pp 157-158.

[cxxii] Plus, Mark. *Henry Knox Visionary General of the American Revolution.* New York: Palgrave MacMillan. 2008. Page 160.

[cxxiii] Plus, Mark. *Henry Knox* Page 161.

[cxxiv] Ibid. Page 168.

[cxxv] Barker, John. *The Diary of Lieutenant John Barker.* pp. 169-70.

[cxxvi] Philbrick, *Bunker Hill.* Page 171.

[cxxvii] Lossing, Benson J. *Life of Washington: A Biography, Personal, Military, and Political, Volume 2. New York:* Virtue & Co. 1860 pp. 172-3.